# Building a Future with BRICs

Mark Kobayashi-Hillary

(Editor)

# Building a Future with BRICs

The Next Decade for Offshoring

Mark Kobayashi-Hillary
National Outsourcing Association
44 Wardour Street
London, W1D 6QZ
United Kingdom
www.noa.co.uk

ISBN 978-3-540-46453-2          e-ISBN 978-3-540-46454-9

Library of Congress Control Number: 2007936168

© 2008 Springer-Verlag Berlin Heidelberg

This work is subject to copyright. All rights are reserved, whether the whole or part of the material is concerned, specifically the rights of translation, reprinting, reuse of illustrations, recitation, broadcasting, reproduction on microfilm or in any other way, and storage in data banks. Duplication of this publication or parts thereof is permitted only under the provisions of the German Copyright Law of September 9, 1965, in its current version, and permission for use must always be obtained from Springer. Violations are liable to prosecution under the German Copyright Law.

The use of general descriptive names, registered names, trademarks, etc. in this publication does not imply, even in the absence of a specific statement, that such names are exempt from the relevant protective laws and regulations and therefore free for general use.

*Cover design:* WMX Design GmbH, Heidelberg

Printed on acid-free paper

9 8 7 6 5 4 3 2 1

springer.com

*Dedicated to Nobumi and Matilda; thanks for your epic tolerance throughout the production of this book ... and also my nephews Luke, Ben, and Lewis, who will look at this as a history lesson by the time they are able to understand it!*

# Foreword

It's always a great pleasure to comment on a new book especially as this one lives up to the excellent standards of Mark's earlier book 'Outsourcing to India' – so really this a great opportunity for me and the NOA.

The NOA recently celebrated its twentieth birthday. Over that time we have observed several important changes in the way companies contract and work together, but one of the most dramatic changes and opportunities has been the globalisation of services and the growth of offshoring.

The arrival of the Internet in the 1990s, the subsequent reduction in international communication costs and the arrival of the millennium bug all converged to create an environment in which companies started embracing the offshore option, whether by outsourcing to a partner or by going it alone. This has now developed to such an extent that many analysts believe that India has the highest quality software industry anywhere in the world, regardless of cost.

Forward-thinking economists are all in agreement about the importance to the entire world of growth in the BRICs region – not just for outsourcing services, but because these countries are developing from being relatively poor to being the economic champions of the twenty-first century. Mark's book has taken the BRICs hypothesis and asked what it means for outsourcing and services as these regions develop and offer services to the world. Listen carefully to the views expressed in this book as the Chief Executives commenting here have clearly spent a great deal of time thinking about the direction in which their industry is headed.

It's a valuable contribution to our understanding of the international outsourcing marketplace today and I offer my congratulations to Mark and Springer for publishing another book that helps us all understand this important subject.

July 2007

Martyn Hart
Chairman, The UK National Outsourcing Association
www.noa.co.uk

# Preface

I would like to thank you for choosing to purchase, borrow, or steal this book. I hope that you find it a useful addition to the wealth of knowledge and opinion on global technology-enabled services and offshoring. This is an area of international business that has exploded in importance since the millennium and I hope I can play a small part in the process of documenting what is going on and where we may be headed.

Why the BRICs region? Well, it helped that the Goldman Sachs analysis had focused so much attention on this region. Many economists have counter-argued that it is impossible to artificially connect the fate of these countries, yet to be honest I am not too worried about this. The BRICs analogy is better thought of as the economic development of those regions that are less developed – becoming wealthier and destroying poverty. The ongoing globalisation of services is creating a wealth of opportunity for regions to interact on a grander scale.

I don't think too much attention should be focused on the statist nature of the debate. We are not literally looking at a China versus India debate. The Indian government is now very supportive of the hi-tech industry there, but we all know that it is really the work of intelligent entrepreneurs such as Narayana Murthy who started this process despite the government - not because of it. Chinese companies will compete against Indian companies and they will compete against Brazilian companies and Russian companies, yet they may also buy from each other and collaborate. There is no black and white or agreed corporate behaviour based on national borders.

I put this book together because I felt that it was important to capture some important board level opinion on where the industry is headed. My own views are captured in the introduction and summary. As I am always meeting IT and outsourcing leaders and interviewing them, as well as working in various parts of the industry myself, I have developed some strong – and I believe, well-founded – opinions. I did not feel that there was anyone out there capturing this moment in time. We are at an important shift in emphasis now after the rapid growth spurt since the millennium. Offshore outsourcing is likely to change a great deal inside the next decade and those companies who still believe that the future is merely an extrapolation of the past are going to be left by the wayside.

A few people have been really instrumental in helping me to form some of these views. My friend Mahesh Ramachandran of fxaworld.com continues to give me new ideas all the time. I'm sure we will eventually write something together and enjoy even more nice dinners at *Sangeetha* in Harrow – possibly the best south Indian food in London. Dr Richard Sykes and I spent much of 2006 and early 2007 working on a book for the British Computer Society *'Global Services: Moving to a Level Playing Field'* (BCS 2007) and this has helped to hone many of my thoughts. Arun Aggarwal at Tata Consultancy Services – their EMEA head of consulting – gave me a great insight into what is going on in the industry from the viewpoint of a consultant, which is not really my natural environment. I grew up from the technical side of the business and never spent time huddled over 2x2 charts until I did my MBA!

The book flows together in a logical way. I introduce the topic and look at the Goldman Sachs research plus my own views on the potential influence of the BRICs – and offshoring in general. Then twelve senior executives give their view on the industry; first the Brazilians, then the Russians, then the Indians, and finally, the Chinese. I then conclude the book with a summary of the key thoughts from the contributors.

This book really focuses on the information technology industry and services that are enabled by IT. Although the original BRICs analysis was an economic study and prediction this is not really a book about economics – the focus is on the topic now known as 'offshoring' (or offshore outsourcing, there is a difference between outsourcing and offshoring, but they are related) and where this trend might be headed. The key information offered within this book is the board-level opinion from companies in all four regions of the BRICs – plus my own 'European' summary of it all. You can read the book straight through for a complete picture of the BRICs, or single out key chapters that might be of most interest to you based on the company or region.

As I have also written in my recent BCS book, writing a book is a thankless task. It means hours of solitary research and writing that stretch into days, weeks and months of effort even before worrying about whether anyone will actually like the result. To work on more than one book in a year is almost masochistic. For this book I even checked into a Brighton hotel for a week so I could get some editing done without any distraction, other than my iPod. Editing a text might seem easier than writing the entire book yourself – after all it's the contributors who do the research and write the text – yet the process of finding people, getting them on board with the project, guiding them, chasing them, and editing the final submissions from each author was immense. I never imagined how much work would be required to pull this together and so I expect my next work to be one in which I can lock myself away for a period of time and write without worrying about anyone else at all! I'd like to thank Katharina Wetzel-Vandai and Gabriele Keidel at Springer for being flexible about the manuscript delivery and helping to make this book a reality. It all took a lot longer than planned, but Springer was supportive enough to help out when it mattered – they probably see it from apologetic authors all the time.

Although I have just complained about how I needed to chase them, I'd like to thank all of the contributors, their assistants and their marketing teams. It has really been a great experience to become closer to all these organisations through our interactions and I appreciate their help. None of the organisations that contributed to this book paid me or were paid for their efforts. I chose the companies I wanted to include and approached them directly. Of course, a few companies got away because they did not have the resources available to put the chapter together within the timelines I offered them, but that's life. I managed to get a dozen great company leaders to invest time and effort in thinking about this industry and writing their thoughts from their own perspective.

It's always hard to draw up a list of the people who helped me to produce this book. I'm always talking to so many people all the time and travelling around the world, so I hope you will forgive me if I have forgotten something you said to me that I ended up using in some way. I like to thank my parents and my brother Rob and sister Caroline, Matilda, Ourah, Jadoo, Ben, Luke, and Lewis, John and Carol Uncle, my friend Siu Ling Choi, Sean Cook at Level 3 Creative, the British Computer Society, Intellect, The National Outsourcing Association, Professor Leslie Willcocks and Professor Patrick Humphreys at the London School of Economics, all the LSE Institute of Social Psychology PhD students, Dr Frédéric Adam at University College Cork, George Bell and Alan Hovell at London South Bank University, Professor Phanish Puranam at London Business School, Anil Kumar and BM Suri at CTR Manufacturing in Pune, Elizabeth Sparrow at the BCS, Hilary Robertson at Xansa, Andrew Fairburn at Hill & Knowlton, Kully Dhadda at Flame PR, Dr Mohan Kaul at the Commonwealth Business Council, Lord Karan Bilimoria and the Indo-British Partnership Network, Labour Friends of India Chair Stephen Pound MP, Vijay Kumar at fxaWorld plc, Vikas Pota at Saffron Chase, Mr S Jagadeesan at the High Commission of India in London... the list could go on because so many have helped, but at some point Springer would like the manuscript! Many apologies if you have helped me in any way, but have not enjoyed a mention ...

Special thanks need to go to Carl Stadler and Ravi Pandey at NIIT Technologies for once again supporting my writing efforts and funding the London launch party for this book. Once again, NIIT has demonstrated strong leadership in promoting their brand that is more astute and forward thinking than many other larger Indian companies. Rajendra Pawar had even insisted on personal meetings to discuss his chapter, even though his busy schedule whenever visiting London meant that a hotel breakfast room would be the only place we could meet.

Sunil Mehta of Nasscom died just before Christmas 2006 and I'd like to express a note of remembrance for him and his family. I had often interacted with Sunil on areas of research into India and the technology industry and for him to die so suddenly at the age of 41 is a reminder to us all of how precious each day really is.

Of course, the most special thanks must go to my long-suffering wife Nobumi. She has really helped me to get this book from idea to publication, even as she was completely swamped by her own research for the Open University in Milton Keynes. Thanks Nobby – domou arigatou gozaimashita!

London, August 2007                                  Mark Kobayashi-Hillary
                                                     www.markhillary.com

# Table of Contents

Foreword ................................................................. VII

Preface ..................................................................... IX

**Introduction**

*Mark Kobayashi-Hillary*

The BRICs Report ......................................................... 2
Offshoring 2.0 ............................................................. 4
Virtual Servers ............................................................ 6
Virtual Applications ..................................................... 6
Virtual Architecture ..................................................... 7
Virtual Communications ................................................ 7
Virtual Services .......................................................... 8
Summary .................................................................. 9
The Web 2.0 Generation ............................................... 10

## PART I: BRAZIL

**An IT Giant Goes Global**

*Dalton Luz*

The Origin of the IT Industry in Brazil ............................. 18
Expertise in Banking Systems ........................................ 18
Brazil's Advantages as an Offshoring Destination ............... 19
Reasons Why Brazilian Companies Are Expanding Abroad ..... 21
Clouds on the Horizon ................................................. 23

## Driving Value Up
*Thiago Turchetti Maia*

Introduction..........................................................................................25
The Trend Towards High-Value Services .........................................26
Service and Relationship Models ......................................................28
Vendor Selection ................................................................................34
Brazil's Path to Becoming a Global Player ......................................38
References..........................................................................................40
Acknowledgements............................................................................40

# PART II: RUSSIA

## Reflecting on the Future to Understand the Present
*Arkadiy Dobkin*

The Origins of Offshoring .................................................................43
Offshoring at Present .........................................................................44
What the Future Holds for Offshoring..............................................46
Russia's IT Industry at Present .........................................................49
Prospects for Russia's IT Industry....................................................54

## Outsourcing as a Strategic Business Model for "Futurised" Organizations
*Dmitry Loschinin*

Introduction........................................................................................57
The Outsourcing SuperHighway .......................................................58
To Russia, with Love.........................................................................60
But Why Russia? ...............................................................................61
IT Focus..............................................................................................61
Economic Flexibility .........................................................................62
Outstanding Talent.............................................................................63
Faster Time to Market .......................................................................63

Futurised Outsourcing Firms Map to Futurised Companies ...................... 64
Building an Industry BRIC by BRIC ........................................................... 65
Caution: Changing Road Conditions Ahead ............................................... 67
Acknowledgements ....................................................................................... 69

## Eastern Europe as Most Promising Market
*Alexander Egorov*

New Old Opportunity .................................................................................. 72
Russian Federation Economic Overview ................................................... 77
Russia in the Global Economy .................................................................... 79
Living Standards in Russia .......................................................................... 80
Business Culture in Russia .......................................................................... 81
Government Support for Software Exports ............................................... 81
Maturing Trends ........................................................................................... 82
Conclusion .................................................................................................... 83

## Dreaming with BRICs
*Dmitry Ponomarev*

Review of the BRICs Economic Predictions ............................................. 87
Why BRICs? .................................................................................................. 89
The Russian IT Industry in Numbers ......................................................... 91
Russian IT Export Industry Expansion to the Regions ............................ 97
Conclusion .................................................................................................. 101

# PART III: INDIA

## Globalisation – There Is Much to Gain
*Shiv Nadar*

Globalisation: What Does It Mean for You? ........................................... 106
Unparalleled Growth, Increased Inequality ............................................. 107
How Deeply Is the World Integrated? ...................................................... 107
Advanced Economies Can Help ............................................................... 108

Promote Globalisation, Promote Peace ................................................. 109
India Can Make the Difference............................................................. 109
India and HCL: Having Run the Marathon, Now Ready to Sprint.......... 112
Leadership Through Value-Centricity .................................................... 113
Beyond the Numbers ............................................................................. 114
Does Globalisation Reduce National Sovereignty?................................. 115

## Sourcing Without Borders – Sourcing in a Flattening World
*Nandan M. Nilekani*

From Offshore Outsourcing to Strategic Global Sourcing ..................... 118
Sourcing to Compete in the Flat World ................................................. 120
Becoming a Flat World Service Provider .............................................. 124
The Next Level of Global Sourcing........................................................ 130

## The World's BPO Hub
*Ananda Mukerji*

An Emerging Global Power................................................................... 133
Rightshoring .......................................................................................... 135
Standardisation of Services.................................................................... 136
Higher Value Outsourcing...................................................................... 137
Challenges to India's Supremacy ........................................................... 138
Reliance on Established Markets............................................................ 139
India's Internal Challenges .................................................................... 140
Overcoming Common Misconceptions and Attitudes............................ 141
Security .................................................................................................. 143
The Future for Outsourcing ................................................................... 143

## Indian Offshoring – Building Sustainable Excellence
*Rajendra S. Pawar*

The Century of the Mind: India's Rich Heritage ................................... 148
Mind Power, the New Reality................................................................ 150

Education: Revolution Through Pioneering Partnerships.........................151
The Importance of the PPP Model..................................................................152
Work: Mentality of Service and Excellence ................................................154
The Changing Customer Climate ...................................................................154
Innovation: Leading the 21$^{st}$ Century Organisation.................................156

# PART IV: CHINA

## China – An Offshoring Leader?
*Remi D. Vespa*

History of China ..................................................................................................164
Economy ................................................................................................................166
Country Infrastructure.........................................................................................169
Population and Workforce .................................................................................170
The Diaspora and Their Impact .......................................................................172
The IT Market in China .....................................................................................172
Panorama of Chinese Suppliers ........................................................................174
Conclusion .............................................................................................................175

## The Second Shift to China
*Jiren Liu*

The Second Shift..................................................................................................177
Why China? ..........................................................................................................179
The Time of Integration .....................................................................................181

## Conclusion
*Mark Kobayashi-Hillary*

Brazil.......................................................................................................................185
Russia......................................................................................................................186
India ........................................................................................................................188
China.......................................................................................................................191
Outsourcing Developments................................................................................192

Process Requirements ..................................................................... 194
Tactical Outsourcing ..................................................................... 195
Strategic Outsourcing .................................................................... 196
Transformational Outsourcing ...................................................... 197
The Key Drivers of Outsourcing Today ........................................ 198
A Final Word ................................................................................ 208

**Bibliography** ................................................................... 209

**About the Editor** ............................................................ 211

**About the Contributors** ................................................. 213

# Introduction

*Mark Kobayashi-Hillary*
*National Outsourcing Association, London, UK*

*"BRIC or BRICs are terms used to refer to the combination of Brazil, Russia, India, and China. General consensus is that the term was first prominently used in a thesis of the Goldman Sachs investment bank. The main point of this 2003 paper was to argue that the economies of the BRICs are rapidly developing and by the year 2050 will eclipse most of the current richest countries of the world."*

Extract from the Wikipedia entry for 'BRICs'

How can a subject such as the BRICs be introduced and summarised in a way that will not date immediately? It's a question I have asked myself as I prepared to put this introduction together. Of course, I am focusing only on the technology and technology-enabled services sector – the hi-tech offshoring that has enabled India to develop a reputation for technology – rather than just curry – amongst the western public.

The millennium bug was the catalyst that sparked this great wave of change. Because every company in every country using any form of computing equipment could not be quite sure of whether it would be working correctly on January 1, 2000, there was a requirement to check everything. With a deadline that could not be changed that meant that there was a resource crunch – quite literally there were countries such as the US with not enough skilled people to check the systems. Enter India and the rest is history, as the share prices of the major Indian service companies since that time clearly demonstrate. Once they got a foot in the door and demonstrated the ability to serve customers remotely, there was no going back.

Yet, this trip down memory lane merely explains that India is now a dominant force in offshored technology services and does not indicate the importance of other regions and their potential, not least the other members of the BRICs.

This book is really all about the twelve senior executives who took the time out from their schedule to contribute. It's a great pleasure for me to be able to marshal together their views into a single volume in this way, as they are the people really changing the industry – not the commentators or analysts. There is a great detail of debate on the ongoing development of the BRICs region, and the combined might of India and China – 'Chindia' – in particular. Before moving on to the contributed chapters, I want to briefly introduce the original BRICs analysis by Goldman Sachs. I will then explore some of the present trends in global sourcing and finally will explore some ideas on the changing nature of the industry. Offshoring technology itself is very much tied to the industry that it serves and there are a number of innovations changing the entire concept of global services and company interaction with customers that I feel will impact on the development of this market.

## The BRICs Report

On the first of October 2003, the global investment bank Goldman Sachs published a research report titled 'Dreaming with BRICs: The Path to 2050'. Jim O'Neill, a global economist at Goldman Sachs, led this research programme and has been credited as the father of the BRICs acronym, although it is worth stating that Dominic Wilson and Roopa Purushothaman are the credited authors of the report. Though there are examples of the term CRIBs being used by academics before and since, it is O'Neill's version that has become shorthand for the new economic superpowers.

The report forecasts that the BRICs region would encompass over forty percent of the world population and hold a combined GDP [PPP] of 14.951 trillion dollars over the projected timescale – which is to the middle of this century. Goldman Sachs never presented the BRICs as a potential economic or political trading bloc, but the exercise of studying their projected economic growth and global contribution over the decades to come does indicate that this is a region to watch.

One of the major reasons is the way the four countries slot together in different ways. China and India are already beginning to dominate global manufacturing and services, with that dominance set to grow. Brazil and Russia have abundant supplies of raw materials (soy, iron ore…) and energy resources (oil, natural gas…). Combine all four nations and you create a powerhouse than can supply energy and raw materials, to the world and also operate as a back office and manufacturing hub to offshore companies. The governments in all four countries have recognised this potential for growth and are all engaged in various measures, the most basic of which is to embrace western capitalism as a way of doing business. The concept and adoption of democracy is variable between the four, with China being the most obviously removed from western ideas of democracy, but this has not prevented Chinese companies from doing business with international clients.

If the BRICs were to join together and form a unique trading bloc of countries that are not even geographical neighbours, but complementary in other ways, then they could create a formidable rival to the present world-order and established power structures.

The initial report stresses that the demographic situation in India gives the country the potential to grow fastest. Working-age population decline in Russia and China will take place much earlier than in India and Brazil, with India enjoying the most favourable ratio of working-age citizens to others.

In 2004, Goldman Sachs released a follow-up report to the original study titled 'The BRICs and Global Markets: Crude, Cars and Capital'. This update went a step further and examined how the growth of these four nations would impact on global markets generally. This report estimates that the BRIC economies share of world growth could rise from 20 per cent in 2003 to more than 40 per cent in 2025. An interesting estimate that gives a clear indication of what this growth could means for citizens of these countries is the Goldman Sachs assertion that between 2005 and 2015 over 800 million people in these countries will have crossed the annual income threshold of $3,000. In 2025, it is calculated that approximately 200 million people in these economies will have annual incomes above $15,000.

Just think about that increase in wealth, and on the immense scale that we are considering here – India and China alone comprise a third of humanity. There will be an extreme increase in demand for luxury goods and non-essentials, especially attractive branded products.

Although this growth indicates immense economic might on national terms, some of this can be attributed to the large population of the BRICs region. Goldman Sachs estimates that by 2025 the income per capita in the G6 region will exceed $35,000 – only 24 million people in the BRIC economies will have a similar income to this, so levels of worker pay are not about to harmonise.

The report goes into more detail on the use of energy – and waste of energy in countries such as India – and the relative unimportance of the capital markets in these countries when compared to the bourses in the US and Europe. However this book is more of an attempt to examine the importance of growth in the BRICs region for the global trade in technology enabled services, so there is little value in repeating the economic predictions verbatim. All the Goldman Sachs analysis is freely available from their website: www.gs.com. What is of more concern in this context are the issues and trends taking place within the international sourcing marketplace.

## Offshoring 2.0

In 2006, IDC reported that the global spend on technology – including IT services, BPO, packaged software, and hardware – was around $1.5tr. That figure grew by 7.7 per cent since the previous year and IT services plus BPO account for about 70 per cent of the entire total. Clearly the market for IT services, and services enabled by technology, is huge and continues to grow.

But this is not really a book about immediate trends, the aim is to explore the BRICs hypothesis within the context of IT services. The Internet is potentially a better source of information on the availability of staff in any particular city or location. However, do I want to explore some ideas I have on changes in the underlying business model of IT services. There are changes in hardware design, software design and the way remote services are marketed and priced that could change the direction this industry is headed. One important mantra that I think needs to be considered by anyone considering offshoring is:

> Country, Company, Change.

These three 'C's are important to remember, as the debate of offshoring is often reduced to discussions on which country is more suitable than another for a particular business. This is generally too simplistic. Every company seeking help with a process and considering offshoring as a solution must at the very least consider the country criteria (tax regime, stability, employee supply etc.) alongside the actual companies being considered.

Companies contract with companies, not countries, so it's important to remember this in the approach to an offshoring decision. I have certainly experienced the same question over and over again – "I am flying to India next week, can you recommend a company that can perform service X?" This is a concern because it demonstrates a lack of due diligence on the part of the company trying to decide how and where to offshore. If organisations can be so casual about the search for a partner then they have probably not analysed their processes on the inside either, so a situation where ill-defined plans meet less-than-suitable partners is very possible.

In the context of this book, my CCC concern is that companies such as Politec or Luxoft may not even be considered for some contracts – simply because they are not Indian. I'm all in favour of a more genuine level playing field where each company can compete with the other, regardless of where they are headquartered. I'm sure that Dalton or Dmitry would be able to promote their advantages in any head-to-head comparison with NIIT or HCL.

The third C – change – could also be termed innovation. This industry moves fast and expectations from consumers change even faster. Although IT services is essentially a business to business (B2B) environment, the consumer has embraced the Internet and turned it into a robust platform used for all manner of services – the B2B world needs to learn a little more from the changes taking place online at present so some of these innovations might change service delivery from remote locations. Some specific changes taking place right now that are certain to have an effect on this industry are virtualisation and interactivity with service consumers.

Anyway, what kind of technology does the modern enterprise need today? Let's think back just a few years to the distant days of the 1990s. You would certainly need some PCs, servers and a local-area-network to offer storage and print capabilities, fax hardware, telephones and a PBX for the telephone extensions.

It sounds like quite a lot, and that's before starting on the software requirements. All those pesky licenses for office automation software and email clients.

What about the modern environment? If you started a new company today then what infrastructure would you install? You could probably get away with nothing more than a fat pipe to the Internet, plus laptops using wifi and mobile phones.

Services such as Skype or Vonage can utilise the Internet bandwidth for telephone calls with the mobile as a trusty last resort. Storage and backups can use the facilities of your ISP and if you start using online office tools, such as the office and email suite provided by Google then your co-workers can share documents and email clients using a robust delivery platform known as the Internet. This isn't a dream; it's a reality for every small knowledge-based company that has started over the past couple of years. If you could start from scratch would you buy licenses for each user in the way larger companies often seem to?

There is an increasingly virtual environment within modern technology. I would like to outline some of these virtualisations, and thank Dr. Richard Sykes as this is essentially a great deal of his thought. The virtual environment has been developing across five key areas of technology:

- Virtual servers
- Virtual applications
- Virtual architecture
- Virtual communications
- Virtual services

## Virtual Servers

The first impact of the new diversity of specialised software systems has been to enable the virtualisation of the server. Classically, a server has always been run on one operating system – whether proprietary such as Windows, Mac OS X, or an open system such as Linux – and the applications running on them have been accordingly restricted. In practical terms, virtualisation now means that different operating systems and the applications that run on them can now be managed on a single machine – or flexibly across a number of machines.

Virtualisation software manages the computing power available in a highly flexible fashion against operating rules designed to optimise the use of capacity. The computing engine can be transformed from a rigid to a flexible resource allowing it to change and respond rapidly while still offering high levels of productivity.

## Virtual Applications

The second impact of the new diversity of specialised software systems has been to enable a similar virtualisation of the design and structuring of the applications systems. This emergent software capability, known as Business Process Management (BPM), is a framework of specialised software systems that enable business processes to be both monitored and managed – automatically or by manual intervention, as needed.

BPM can enable the easy integration of business transactions across multiple application systems, delivering their end-to-end alignment as and when required. The important capability to deliver straight through order processing, as one concrete example of this approach in action, can now be implemented with relative ease.

By breaking the stranglehold of tightly coupled business applications BPM allows a flexible structure of loosely coupled processes, the applications equivalent of the first virtualisation.

## Virtual Architecture

The third impact of the new diversity of specialised software systems has been to enable the virtualisation of the architecting of the diversity of components that are assembled to create the contemporary IT infrastructure – processing power, data storage, and network bandwidth. This emergent structure of industry standards is labelled Service-Oriented Architecture (SOA). It is in essence an application architecture, in which all functions are defined using a descriptive language, with interfaces that can be invoked, or activated, to create interconnecting applications delivering business processes. Each interaction between the functions is designed to be independent of each and every other interaction – and the interconnecting protocols for communicating devices are specified to be interface-independent and interfaces themselves are computing platform independent.

SOA focuses on the business solution and not the IT platform. Clearly it is a key enabler of the BPM promise – the former creating the means for the latter to be delivered. The working assumption of both is a move from tightly coupled to loosely coupled systems. More importantly, the combination of both creates the environment for the architecting of systems around the specific requirements of the business objectives to be delivered.

## Virtual Communications

The virtualisation of data communication across a wide diversity of frequencies from cabled to wireless has changed the communications environment. Tools such as Wifi, wimax, Bluetooth and emerging Voice over IP standards are all shaping new innovations in communication.

The speed of innovation and development here is shaped by a complex mix of hardware development, software development and the development of agreed industry standards and protocols and, in the wireless world, regulatory regimes around the exploitation of the radiofrequency spectrum.

Exploitation of Internet data transmission protocols and new software structures has brought to market the 'Voice over IP' capabilities being exploited by recent business start-ups such as Skype and Vonage. These systems exploit the operational reality that the digitisation of voice as data packages to be switched and transmitted over the Internet (loose coupling) is so much more efficient in utilisation of the fixed assets of the telecoms network than classic open-line analogue telephony that it can competitively undercut established services by major margins. The telecommunication companies are responding with major programmes of reinvestment in new-generation digital networks based on the exploitation of virtualisation to allow very much higher productivity operations.

## Virtual Services

The web has matured as a robust public utility. The consumer imperative for new and improved services has been the prime driver behind this process. The prime enablers have included the development of increasingly reliable sever farms and data centres whose costs of operation have plummeted; increasingly reliable network capabilities, capacities, and asset productivity driving down bandwidth costs sharply.

At the same time, the consumer imperative has speeded the development of broadband access to the web. Competition between the cable and telecommunications industries has accelerated the process. Broadband access has now become essentially free in the UK, with TV providers such as Sky bundling access to any TV subscriber or retailers such as Carphone Warehouse offering it to phone customers in bundled packages.

Whether access is by wired or wireless means, the web has emerged as a natural delivery highway for a diversity of relatively straightforward digital consumer services – the transmission of email to music files to films and video and so on, to the remote accessing of online services such as Google. This has in turn promoted and fostered a range of new industry standards and protocols designed to further improve and extend the web's operational flexibility in servicing a wider arena of more complex and sophisticated digital services – this fifth virtualisation.

These new open standards and protocols have created a framework that allows web services to share business logic, data and processes (the structured core of business applications) through interfaces across the web – applications interfacing applications, rather than users. The standards and protocols ensure that different applications from different sources can communicate with each other without time-consuming custom coding, and because all communication is in the web language of XML, web services are not tied to any one particular operating system or programming language. These open standards allow data to be tagged, transferred through a messaging protocol that is operating-system independent, and provide standard languages to describe and list the services available on central catalogues. So web services allow corporate organisations to intercommunicate business logic, data and processes without any requirement for a specific knowledge of what systems lie behind protective firewalls.

These same standards are in the process of being actively developed to provide security structures for web services, including encryption and digital signatures. Computers can now talk to computers in a far easier and more open way, allowing services to be more easily constructed and merged with others. Typically the merger of online services in this way is termed a 'mash-up'. Examples include services such as the classified advertising site CraigsList using Google Maps to help users find where that rental property they are reading about is located. Another very common service deployed in this way is credit card authorisation; why construct all the technology required to perform this process when open standards allow your own site to call on the services of another?

A leading example of the potential for web services in the corporate arena has been the success of Salesforce.com, who offer a family of integrated and fully customisable customer relationship management services that are available on demand – all delivered over the web. The core services include the range of capabilities required to support effective sales work, including sales force automation, customer service and support, analytics, offered within a framework that allows straightforward assembly and self-customisation. The architecture of the computing platform that Salesforce.com utilises ('AppExchange') has more recently been exploited to allow an a widening range of third-party software vendors to both customise and integrate the Salesforce.com applications and to build, publish and share their own enterprise applications as services on the Saleforce.com platform.

## Summary

These five various forms of virtualisation lie at the root of the switch from being dependent on technology – and the limitations of specific technology – to the ability to start thinking more in terms of business services. The combination of BPM and SOA changes the game for enterprise software and hardware design. Business requirements start shaping IT design in a way that should have happened many years ago, but it now forced because of the way the architecture is constructed.

The communications revolution liberates the individual worker to operate to their best advantage in both time and space. The shift from the paradigm of the tightly coupled to the loosely coupled not only enables this greater flexibility, agility and responsiveness, but also provides the means of working assets harder and to higher levels of effectiveness and efficiency.

There is a major revolution in business IT taking place around us right now and it is the shift to virtualisation, in its many forms. The consumerisation of IT since the late 1990s (acceptance of the web) has speeded the development of the Internet as a public utility; a platform for genuine service access and delivery.

The five virtualisations have been releasing the world of applied IT from the historic constraints that ensured technology-specified application scope, restricting the opportunity for business-shaped, business responsive application systems. The new freedom to deliver application-specified technology scope are – in parallel – enabling the development of new generations of flexible enterprise business systems deliverable as services, including over the net.

## The Web 2.0 Generation

Myspace, Bebo, Facebook, Youtube, Flickr, Blogs, Second Life, Podcasts. Is your company actively engaged in the 'blogosphere' or do you still think that interactive social networks are for teenagers to burn the hours they used to spend watching Neighbours on TV? Is it even possible for corporate IT to engage with social networks without selling out and possibly even causing brand damage in the headlong rush to 'keep it real'?

Key attributes shared by all of these sites and methods of sharing information include transparency and immediacy. That's exactly what Mike Scott, UK head of innovation for Tata Consultancy Services, was looking for when he wanted to find a way of keeping customers informed about research at the Peterborough-based innovation lab he heads: "We could have started publishing yet another glossy corporate newsletter, but they usually go straight into the bin, they are expensive, and the information flow is one-way."[1] Scott produced a new blog to not only update customers on what TCS is doing, but to also stimulate online debate on innovation. He hired technology journalists to contribute and encouraged TCS executives to comment, both on the blog and through audio podcasts.

In their book 'Wikinomics' authors Don Tapscott and Anthony D. Williams (Tapscott & Williams 2006) argue that increasing interaction with clients through interactive web technologies encourages a transparency that can have positive long-term business benefits: "Recently, smart companies have been rethinking openness, and this is beginning to affect a number of important functions, including human resources, innovation, industry standards, and communications. Companies were closed in their attitudes towards networking, sharing, and encouraging self-organisation, in large part because conventional wisdom says that companies compete by holding their most coveted resources close to their chest." Tapscott and Williams go on to argue: "Today companies that make their boundaries porous to external ideas and human capital outperform companies that rely solely on their internal resources and capabilities."

This resonates with the experience of Scott at TCS: "For a very low initial investment we have created an extremely collaborative environment. Globally we have nineteen innovation labs and interaction between them has improved because of the blog, along with the improved communication with those reading the information – who might never have interacted with TCS if this was on glossy paper."

It's not just companies that are exploring this potential for reaching out to interested collaborators; politicians are dipping a toe in the water too. British MP and would-be leader of the Labour party Michael Meacher ran his ultimately unsuccessful MM4PM campaign almost entirely on various social networking sites. Meacher's campaign manager Dan Judelson expains: "The Labour leadership election will be the first major party oriented contest involving social network sites. We can expect all three major political parties to draw lessons from them for the next general election campaign. The interesting thing about Facebook, Live Journal and Myspace is that they have the potential to put campaigns in places where a target audience already is – we are going to them, rather than designing an expensive looking platform with any number of interactive plug-ins to make it look more interesting and hoping voters will turn up. The test will be to see if political campaigns are accepted in social network sites and

---

[1] Mike Scott, Personal interview with the author, April 2007.

how many people attracted to online campaigns will be attracted to knocking on the doors of voters on polling day."[2]

Meacher's tenacity and willingness to explore new ground has to be admired, especially when his myspace page does not hide the fact that he is 67, rather than 17. On opening, his myspace launches into the song 'I have a dream' by Brixton hip hop artist Logic, and one of his other musical favourites is 'Hospital Beds' by the Cold War Kids.

But beyond the use of blogs to reach out to interested consumers or voters, how else can companies use a collaborative web environment to their advantage? Mahesh Ramachandran, a non-executive director of foreign exchange currency firm FXaWorld explains the rationale behind an initiative his company has launched on youtube: "We decided to run an online competition that utilises youtube as a delivery platform. Basically, we asked the online community to upload their own videos to youtube with the promise of a ten thousand dollar cash prize for the video that best captures the spirit of our company."[3] As a peer-to-peer company that directly connects a currency buyer to seller using the Internet, FXaWorld can already be viewed as an innovative organisation, but wasn't Ramachandran afraid of people making spoof videos or in some way abusing the competition? "Not at all. We have seen some excellent videos being produced, which we can now use for our own marketing purposes. If anyone wanted to go to the effort of making a negative spoof then it would in fact be quite complimentary – all online publicity is good publicity!"

But the networking and collaborative possibilities of the Internet don't have to be harnessed from the boardroom for the initiatives to be useful. A Californian college student and former Starbucks employee, Andrew Gonis, created a myspace group named 'Starbucks HQ' 18 months ago – now he has 4,000 members. The group was not created or endorsed by the company itself, Gonis wanted to create an unofficial environment where colleagues could connect with their international peers and share experience and ideas.

Gonis explains his motives: "I think there is no way you can go wrong when you connect employees who share the same passion for your company. When you put people like that together, their passions ignite and they feed off one another." He goes on to say: "Myspace and similar sites 'humanise' your brand or company. Rather than having to look at a corporate 'dot com', the viewer is on equal ground with the company because

---

[2] Dan Judelson, email interview with the author, April 2007.
[3] Mahesh Ramachandran, personal interview with the author, March 2007.

myspace is something they can identify with. I love the company. Even though I am not employed by Starbucks at the moment, I still feel connected for some reason."[4]

Tony Virdi is a managing director in the consulting division of IT services company Atos Origin. He recently asked one of the new graduates entering the company to study the online virtual world 'Second Life' to see if there is any value in them getting more involved in this virtual society.

The initial study proved positive and now Tony is recruiting a larger team of researchers to live and breathe Second Life, and report back on longer-term opportunities in this new world for Atos Origin.

Tony explains his reasons for taking such a methodical approach to what many might still see as an unimportant 'virtual' community: "The first thing about this is that we are continually looking at our solution portfolio. We look at the ideas that are winners and losers and this idea is closely linked to product innovation. Second Life is just a different way of dealing and working with people and businesses. We have observed some other technology companies on there – though not too many yet – and some product-based companies such as Reebok are advertising there."[5]

Tony doesn't have a specific objective for the Second Life research project, Atos Origin just wants to understand what is going on: "We have looked at the environment in some detail already and realised that a lot of real money is transacted within Second Life. I don't really know where all of this will lead, but there is something in it; so many people are involved and interacting in this environment. I think that those of us used to a certain way of doing business are just not attuned to this environment yet."

Atos Origin has already created a virtual group of existing employees who are regularly to be found living out an alternate existence within Second Life and they are actively recruiting full-time researchers for their detailed examination of the real possibilities of the environment – beyond the usual media hype. They want to determine how to purchase some real estate in Second Life and what kind of services can work for the organisation in a virtual space. Tony said: "We need to do this detailed research ourselves to really tap into the way it works, not just gather some opinions from a newspaper. I know that my daughter is fifteen and she is on all the social networking sites. The way that kids interact with each other through this medium is amazing – this is the way people are going to do business in future."

---

[4] Andrew Gonis, email interview with the author, March 2007.
[5] Tony Virdi, telephone interview with the author, April 2007.

It's clear that online collaboration is the next killer app. Web 2.0 has already arrived and whether you are a B2B organisation with a maximum of 100 possible customers, or a retailer with millions of customers, tapping into the creativity of your employees and customers through established web platforms is an essential key to future innovation. The Web 2.0 phenomenon of interactivity and collaboration that allows viewers to create and improve the web sites they interact with can be of immense use to organisations, provided they learn how to engage in an open and transparent manner. Corporate blogs that capture the ongoing thoughts of a senior executive can be a fascinating insight into an organisation, but the turgid style of some suggests a triple-layer editing process to ensure nothing damaging (or interesting) is published. If you can't embrace openness then attempting to interact with a social networking environment as a company will probably fail. There are many benefits to making it work:

- Encouraging interaction at all levels of an organisation, particularly useful in large multinational companies.

- Encouraging collaboration with business partners and end-consumers through easy and direct channels – anyone can access the web to read a blog or view a video on youtube or picture on flickr.

- Encourage more active participation and two-way information flows between company and customer.

- Reduce the cost of collaboration and information. The required tools already exist on the public Internet and are robust enough to be deployed as corporate solutions.

- As Tony Virdi suggested, sometimes there is no immediate benefit, but just a feeling that a particular technology is going to go *somewhere*. If you are not actively exploring what is going on then you will only ever follow the curve – if you survive the change.

So there it is. I think the IT services industry is being changed through a combination of Countries, Companies, and Change. The change is immensely important as it transcends the region of delivery and company offering a service. However, the BRICs concept remains important as shorthand for us to understand who are the new regional players in global services. In the nineteenth century, Britain dominated global trade, culture and politics. In the twentieth century this was achieved by the United States. We are just entering the twenty-first century now, but it already looks like this could be the BRICs century.

# Part I: Brazil

# An IT Giant Goes Global

*Dalton Luz*
*CEO, Politec USA, Reston VA, USA*

Brazil's economy does not always garner the same attention in the press as China and India, the largest and fastest growing of the BRICs economies. The picture is worse when it comes to Brazil's IT sector, which is surprisingly close in size to India's in revenue terms. Nonetheless the Brazilian economy, and particularly its IT sector, is clearly important enough to merit the same attention as China, India, and Russia when studying the world's leading developing economies.

The BRICS report finds that Brazil's economic growth in the coming decades is likely to be substantially slower than growth in the other BRICs countries. In itself this is not that surprising, since Brazil's economy is already fairly well developed in comparison with the other three countries. But the report goes on to state that even to achieve the relatively modest growth assumptions made in the report, significant structural changes will be needed to Brazil's economy.[1] Since the BRICs report was published in 2003 – the same year Brazil's current president took office – overall economic growth in Brazil has not only remained substantially lower than that of the other three BRICs countries, but has also lagged behind much of the rest of Latin America. A big reason for this is Brazil's huge and growing public sector, which keeps the country's interest rates high. To date, the country's current administration has done nothing to reverse this trend. Brazil's economic growth doesn't need to match China's in order for the country to be successful, and the growth of Brazil's GDP does not necessarily correlate with the growth of the IT sector, particularly where service exports are concerned. Nonetheless the current macroeconomic picture in Brazil influences our own outlook and decision making, and like the authors of the study we remain guardedly optimistic.

---

[1] Wilson, D., Purushothaman, R., 2003. Dreaming with BRICs: The Path To 2050. Goldman Sachs.

## The Origin of the IT Industry in Brazil

The Brazilian IT industry has developed along a quite different path from the other three BRICs countries. Unlike the IT industries in most developing countries, which have grown by focusing on exports of software and services, the vast majority of IT services and products developed in Brazil have up until now been aimed at the Brazilian market. This is highlighted by the fact that by 2001 the Brazilian software industry was valued at around $7.7 billion, on par with the Indian and Chinese markets, but exports were just $100 million, or about 2 per cent of the total market.[2]

The roots of the Brazilian IT industry can be traced back decades, and in fact Politec was founded in 1970, not long after the beginning of the mainframe era. Most of the rapid growth in the sector in Brazil occurred during the 1990s, following the liberalisation of the economy in the first part of the decade and the introduction of the Real Plan in 1994, which rapidly stabilised the economy and brought inflation down to reasonable levels. As barriers to foreign competition were reduced or eliminated, Brazilian firms were forced to focus on core competencies to stay in the game, and as a result began to outsource software development of custom applications and other important IT functions. Hardware prices also dropped as import tariffs dropped, fueling even more demand for software.[3]

Of course economic liberalisation in the 1990s also made software imports cheaper, and by 2001 these imports had grown to about $1 billion annually.[4] But software imports to Brazil still consist largely of off-the-shelf applications, while Brazilian firms have been able to expand their share in business-critical custom applications and related consulting services.

## Expertise in Banking Systems

A good example of critical custom application development by the Brazilian IT sector is the country's payment and check clearing system. By 1993 the annual rate of inflation in Brazil was close to 2,500%, or about 50% a month. The Brazilian government initiated a structural solution to hyperin-

---

[2] Botelho, A.J., Stefanuto, G., and Veloso, F., 2005. The Brazilian Software Industry. In Arora, A. and Gambardella, A., From Underdogs to Tigers: The Rise and Growth of the Software Industry in Some Emerging Economies. Oxford University Press.
[3] Ibid.
[4] Ibid.

flation with the Real Plan in 1994, but prior to that a technical solution had been developed. The indexing of bank accounts and other financial instruments to inflation drove demand for a highly automated and efficient mechanism for making payments and transferring funds – in other words for getting rid of cash as quickly as possible.[5]

In 1993, just before the Real Plan took effect, the Brazilian payments system cleared about 350 million checks per month, and checks drawn and presented in most larger cities were cleared within 24 hours.[6] The efficiency of Brazil's 1990s-era payment system remains unmatched today even in much of the developed world.

An even more ambitious new payments system went live in April 2002. Whereas the original system was primarily focused on increasing speed and efficiency, the new one aimed for further efficiency gains while simultaneously reducing risks. At the heart of the new payments system is the STR – Sistema de Transferência de Reservas (Reserves Transfer System), which handles real-time interbank funds transfer and is operated by the Brazilian Central Bank.

The development of the new payments system took only 1 year and 9 months. Brazil's indigenous IT skills and, ironically, experience with hyperinflation have been cited as key success factors for the initiative.[7] Brazil's expertise in IT solutions for financial services has recently been singled out by A.T. Kearney as one of the country's key strong points in the global outsourcing market.[8]

## Brazil's Advantages as an Offshoring Destination

Brazil is not typically the first location that comes to mind when one considers destinations for offshore IT work – but a number of unique factors set it apart from the competition in the offshore market, including the other BRICS countries. These factors include Brazil's geography, workforce

---

[5] Listfield, R., Montes-Negret, F., 1996. Brazil's Efficient Payment System – A Legacy Of High Inflation. The World Bank.

[6] Ibid.

[7] Larbalestier, B., Danbury, M., 2005. Brazil – Building A World Class Payments Infrastructure. The Association for the Promotion of the Brazilian Software Excellence (SOFTEX).

[8] Desenvolvimento de uma Agenda Estratégica para o Setor de „IT Offshore Outsourcing". A.T. Kearney, unpublished study for BRASSCOM, November 2005.

demographics, the sophistication of its IT environment, and the country's relatively well-developed market for goods and services.

## Time Zone

Most of Brazil is only two time zones away from the US East Coast, putting Brazil far closer to the US in terms of time than any of the other BRICS countries. Brazil's time zone creates a number of distinct advantages for the US market. First, since more of the working day overlaps between the US and Brazil, real-time collaboration becomes much easier than it is between, for example, workers in the US and India – which lies 10.5 time zones east of the US East Coast. Ad-hoc collaboration, consultation, and emergency response are all much easier when onshore and offshore teams have similar natural schedules. Nightshift staffing, as Indian firms must do to service US clients in real time, is only a partial solution, as nightshifts not only increase costs, but also are unattractive to most workers. Executives travelling between the US and Brazil also experience little or no jet lag, and while this seems a minor point relative to the other factors involved in an outsourcing project, we know from experience that this point alone can be enough to make or break a business deal.

## Geopolitics

Unlike each of the other three BRICS countries, Brazil has no ongoing military conflicts or major territorial disputes with any of its neighbours. Regional tensions impact not only foreign investment decisions but also currency markets and credit ratings – and of the four BRICs countries, Brazil is arguably the least likely to become involved in a major regional or international conflict in the next few decades.For many of our clients, minimising geopolitical risk means having operations in more than one region of the world. As a result, there is room in the market for Brazilian companies to provide services to firms that already have substantial and successful offshore operations in other parts of the globe. This trend has not gone unnoticed by the major Indian players in IT outsourcing – Tata Consulting Services has already launched a joint venture with Brazilian firm TBA. As of 2006 the operation has about 1,000 employees, and according to the company is the fastest growing division outside India.[9] For the

---

[9] Teletime Editors, 2006. Tata quer duplicar equipe na América Latina. www.teletime.com.br.

same reasons Politec has recently entered cooperative agreements with outsourcing firms in both China and India.

## Demographics

While Brazil is only the third largest of the BRICs countries, its working age population is projected to continue increasing to about 2020, longer than China's or Russia's.[10] This also means that the number of graduates entering the workforce will continue increasing as the number of new graduates decreases in China and Russia. However India's working-age share of population is projected to increase longer than any of the other BRICs countries, and decline more slowly as the Indian population continues to expand. However Brazil bests India in at least one important workforce statistic: employee turnover. Despite continuous double-digit growth at Politec in recent years, our employee turnover has held steady at under 5% per year since the mid-1990s – and based on conversations with our peers, we believe this extremely low turnover is more the rule than the exception in the Brazilian IT sector. Turnover can run 30-40% annually at IT firms in India, according to a recent report by the Economist.[11]

Brazil's ethnic Japanese population represents another demographic advantage. São Paulo boasts the largest Japanese community of any city outside Japan, and the city's correspondingly high number of Japanese speakers make it an ideal location for IT and business process outsourcing work for the Japanese market. Politec opened a sales office in Tokyo recently to capitalise on this unique advantage.

## Reasons Why Brazilian Companies Are Expanding Abroad

The Brazilian IT services sector, unlike those in India, China, and Russia, has reached its current size – around $10 billion annual revenue – almost entirely by providing outsourcing services to the local market. While there is still room for growth in the Brazilian market, the largest Brazilian IT firms are at this point so well established in our home market that future growth within Brazil will soon be limited by the growth of the Brazilian

---

[10] Wilson, D., Purushothaman, R., 2003. Dreaming with BRICs: The Path To 2050. Goldman Sachs.
[11] Watch out India. The Economist, May 4, 2006.

economy itself – which at this point is lagging behind expectations. By expanding internationally we can take advantage of the continuing shift towards offshore outsourcing in the US and elsewhere. The market for lower-cost offshore solutions has the potential to grow much more quickly than our home market in Brazil. Furthermore as discussed earlier, the Brazilian IT sector has developed world-class expertise in certain areas like banking technology. If we believe some of our technology to be the best available anywhere, why shouldn't we market it abroad?

### How Can Brazilian Firms Effectively Expand?

The unique history of the Brazilian IT sector calls for a very different approach to the offshore outsourcing market if we are to succeed. Politec has chosen to initially focus on the offshore market for Application Lifecycle Services, which we believe to be the best approach to leverage both Brazil's specific advantages as an offshoring destination, and Politec's own expertise and experience with the outsourcing market in Brazil. Application Lifecycle Services consists of three distinct components – application development, application maintenance and legacy transformation. Many large companies in the US – as in Brazil – have custom computer applications that have been developed and perfected over time and are critical to the company's operations. But as important as they may be, the work of keeping these applications running smoothly often is not one of the company's core competencies, and may require a sizeable, dedicated IT staff. US companies can realise significant savings by sourcing this sort of maintenance offshore, and our decades of history providing the same kinds of services to Brazilian customers mean that Politec has more experience performing application development and maintenance than companies in any other major IT offshoring destination, including India.

Legacy transformation refers to taking a custom application that was originally written in a language like COBOL to run n a mainframe environment, and updating it to run on a modern platform like Java or .NET. Legacy transformation can drastically reduce maintenance costs, and can also reduce or eliminate dependence on obsolete or more expensive mainframe hardware. Politec has substantial experience in many other areas of IT services for the Brazilian market, including higher-value-added services like custom application development. But application development usually requires substantial onshore resources to assess application requirements and perform the high-level design of the new application, and since personnel working onshore offset the offshore cost advantage, offshore application development makes the most sense for very large projects. Offshore application development, maintenance and legacy transformation can offer substantial savings for clients – and profits for service providers – on projects of virtually any size. Brazil's favourable time zone represents another advantage in performing maintenance services for North American clients. As most of the major cities are only two time zones west of the US East Coast, normal working hours in both countries largely coincide. As a result it is much easier to provide real-time support for US clients from Brazil than from most other major offshoring destinations, including the rest of the BRICs. Thousands of US companies – including more than 400 of the Fortune 500 – already have operations in Brazil, and this helps to create an additional natural market for Brazilian IT services.

## Clouds on the Horizon

The BRICs report lays out three specific challenges the country must overcome if the country is to realise its full growth potential:

- *Brazil is much less open to trade.* The tradable goods sector in China is almost eight times larger than in Brazil, when measured by imports plus exports.

- *Investment and savings are lower.* Savings and investment ratios are around 18-19% of GDP compared to an investment rate of 36% of GDP in China and an Asian average of around 30%.

- *Public and foreign debt are much higher.* Without a deeper fiscal adjustment and lower debt to GDP ratio (currently at 57.7% of GDP on a net basis and 78.2% of GDP on a gross basis), the private sector is almost completely crowded out from credit markets. China's net foreign debt and public debt are both significantly smaller.

While these three obstacles together are potentially serious impediments to Brazil's overall GDP growth over the coming decades, they will not necessarily affect the prospects of the Brazilian IT sector. To consider each of the points from the BRICs report in turn: *Brazil is much less open to trade.* While Brazil's relative lack of international trade compared to other large developing countries is in part a result of past and current trade policies, it is worth remembering that Brazil's domestic market for many goods and services is already very large, even compared to the other BRICs Brazil's IT sector has already grown to over $15 billion, almost entirely from local demand. (BRASSCOM) *Investment and savings are lower.* While this is certainly true from a macroeconomic level, an important consideration for the development of the industry is how much the companies themselves are investing. Politec invests about 5% of annual revenue in future growth.*Public and foreign debt are much higher.* Of the three factors listed in the BRICs report, Brazil's high public debt is likely to be the one with the greatest potential impact on the development of the IT sector. As a result of Brazil's high level of public debt, interest rates in Brazil are kept high to control inflation, and credit is difficult to come by in the private sector. On the other hand, growth of the IT sector in the Brazilian market is still strong – Politec grew by about 10% in 2006 – so for the time being we can finance our international expansion through our existing operations. But easier access to credit would certainly speed the growth of the Brazilian IT sector in international markets. The growth of the BRICs economies in the coming decades will impact costs in two ways: first by currency appreciation, and second as incomes in each country rise. The amount by which each country will grow in the coming years is of course a matter of great debate, but one point that's clear is that the faster the BRICs countries grow relative to the US and other large markets for IT services, the smaller the difference in cost between onshore and offshore alternatives. To address this issue Politec has taken the same approach that many Indian firms have – as costs increase in major cities, we are opening development and maintenance centres in lower-cost locations within Brazil that nonetheless have world-class infrastructure and large technical universities.Few countries in the world can match India for sheer annual output of IT graduates – about 150,000 per year according to one recent study[12], and India has clear advantages over just about any other location in sheer workforce scalability. Brazil's output of IT graduates is only about one third that of India's (BRASSCOM). On the other hand one of the results of the enormous number of graduates each year in India is that companies and recruiters often must sift through thousands of resumes for each open position. In our experience at Politec, we typically see only need to see about half a dozen resumes to find a qualified applicant for a given position. A final area that needs improvement in Brazil is the level of English for IT workers – but we feel this issue can be largely mitigated, within a generation, by the right combination of public- and private-sector initiatives.

---

[12] Strengthening the Human Resource Foundation of the Indian IT Enabled Services/IT Industry, KPMG/NASSCOM, 2004.

# Driving Value Up

*Thiago Turchetti Maia*
*CEO, Vetta Technologies, Belo Horizonte, Brazil*

## Introduction

The offshore outsourcing market has grown and evolved tremendously ever since outsourcing became an increasing trend in corporations worldwide. The potential for future growth in this market is just as large as are the transformations it undergoes in the process. As the demand for offshore services changes, so must the supply. While existing providers must constantly innovate and differentiate themselves, new players from different locations arrive at the scene to challenge old service models and claim their share of the market.

The offer from traditional players in the offshore outsourcing market already shows signs of wear, with rising costs, limited scalability, and difficulty to offer services with specific requirements. Buyers seek alternative locations not only looking for new skills and new competences, but also trying to diversify their sourcing strategy to mitigate risks. There are many opportunities being created, and new players have a chance to gain market share using their countries' competitive advantages as well as their own.

The has been a lot of attention to the so-called BRICs – Brazil, Russia, India, and China – developing countries with emerging economies that are expected to be the leaders in this fast growing and fast changing market. India has been the traditional leader, combining a mature offer with large-scale delivery capabilities. With an enormous potential for talent together with competitive rates, China is quickly gaining terrain. Within the BRICs, Russia and Brazil are still to catch up. Russia has a good talent pool and competitive costs, but lack of government support and infrastructure are still severe holdbacks. Brazil has its own obstacles and challenges as well, but has on its side a large, well-developed internal market, along with several other advantages that will be covered later. Outside the BRICs, special mention should be made to Canada and Ireland which, alongside India, are the world's largest outsourcing providers, dominating the market.

Although comparisons to fellow BRICs and other countries are often made, this chapter is focused on Brazil. First, how global corporations may take advantages of Brazil's unique characteristics and service offers. Second, how Brazilian companies should respond to that demand and use the opportunity windows in the outsourcing market to leverage its exports and make the country a global player.

Throughout the remainder of the chapter, we will examine the trends in outsourcing services, models, relationships, and what to expect from both buyers and vendors in the future. In parallel, we examine how these new trends create opportunities for Brazilian companies. Overall, we make the general claim that the best opportunities for Brazil are centred on higher-value services, whether by renewing and adding extra value to existing models, or by offering new types of services. This claim is backed by Brazil's unique position of having a strong and mature internal market, which is locally serviced at the state-of-the-art in many verticals. As the offshore outsourcing market evolves, Brazilian companies have their chance to export the experience and competences they have already earned, as the country differentiates its offer through value.

## The Trend Towards High-Value Services

There has been a dramatic change on the way corporations deal with outsourcing, especially offshore. What once was a race against costs has now become a powerful tool to add value, not just by reducing expenses, but also by bringing in new competences, creating more efficient processes, and increasing overall performance. As a result, corporations now seek to outsource not only low-value, high-volume operational services, but also high-value, strategic services.

This does not mean operational services will not continue to be outsourced, on the contrary. The market for operational services outsourcing is growing as fast as ever, as both demand and supply gain maturity and more companies take advantage of it. But even operational services must joint the everlasting quest to add more and more value to the buyer. Today's minimum offer should start with low cost, high quality, high productivity, and service level agreements. These are now service commodities. In addition, operational service vendors should enrich their offer with innovation, flexibility, adaptability to changing environments, predictability of demand, extreme scalability, and technology alignment.

The same value crusade drives other services as well. Traditional software development services are giving room to application portfolio management. IT and business consulting are being replaced by the outsourcing of entire operations. Low costs and high service levels set the standard, while providers are expected to comply with changes in the short-term as well as keep their operations aligned with long-term strategic goals.

This tendency to innovate and add extra value to existing models, together with an increasing global competition, means that offshore providers are at constant pressure to reposition their offer and secure market share. Figure 1 outlines this trend. Consider the current available supply of services offered in a given market. If one plots the cost of possible service contracts against the value that they would actually add to their buyers, one obtains an efficiency frontier, as shown in Figure 1. In theory, new contracts closed above this frontier are overpriced, therefore with conditions against the buyer. Analogously, new contracts below the frontier are under-priced, conditions against the provider.

A contract lying away from the efficiency frontier may have been either closed under special circumstances, or the frontier itself may have shifted. There are many forces acting upon the frontier, in most cases favouring the

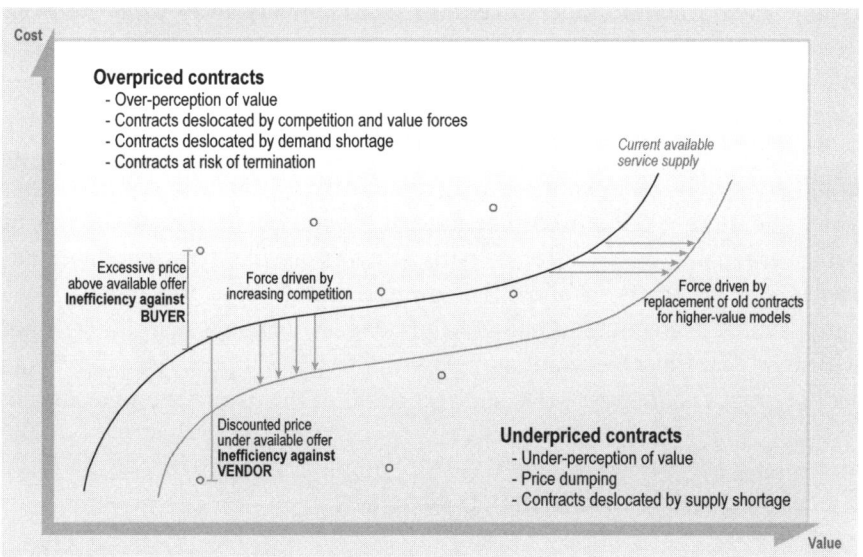

**Fig. 1.** Forces at work on cost / value relationship for outsourcing contracts

buyer. The trend towards higher-value services will trigger the replacement of old contracts by new, higher-value models, hence driving the frontier to the right. Meanwhile, demand shortages or increased competition will pressure for lower prices, thus pushing the curve down.

Although the global IT services market is estimated to steadily grow at average rates between 5% to 7% per year, the effects of the laws of supply and demand must not be overlooked. As the market increases, so does the competition, coming from in and out of the BRICs. Not only there is an increasing number of new players trying to penetrate existing markets, sudden currency fluctuations may compromise service rates, pushing the frontier further down overnight.

There are many reasons why a contract may have been closed away from the efficiency frontier, most having to do with the perception of value from the customer. Specific characteristics of the vendor may increase or decrease value perception without necessarily changing the value added by the contract. For instance, a given customer may agree to pay a premium for a selected vendor with proved expertise in his domain, even if the vendor will assemble a new and inexperienced team to service the customer. Country features may also alter the perception of value. For instance, we may expect a sudden value drop in services from a country that has had recent political instabilities or has engaged in military conflicts.

Other factors such as price dumping practices and risk aversion to change established providers may also pull contracts away from the frontier, usually in the short-term. In either case, though, these differences tend to vanish in the mid to long-term, as the market stabilises and customers terminate old contracts seeking efficiency.

Whenever a contract is far from the efficiency frontier, either due to its initial conditions or to shifts in the frontier itself, it is at risk. The further away, the more it is exposed. The more it is exposed, the greater its risk of being terminated by the affected party. Buyers are likely to seek more advantageous contracts should their arrangement diverge too much above current market practices. Analogously, vendors' contract margins will not withstand significant deviations below the frontier, as the rise of average service prices is, in most cases, a direct result of the rise of average costs.

## Service and Relationship Models

In order to back our initial claim that Brazilian providers and global corporations should embrace in higher-value services, in this section we explore how different service and relationship levels impact the value of service contracts. We show how the Brazilian offer is well suited for this, and how Brazilian companies may use value to differentiate themselves from foreign competitors.

Let us start by extending Figure 1, where the cost of outsourcing contracts is plotted against their value added, and replace individual contract instances by their service model. The result in Figure 2 shows a balanced line between cost and value for different types of service. In the lower left-hand quadrant we have different lower-value services. In the upper right-hand quadrant we have higher-value services. These two quadrants resemble the surface shown in Figure 1. It is easy to see that services that diverge too much from these two quadrants, or from the frontier from Figure 1, inflict a penalty on either party. In the upper left-hand quadrant, the inefficiency is against the buyer, who pays too high a price for services that do not add as much value. In the lower right-hand quadrant, the inefficiency is against the vendor, which is forced by various reasons to practice lower rates for services that are generally worth more.

Since we have preserved the same axis, the forces that put pressure on the efficiency frontier from Figure 1 are drawn in Figure 2 as a friendly reminder that the equilibrium between cost and value for all types of services, low and high-value, is always at stake. That is exactly where innovation strikes, creating new service models that offer more guarantees, more flexibility, and more efficiency to buyers.

Generally, old practices and poor execution will drive down the value of existing services. One of the most classical examples of a value-destroying, yet popular practice is the old time-and-materials model. There are many existing contracts for various types of services that are solely based on timely charges, and definitely there will be many more closed in the future. In this type of relationship, all execution risks are on the buyer. Project problems, low productivity, turn over issues, or any other difficulties that so often arise during the execution of an outsourcing contract will result in financial losses, and all of them will be charged on the buyer's account. I am not pledging that timely charges should be abandoned all together, not at all. Especially for small, short-term contracts, its simplicity and flexibility make it a good choice. For anything other than that, though, simple time-and-materials relationships destroy value, as providers fail to shift operational risks from their clients to themselves. Providers should at least offer guarantees and minimum service levels on productivity, turn over, milestones, or any other set of metrics of the operation. The buyer is When a service model is not robust enough to ensure value is not destroyed,

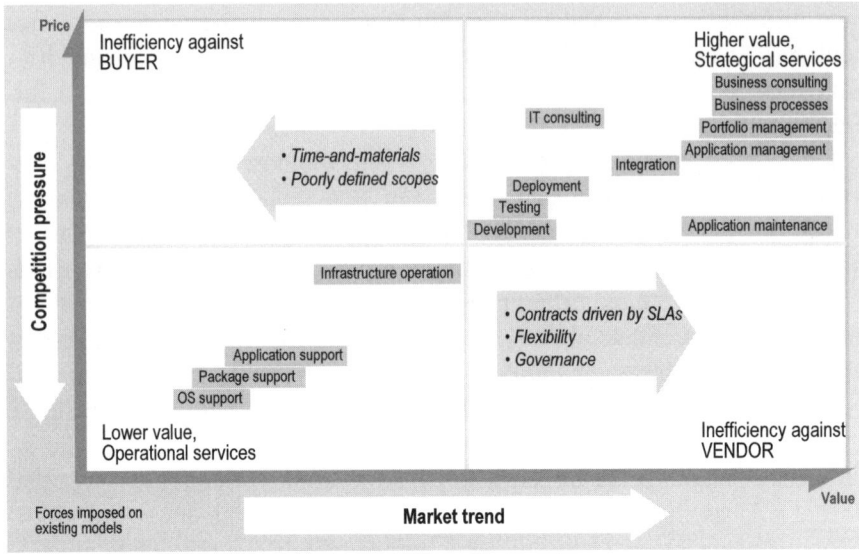

**Fig. 2.** Service models and value drivers

both parties should pay extra attention to the execution of the contract. It is amazing to see how relatively simple steps are often overlooked, such as making sure there is a clear scope definition. When scope is not automatically defined by the model, either by being fixed or by designing terms to cope with flexibility, we have the potential for disaster. When buyers and vendors do not agree on the scope of services, especially after an operation has already started, we will have an uncomfortable situation ranging all the way from contract renegotiation to the buyer not being properly serviced, financial losses to the vendor, loss of mutual trust, and even contract termination.

Scope definition is an essential part of a services contract. It should be jointly addressed by the service model and by operation management, both filling in the gaps that the other left out. Along with a clear scope, contract visibility and governance are crucial to avoid differences in expectations and undesirable mishaps. During the negotiation of contract terms, should the model not already be based on key indices that extract the performance measures of the operation, the buyer must ensure he will have proper access to information. Receiving management reports is but a minimum. The more visibility and access to information the buyer has, the more comfortable he will be if it ever comes to the point where the contract must be extended, or its terms must be renegotiated to accommodate an unforeseen scenario.

Service levels, pro-activity, scope definition, governance, flexibility. The list of contract best practices goes on, and is of no secret to buyers and vendors. This point is not knowing what the best practices are, but ensuring that they are correctly applied to add value to an outsourcing service contract. This is one of the aspects where the Brazilian offer excels. The Brazilian culture is much too creative in general. In business, this creativity is immediately translated into innovation and flexibility. We have seen many contracts awarded to Brazilian companies not because they were the lowest-cost provider in an international quote, but because they managed to understand the value drivers and stakeholders of the deal, and offered unmatched guarantees, terms, and even customized service models. If we refer back to Figures 1 and 2, what these companies did was nothing but generate extra value through innovation, and shift contract instances towards the right. From the buyers' point of view, they agreed to pay a premium for contracts that serviced them better. From the providers' point of view, companies effectively differentiated their offer from those of other providers. This strategy will work well for as long as there are buyers shopping for something other than the lowest cost.

Brazilian companies are able to add value to service contracts not only during their design, but also during their execution. Together with flexibility and creativity, the Brazilian offer is marked by its maturity and delivery capabilities. Brazil has a well developed internal market, the IT segment yearly answering for approximately 10 billion USD. Brazilian companies have a tradition for high quality software and IT services, and for some verticals they set the worldwide benchmark. As more Brazilian companies hit the offshore market, there is an increasing trend towards process improvement and international certifications. Although Brazil is still far behind some of its fellow BRICs in the number of certified organizations or professionals, Brazilian IT companies are generally acknowledged by the quality with which they service their customers, domestic and international.

Yet another way to understand and differentiate between offers from different players is to analyse the way they establish and maintain relationships with their clients. If we create a scale to measure the intensity and level of customization of relationships that different profiles of companies are willing to engage, and plot it against the value that these relationships add to the buyer, we come up with Figure 3. For this analysis, we may see value as the relevance of the processes that these relationships influence. From both ends, the buyer's and the vendor's, the relationship level measures the corporate effort required to support the operation, for instance considering the number of hours dedicated by management, purchasing, and operations needed every month. The larger the level of relationship customizations, that is, the more it requires specialized processes, the larger the effort. As the intensity of the relationship grows, so does the internal investment demanded from both parties.

As with other value plots from Figures 1 and 2, most activity is located along the main diagonal of Figure 3. Intense, customized relationships will add more value – or have the potential to add more value – to the buyer than undifferentiated ones. On the upper left-hand side of the plot we have an unfeasibility zone, as it is unlikely to obtain a lot of value from occasional, preformatted relationships, often meant for large customer pools. On the lower right-hand side we have the opposite situation, which unfortunately is found more often. In this over-investment zone, relationships fail to return as much value as they could, largely due to inappropriate service models and poor contract designs.

On the far, lower left-hand corner of the plot, we have fixed relationship models, often targeted at large customer bases, and which require little additional effort. As expected, they are not capable of adding much value to the buyer. Good examples of such relationships would be those between common application vendors and their customers. The additional effort required from the buyer is minimal, in most cases not exceeding the installation and management of these applications, and less often some

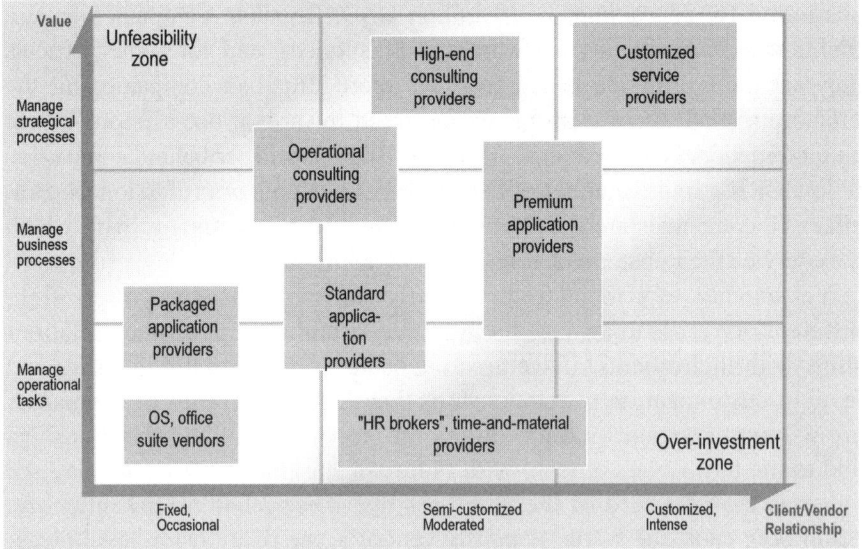

**Fig. 3.** The effect of client / vendor relationships on value

training courses for the target staff. The purchasing process itself is also simple, probably involving an initial transaction and periodic subscription renewals. The return brought by the relationship is then the availability of standard, generic applications to assist users in their activities. For future comparison, consider the problem of managing a few specific business processes, where users would use documents and spreadsheets to help them keep track of things, and report results to their superiors.

The opposite situation lies on the upper right-hand corner of the plot, where we have highly demanding, tailored relationships, with the potential to add a lot more value. Using the same context example, this is the profile of application portfolio management service providers. In this type of contract, the provider becomes responsible for the complete life-cycle of all business applications required by the customer, from business analysis and requirements to maintenance and user training. Clearly, managing such relationship from the buyer's end requires a great deal of effort from key users, infrastructure, IT, and management. Even purchasing is highly demanded, first to plan and produce a proper request for quotation, then to evaluate different proposals with different models and terms, and finally to keep track of variable service items and control service-level agreements. All this investment must yield its return, though, which is exactly the availability of customized and well maintained applications that would ultimately manage the business processes mentioned earlier, control their workflow, allow collaboration between users, and automatically report results.

Although this is a naïve example, it illustrates well couple of interesting things. First, that higher-value services often require more effort from both parties, buyers and vendors. These investments should be factored in not only by the vendor if this is his business model, but especially by the buyer, which often overlooks the additional burdens required to manage an advanced outsourcing contract. Second, that different problems and different corporations demand different levels of relationships and their associated value. It is easy to see in our example that the number of users managing our fictitious business processes is a decisive factor in deciding what strategy to follow. Whether there are only a few people involved, or if there are a few thousand people involved, is likely to suggest strategies at both ends of the spectrum.

Following the same trend seen for higher-value service models, Brazilian providers are particularly capable of engaging in intense, customized relationships. The first and foremost reason for this is the Brazilian culture. Brazilian companies are particularly able to drive value into services through innovation, and in the case of relationships, adapt their business model and offer highly customized contracts to suite specific needs. Also, the Brazilian culture itself is much too similar to that of the United States and Europe, which makes interaction, decision making, and negotiation smooth and straight forward. The second reason is Brazil's geographic features such as close time zones, proximity, and short flights. This means that whenever personal interaction is required, it can be efficiently done in conference calls, video conferences, or even by paying a short visit. More on these factors ahead, where we discuss specific features of the Brazilian offer.

## Vendor Selection

Several factors, internal and external to service providers, may add or destroy value to service contracts, regardless of the model they adopt. These factors should be carefully analysed by the buyer during the vendor selection process, as they are not likely to change in the short to mid-term. Internal factors are specific features from each vendor which will somehow contribute – or cause difficulty – to the execution of a given outsourcing contract. External factors are features of the environment where the provider is located. External factors are often compared in country matrices that attempt to distinguish between different offshore locations. In this section we discuss how country and vendor factors influence value. In parallel, we provide information about the Brazilian offer, giving both global and local information for selected locations.

For most vendor and country factors discussed below, when a given factor adds value to a contract, its antonym will analogously destroy value, and vice-versa. For instance, process maturity certainly does add value, while its absence is likely to destroy it. Some antonyms may not make sense, for instance, the absence of tax breaks will not necessarily destroy value in a contract. Figure 4 shows several vendor and country factors, along with their relative impact on value. Antonyms are avoided as much as possible, unless their effect is somewhat significant. We start our discussion with vendor factors.

Vendor factors may be grouped into four main categories, namely capability, best practices, infrastructure, and human resources. Capability factors consider domain expertise and experience, that is, how well prepared a vendor will be to execute a specific outsourcing contract. These factors are opportunity-dependent, varying from contract to contract for each vendor. Also, when these factors are decisive on vendor selection, the buyer must ensure that they are actually carried out to the execution of the contract.

For example, if a vendor is selected for his experience in a given field, he must bring in selected resources not only with this specific skill, but also with a track record of successful related engagements done under the vendor's own management. As far as capabilities go, the Brazilian offer is far too rich to be properly detailed in a short text. As a reference, though, there are some segments where Brazilian companies do excel, servicing multinational corporations at the state-of-the-art. For these segments, namely finance, energy, steel making, oil & gas, manufacturing, telecommunications, aviation, education, e-government, and health, the Brazilian offer is mature and widespread.

Best practice factors consider the general capability of a vendor untied to specific domains or technologies. They encompass maturity models, project and risk management, flexibility, visibility, and governance. These will add value to contracts as much as they will destroy should the vendor fail to aggregate them to their offer. Despite being so critical, these factors are also hard to evaluate during the vendor selection process. Except for certifications, which give good yet not 100% guaranteed indication of a vendor's commitment to quality, the buyer should spend considerable effort understanding how a provider plans to offer visibility, governance, and even how flexible the contract will be to accommodate scenario changes. If the buyer rushes into the deal with no clear indication of those settings, he will only discover how well or how poor they have been implemented after the contract is being executed. For this whole group of factors, the Brazilian offer is already strong and gaining a lot of momentum. There has been much activity aiming at process maturity and capability in Brazil, including a lot of government support. There is even a new made-in-Brazil maturity model, MPS.BR, a CMMI-compatible alternative made for Latin American countries, sponsored by the Brazilian government and the IADB. Formal project management skills are also widely available, and, together with maturity certifications, are quickly becoming mandatory requirements to service the Brazilian domestic market.

Infrastructure factors consider the provider's own structure for IT and telecommunications, as well as its locations' quality and availability of basic utilities, hotels, and transportation. Although they may severely impact contract value, these factors are usually easily verifiable, as they are dependant on tangible, physical elements. The Brazilian infrastructure in large centres and densely populated areas are as advanced and as available as those found in developed countries. There are no such problems as power outages, or difficulties to get hotel rooms. As for the specific infrastructure of vendors, most will have complete data-centres with assorted levels of physical and data security policies. And those who do not have such structure in-house, will definitely have access to a domestic infrastructure outsourcing vendor. There are many large providers available in the country, and there is an increasing trend for Brazilian corporations to outsource their IT infrastructure to specific providers.

Finally, human resources factors consider all aspects having to do with talent, including its availability, scalability, skills, training programs, and retention strategies. This is one of the most important groups to be considered, not because of its potential to add extra value, but due to its potential to destroy it. Worst of all, these factors are not easily perceived by the buyer unless a thorough selection process is undertaken. There are many large talent pools in Brazil, mostly located around large university centres and technology parks. The largest centres, such as São Paulo and Rio de Janeiro, all have significant talent pools, strong local universities, and well-developed markets to retain talent. Other cities, like Belo Horizonte, are traditional talent exporters, and have increasingly attracted companies like Google Inc. due to its resource availability. Other centres worth mentioning are Recife, on the northeast of the country, and Porto Alegre, on the south, as both have managed to create large technology parks backed by strong universities. There are other examples of strong talent pools, especially in south-eastern and southern states, and within 100 km radii

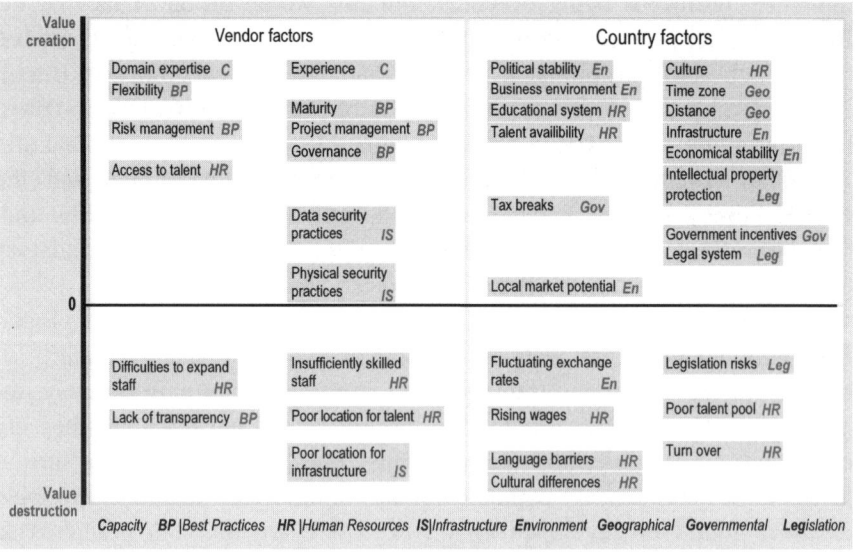

**Fig. 4.** Vendor and country factors: differentiating through value

around most capitals and large cities. Overall, talent is largely available, as will be discussed ahead in the context of the whole country.

Next, we discuss country factors. We may classify country factors in five groups, namely environmental, human resources, governmental, legal, and geographical. Environmental factors include political and economical stability, infrastructure, local market potential, and the general business atmosphere at the location. Brazil is a well-established presidential democracy, with a handful of major parties that share seats across the Senate and Congress, and healthily alternate power in the Federal Government. Since the early 1990s, the Brazilian economy is equally stable, with inflation rates lower than many developed economies. There are no external political conflicts nor the risk of war, which has not been part of the Brazilian history since the 19th century. On the contrary, Brazil plays a leading role in Latin America, being its largest country in terms of land, population, and economy – the world's ninth – which additionally creates a lot of potential for foreign companies to settle in. Overall, Brazil has attracted multinational companies from all over the world, as much as it has been acknowledged for its friendly-to-business environment.

Human resources factors, as before when we discussed them on the context of the vendor, encompass all aspects related to talent, this time seen from the country's perspective. They include factors like talent availability, educational system, wages, quality of the talent pool, turn over, as well as others like culture compatibility, and language. In Brazil, there is a wide educational network, with solid technology and business schools. Although the country may not provide as many graduates each year as other fellow BRICs with much larger populations, turn over rates are much lower than most other offshore locations. The Brazilian culture is also very similar to that of the United States and Europe, including its western business practices. This is certainly one Brazil's major advantages, especially for providing higher-value services to these markets, as cultural similarities favour efficient communications, interactions, avoid misunderstandings, and ultimately avoid the destruction of value.

Governmental factors consider whatever incentives each government has granted to foster its service exports. In Brazil, information technology has been nominated one of the four priority sectors whose development has been specially assisted. Through many agencies, the Federal Government has started different programs to assist IT companies with different profiles, including a nationwide quality and process improvement program, many financial grants aimed at process improvement, research and development, innovation, foreign marketing & sales, among other goals.

Additionally, the Federal Government has reduced to zero some taxes on exported services and goods. Following the same line, several Municipalities have also drastically cut or dropped taxes applicable to service export contracts.

Legal factors consider the maturity and efficiency of the legal system, legislation risks, and intellectual property protection. Along with political stability, Brazil's political model and its well distributed power across the Senate and Congress dramatically mitigate legislation risks. Brazil is signatory of several conventions, treaties, and agreements, and there is specific legislation to protect intellectual property in several forms, including patents, copyrights, and even software. Generally, Brazil is a safe location for a foreign corporation, which is able to effectively enforce and protect its intellectual property.

Finally, geographic factors consider the country's distance to major markets, its time zone, and even its amenities. Brazil is strategically located between the United States and Europe. This enables local and remote teams to easily cooperate and efficiently work together in joint activities. It is also fairly common for Brazilian service providers to have their offshore teams working under the client's working schedule, maximizing their interaction with remote counterparts. The Brazilian time zone enables not only the direct collaboration between distributed team members, but also follow-the-sun operations for services such as customer support, helpdesk, and other 24-7 activities. Along with the time zone advantage, Brazil is also a night's flight away from the United States and Europe. It is possible to get on a plane in Brazil after dinner and have breakfast in Wall Street. This means that emergencies may be dealt with in person, and also that scheduled visits do not compromise the whole week of key resources. Last but not least, Brazil is a favourite tourist location, with many entertainment options for all tastes. This should not be a decisive factor to select an offshore destination. Still, it is easy to imagine that business trips to places like Rio are likely to be easier on staff morale and motivation than flying them around the globe to other less gorgeous locations.

## Brazil's Path to Becoming a Global Player

What must Brazil do to become a global player in the offshore outsourcing market? This has been a controversial question, with a wide range of opinions. There are some who believe it should follow the footsteps of fellow BRICs, especially India, aiming at large-scale, often lower-value service contracts for global corporations. Our opinion is somewhat different, though.

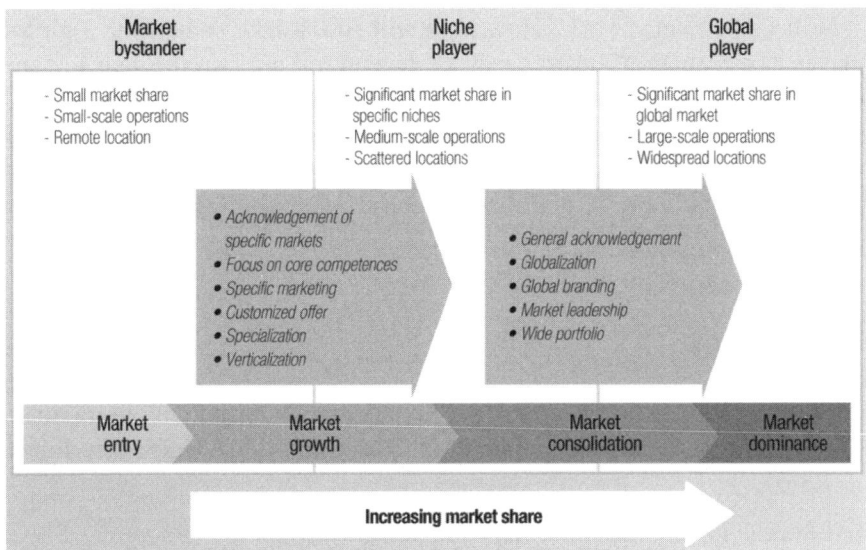

**Fig. 5.** The path towards becoming a global player

Most opportunities in this market, including the majority of large-scale, low-value contracts, are already dominated by market leaders. Also, although Brazil has significantly lower costs than most developed nations, it is still more expensive than the other BRICs and other developing countries. Therefore, attempting to gain market share over well established players with no cost advantage and no clear way to differentiate its offer does not seem to be an effective path, unless competitor's local costs rise significantly or severe currency fluctuations happen at these competing locations.

An alternative approach, which we strongly believe, is that Brazil should look at higher-value opportunities, where companies will be able to differentiate their offer and earn rates compatible with the country's own domestic rates. A possible consequence, should this strategy work to secure some market share, will be an increasing tendency towards specialization and verticalization of the Brazilian offer, as shown in Figure 5. If all goes well, Brazilian companies will increasingly dominate selected niches where their offer is strong and their value proposition is superior to those of other outsourcing locations. In time, the successful consolidation of several niches dominated by Brazilian providers will increase the country's global market share, and eventually promote Brazil to the status of global player.

Will this strategy work? How long will Brazil take to become a global player in this market? These answers depend not only on the status of the offers from other countries, especially fellow BRICs, but also on how Brazil succeeds in differentiating its own offer. As discussed throughout this chapter, Brazil may just be able to do so, not just by adding extra value to existing service models, but also by innovating and transforming the current market.

## References

Offshoring Information Technology: Sourcing and Outsourcing to a Global Workforce, Erran Carmel & Paul Tjia, Cambridge University Press, 2005.

Offshoring in the Financial Services Industry: Risk and Rewards, PWC, report, 2005.

Developing a Strategic Agenda for IT Offshore Outsourcing, AT Kearney, report, in Portuguese, 2005.

Initial Findings on the State of Global Service Delivery, TPI, report, 2005.

Brazil: A Viable Alternative for Intellectual Property Outsourcing, Robert A. West, Guillermo Wasserman, and Renata Poroger, Southeast Tech Wire, 2003.

The Black Book of Outsourcing: How to Manage the Changes, Challenges, and Opportunities, Douglas Brown and Scott Wilson, Wiley, 2005.

Research and Development Outsourcing, Vetta Technologies, whitepaper, 2003.

MPS.BR Website, http://www.softex.br/mpsbr/, in Portuguese.

## Acknowledgements

I would like to thank Mr. Yuri Gitahy, Mr. Ricardo Giacomin, and Mr. Cesar Rodrigues for insightful comments and feedback on the text, Mark Kobayashi-Hillary for the invitation, and all my associates at Vetta Technologies that succeed everyday in making it such a great company.

# Part II: Russia

# Reflecting on the Future to Understand the Present

*Arkadiy Dobkin*
*CEO and President, EPAM Systems, Moscow, Russia*

Some take optimistic projections about the bright future of the BRICs with caution, while others are already considering the ways to invest into the BRIC countries. There are a lot of examples and arguments proving that both the points of view have the right and ground to exist. Brazil's "golden age" has been predicted since the middle of the 20$^{th}$ century and unfortunately still remains only a prospect, while Japan's and South Korea's astonishing growth rates exceeded all expectations.

However, even the highest expectations can turn out to be the minimum of what the future holds. The gap between the forecasts and the facts can go either way.

## The Origins of Offshoring

The international division of labour has been going on for years. As a result, many people believe that the best banks and watches are to be found in Switzerland, the best cars are manufactured in Japan (at least for the last 20-30 years) and that the petrol those cars are fuelled with is most likely produced from the oil obtained in one of the Arabic countries. With the development of communications and information technologies it has become possible to divide labour between the countries in a way that was not thought of before, to convert goods into digital form and to distribute them via global networks. In many aspects, the "global IP revolution" has stretched far beyond the corporate borders of individual companies, and has made an essential impact on the business climate at large. This impact is universally favourable for diverse industries that benefit from reduced tariffs on data, voice and image transmission.

As it has become possible to divide labour into services that can be produced at times and places different from where they are consumed, companies have been enabled to "shop worldwide" for domestically unaffordable or unavailable services and skills. This has become the essence of offshoring, a phenomenon helping both the customers and the service providers to achieve multiple goals. The former get good service at a good price, benefit from flexibility of resources and improve time-to-market, while the latter receive the desired jobs and money along with accelerated development of the hi-tech sector.

Through making the business field international, offshore outsourcing drives unification of business legislation in various countries, contributes to the emergence of a common business environment and thus leads to the improvement of cooperation between the developed and developing countries. The economies of the latter, the hi-tech sectors in particular, get boosted by the resulting cash flow. Thus offshore outsourcing not just drives the costs down for the European and US customers, but it contributes to economic progress of the offshore destination countries.

Yet besides the economic aspect, offshoring has a strong social one. The offshoring industry can be viewed upon as an excellent illustration of the concept of free trade, taken onto a truly global scale, and an effective mechanism of uniting highly skilled intellectual labour, stemming from various cultural backgrounds, around the common professional and, in the long run, social values.

## Offshoring at Present

The offshore services market is undergoing a spectacular growth, beating even the most optimistic projections of the past. The hundreds of millions of dollars that analyst group Gartner was giving in the beginning of the 90s to estimate the offshore software services market looked too optimistic. Back in 1993, when EPAM Systems started its offshore software engineering operations, the very idea of offshoring was still a novelty that many corporate people looked upon with a shade of doubt. At the start of each new deal, we had to provide some clear and convincing evidence demonstrating that the concept really works. Gartner's prediction that the offshore services market was going to be a multi-billion market in 5-6 years seemed just crazy. And we all know what happened next – the market outgrew the most optimistic expectations and today has topped tens and tens of billions.

What we are witnessing now is that the offshore IT outsourcing market is maturing. Among the main tendencies that can be distinguished I would name the growth of demand and its sophistication, coupled with the growth of supply and more distinct specialisation of services provided. The possibility of driving the costs down still remains one of the major arguments making companies consider the offshore alternative but there is clear evidence that customers' motivations are changing.

Today offshore outsourcing has become just "a must" for many companies, while more and more of them are still planning to benefit from services globalisation in the future. The IT outsourcing industry is characterised by a higher level of offshore/near-shore services acceptance in general, clients' readiness to outsource much more complex and business critical projects and, as a result, a growing demand for more specialised skills, knowledge, and expertise. Five years ago EPAM worked just for less than a dozen clients, whereas now our customer base has expanded to more than 150 companies. These companies represent leading global corporations, which are doubling business with us annually and have tremendous experience working in the global model for years as well as emerging technology start-ups which are starting today their operation from selecting the right partner to utilise the model for the first time. As clients are ready to outsource more projects and of higher complexity, their trust in offshore is increasing, there appears a shift of priorities affecting the choice of an offshore vendor whose services now have to be not just the cheapest, but the best in a certain field to be able to satisfy the specific requirements. Happily, customers can now fully use their right to choose. Whereas a few years ago, only a small number of service providers existed for each outsourcing project, there is currently a sea of highly skilled and qualified candidate service providers that exist in any given market – a positive problem that firms are faced with when selecting an outsourcing service partner. This increase in supply from these budding service providers is healthy for competition and results in heightened quality.

Corporations realise that although they must benefit from reduced cost to justify their investment in offshoring, benefits from skill sets and experiences gained provide the ultimate advantage. High quality of service is becoming much more important than low price as the tasks outsourced do not boil down to simple coding, testing or bug-fixing anymore, but are measured by actual value to the business brought by complex services delivered with help of much more experienced and sophisticated outsourcing partners than it was possible just 5-6 years ago. And companies are ready to pay for such specific values, even if it means paying much more.

## What the Future Holds for Offshoring

If we take a wider outlook, what is going on now is that countries are building up expertise in various business areas. Some countries already have, on the global scale, occupied a certain niche in the traditional services/industries and have become a kind of global hubs for these specific niches. As far as the IT industry is concerned, thanks to the tendency of sending IT services across the borders, IT industry on the whole is becoming global as well.

Based on today's analysis, most likely in future the IT services market will include at least three main hubs serving the global market:

1. USA – due to the very strong and advanced practices in IT development, presence of very large global IT companies (like IBM Global Services and Accenture) as well as highly developed software and hardware product industry including majority of global players like Microsoft, Oracle, Intel, Sun, HP, etc. USA can be the IT services hub for the whole North American region potentially drawing on resources from other countries as well.

2. India – due to the current very strong position based on 15 years of investment in building IT services industry resulting in huge current advancements in IT expertise and scale (Wipro, Infosys, TCS, Cognizant, etc). In future India might become an IT services hub for the whole globe but with a stronger focus on North America, Asia and maybe some of Europe as well.

3. China will become an IT services hub due to the huge demand for local services coupled with a strong necessity for local cultural compatibility. The level of investment coming to the country today is also important for the successful development of the industry. Japan is a potential market to be served by China.

4. Russia stands a good chance to become the IT services hub for the Western and Eastern European markets. It will also serve the local market. Its GDP is growing and the domestic demand for IT services will significantly increase. So like China and India its local market will become more and more attractive.

It is absolutely clear that the target markets will, too, undergo significant changes. They will expand and not boil down to just US, UK and a bit of

Western Europe, unlike the current situation The IT services market will become truly global. I believe that in the future it will include:

- the "traditional" targets like US, UK & Western Europe
- BRIC countries themselves, based on Goldman Sachs projections for growth
- Asian countries (like Japan, Korea, Arabic world) which are not really utilising yet the outsourcing model to a full extent
- Eastern European countries (including former Soviet Union countries)
- Latin American countries

The above-mentioned metamorphoses affecting the IT market will inevitably alter the nature of IT vendors. The IT companies will become global multinationals specialising in particular services, with a visible local presence in target markets (local presence in the service industry always will be important to some extent) and globally balanced resources. Each of such companies will have many development centres around the globe working in tact to provide best resources, experience, and skills to meet the client needs.

However, the multinationals of the future will base their resource pools in the countries which manage to become the hubs for the services these companies specialise in. Such regions will be defined by the current and future situation within the IT services industry. Those countries that would be able to accumulate the deepest and vastest expertise, build a strong specialised educational system to support the necessary growth scalability, incorporate the due level of respect into the local culture for the profession, provide governmental and legal support to the industry will win. Such countries will be able to become a brand for IT services, as India has already done.

I am not mentioning lower labour costs among the main characteristics of a country-hub for IT services because the levelling of costs among the IT service providers from different locations will not take long. Even the difference in income per capita in various locations will practically have no effect on the price of IT expertise due to the industry's very high level of ability to "virtualise" (ability to provide services remotely due to the current and future advancements in telecommunication, etc.). Various industries are affected by various factors critical for choosing a location to build a presence there. In heavy manufacturing like automotive, Japanese companies, for example, are producing a lot locally (i.e. in US and EU) due to the cost of delivery and automation. The Construction industry very much depends on the cost of local materials and local labour. As for IT services, most of the tasks can be done remotely by skilled people. This excludes the delivery costs and so on, only labour cost remaining. But local labour costs will not be influencing the wages paid in IT due to the fact that labour costs there will be largely defined by the situation in the global market, not by the economic situation in the region. This will lead to the equalisation of prices for IT services over the globe relatively fast.

With this said, it becomes clear that lower costs for services will no longer remain the main advantage in the market. Firstly because, as I have already said, quality will be more important than lower prices, and secondly, the costs will be levelled.

As for the further prospects of the offshore IT industry, I believe its peak development is still to come. Offshore IT outsourcing is little more than a decade old, and is still rather a "young" industry with a lot of unexplored opportunities for customers and for service providers ahead. However, these opportunities might remain unused if the following hindrances will not be taken care of.

Among the main threats that might hinder the development of the offshore IT services industry I would name a possible sudden rise in costs, potential lack of qualified human resources, possible technology changes (automation), and business model changes.

One of the major and most problematic barriers that might arise on the way of the further progress of offshoring is potential labour shortage that will lead to the rise of offshore service costs before countries manage to accumulate the expertise that would give them an ultimate advantage in comparison to other locations for future competition. The resulting rise of wages can put the brakes on the offshoring trend, because at this stage of global IT market development it will be difficult for service providers in offshore locations to compete with the onshore locations when the prices are practically equal. Thus, to avoid trouble, the BRICs should make sure their educational systems are ready to produce skilled workforce sufficient to satisfy the demand for offshore talent.

What role the BRIC countries are going to play in the offshore industry depends on what future they will face. Goldman Sachs are predicting a bright one for them and I don't see any particular reason for not accepting their projections. If things go as Goldman Sachs predict, the BRICs themselves will become IT markets to be served. It's great that these four countries are on the way to prosperity, but if today's assumptions are correct the offshore future of BRICs is threatened. If the BRICs become the G4 of the future the levelling of prices will take place, i.e. the four countries will not be able to provide services at competitive costs compared to other countries. The costs for their services can reach the level of costs offered by onsite IT vendors. This can be the end of offshoring to BRIC countries if they don't provide customers with advantages (other and) more important than low costs. If the Goldman Sachs projections come true before the BRICs have the time to build up expertise and a stable, mature infrastructure to provide unique services then offshoring to the four countries may cease.

Open source software can also be viewed as a possible factor that might slow down the offshore trend – but not stop it. Open source software will not be able to satisfy custom software development needs. Nevertheless, we can only project from current models. I do not deny the possibility that a completely different concept of software or new technology might eliminate the need to send projects offshore at some future time. Neither can we predict or exclude the emergence of new business models which can radically change the ways IT services are provided today. Another threat might be the lost opportunity where the BRICs divert the focus from offshore outsourcing to other business models or practices.

## Russia's IT Industry at Present

If we take this "brick" out of the BRICs to scrutinise it, the immediate and biggest fact about Russia is that its IT sector develops at the staggering pace of 25 per cent annually, making IT the fastest growing economic sector of the country. I believe this positive trend is likely to continue in the coming years, as there are all the makings of progress in Russian legislative and economic field, which stimulates domestic and foreign demand for IT services. The progress is intensified with the following preconditions for the success of Russian export-oriented IT industry.

- *Human Resources*: Russia is one of the countries with the most skilled and highly qualified labour pools in the world. Given the fact that Russia's IT sector is still in the development stage, the IT labour force costs rise at a relatively slow rate compared to those of the happier Indian IT industry. This brings tangible cost savings to the customers. Driven by competition, Russia seeks new ways to stand out. Thus domestic IT companies apply differentiation in the form of specialisation.

- *Location*: Due to the geographical proximity to the EU and US, Russia boasts cultural proximity and provides full-scale time zone compatibility, unlike the rest of the BRICs. The cultural background shared by providers and their clients is particularly important for more complex business processes.

- *Infrastructure*: With the Telecommunications industry developing rapidly, Russia possesses a good quality and reliable telecommunications infrastructure, including physical and power infrastructure.

- *Legislation*: Given the overall changes brought by the government, Russian laws seem to be generally adequate to support contracting and investment in the hi-tech sector, including IP protection and trade secret laws. According to a report by internaional law firm Baker & McKenzie, the quality of the court system in Russia has much improved particularly in the major commercial centre. Litigation is quick and cheap and the ease of enforcement means it is a meaningful threat to counter misbehaviour.

Thus, Russia's image of a "Wild East" is no longer justified. In terms of business conduct, the structures and documentation norms can be adapted to work here. With proper attention to the legal issues, an enormous and talented pool of quality specialists can be utilised to one's business advantage.

Besides the wealth of benefits that external investors and buyers may reap of the lucrative assets supplied by the region, foreign demand is stimulated by government-facilitated positive tendencies. A lack of governmental support can be removed off the hurdle list for Russian IT sector development.

Russia's over-dependence on raw materials has much been criticised both in the West and locally. After his visit to Indian technology capital Bangalore in 2004, inspired by the impressive results of the transformed Indian economy, President Vladimir Putin instructed the government to elaborate and enact the measures that would help create favourable conditions for exporting IT services in order to diversify the economy by unlocking the country's significant intellectual potential through entrepreneurship and investment in non-energy-related research and development.

As a result a number of government initiatives and projects have been proposed and planned for implementation in the very near future. For instance, the Ministry of Information Technologies and Communications presented its plans by the end of 2006 to create a dedicated authority –

Federal Agency for IT Exports Development. The agency will analyse the exporting potentials, provide marketing support and conduct marketing and PR activities.

The ITC ministry will also run a dedicated Russian Investment Fund for Technologies and Innovations, which is expected to become completely private by 2010 with the state share in the fund making up around 25 per cent by the end of 2007. Some of the British and American financial institutions who invest in IT and know the Russian market well, are ready to make financial contributions. The government plans to organise public relations events around the world to promote the fund – and the Russian technology sector as a whole – to foreign investors.

Another incentive is development of industrial technoparks in the areas of the cities with largely unused human resources and scientific potential. The technoparks will be created with the help of business-driven practices unlike the existing 40 active technoparks that were developed during the Soviet/post-Soviet era and which, therefore, lacked well-developed infrastructure and management, let alone tangible subsidies to finance the innovative projects. As stated in the programme adopted by the government in March 2006, such parks shall be set up in all over Russia – in Moscow, Leningrad, Tyumen, Nizhniy Novgorod, Kaluga Novosibirsk regions, and in Tatarstan. Intensive construction operations are to be launched within the next year, and in two more years time the parks will start to look for investors. At present several technoparks are already being engineered and constructed in St. Petersburg which is set to be one of the most technologically packed zones in Russian IT. In addition, the Novosibirsk region authorities have passed the decision to initiate a large-scale construction of a technopark located in the vicinity of Academgorodok (Academic Town). The project envisages the budget of 17bn roubles and is included in the ITC ministry's federal investment program.

The pilot technopark projects envisage creation of satellite labs and offices concentrated around the scientific centres and universities serving as hubs for the talented youth and highly-skilled specialists. All in all, the industrial parks will be built in a ten-year period. As a result, 19,000 jobs are to be created by 2008, and 75,000 by 2011. The expected total value of the industrial parks output is estimated as approximately $4.38bn by 2011. Already in 2007 the federal budget will finance the further development of technopark infrastructure – investing about $52m. At the same time the government will not invest or hold stakes in technoparks; instead, the latter will be created and operated solely by private companies. However, the government intends to finance around 20 per cent of the feasibility studies and provide other support, including allocating land plots, helping set up telecommunications infrastructure, and encouraging investment into buildings and office space that would later be rented out to IT companies.

I see the new incentives and business oriented approach to the technoparks creation inspired by the real life examples in the Indian IT industry as essential elements facilitating IT industry development.in Russia.

The Russian legislation has also been affected by the positive trend. Amendments to the Tax Code of Russia have been made. Instead of imposing a special taxation scheme for IT companies, at this time the Federal Tax Service agreed to abolish VAT and reduce social security payments. However, this would still represent significant tax savings for IT companies as payroll costs generally account for around 70 per cent of their operating expenses. The tax remissions, which came into force from January 1, 2007, will enable the IT companies to invest more into the business development and increase the production volume.

Following the acknowledged concerns over the business climate in Russia and in an attempt to meet the expectations of investors, the government has given indications of supporting measures that would limit the discretionary authority of the tax administration and decrease the period of contestability for privatisation deals from 10 to 3 years. This way the government reiterates its basic commitment of improving conditions for the private sector as the primary engine of growth and investment.

According to the Troika Dialog research, from the stock market perspective in the short term Russian IT provides more opportunities for private equity investments than for IPOs. The nature of capital investment in the industry is such that company owners do not require external funding to support growth. However, private equity investments may come in handy, should IT companies choose to make acquisitions, which has been a trend lately. The need for external financing is expected to grow quite intensely over the next several years as the sector heads into a period of consolidation.

A remarkable achievement in the field of the investment climate improvement as a result of the initiatives undertaken by the government is the fact that several world's major rating agencies (such as Moody, Fitch Ratings, and Standard & Poor) have awarded Russia an investment grade status with a stable outlook for its long-term foreign currency liabilities.

The current long-term currency rating for Russia by Fitch Ratings is BBB, which stands for "good credit quality", with a stable outlook. At the same time, out of the BRICs, only China boasts a higher credit rating of an A grade with a positive outlook for the long-term currency liabilities, whereas Brazil has a BB speculative (non-investment) grade with a stable outlook, and India – BBB- investment grade with a stable outlook.

Amendments to the law on bankruptcy, the adoption of a new law on credit bureaux, measures to develop the banking system and the reform of the United Energy Systems have all helped strengthen the market system in Russia. This, together with the near-term plans to develop new economic zones to further diversify the economy, has had a positive effect on the investment climate and on IT sector development in particular.

As a result, the foreign investment rate in the first half of 2006 has increased by 41.9 per cent compared to last year, including direct foreign investment that has grown up by 43.9 per cent. This tendency reflects the reaction of foreign investors to the improved investment climate in Russia.With steady growth rates of 6.6 per cent for 8 consecutive years, making it the longest period of growth since the collapse of the USSR, the Russian economy alone paves the way for a more dynamic investment-friendly future. The Kremlin is projecting a significant budget surplus in 2007, and in August 2006, Russia was able to clear its entire $22bn (£12bn) Soviet-era debt to 17 Western countries known as the Paris Club.

Yet the local market is also growing and gaining weight as a potential market to be served. Already in 2002 the Telecommunications industry adopted a program called "Electronic Russia", which set informational guidelines for government institutions. The program focuses on legislation and regulations, Internet infrastructure, e-government and e-education. "Electronic Russia" makes Russia's public sector one of the country's major buyers of IT products and services. The government regularly purchases IT equipment and services, the contracts for which are usually awarded by tender and private companies perform the work. Now the government accounts for at least 30 per cent of Russia's IT spending. The adoption of IT by the government automatically makes each of the 88 constituent entities of the Russian Federation a potential blue chip IT services customer. What is more, the parliamentarians have aired a unanimous opinion to obtain the government's approval on the increase of the programme budget.

Russia's structural reforms take a long time to implement, but the process has been started and the results – for example, the IT sector rapid growth and the understanding of the need for economic diversification – seem to be more plausible than ever.

## Prospects for Russia's IT Industry

The Goldman Sachs forecast refers to a set of core factors that can set the stage for further growth on the national level: macroeconomic stability, institutional capacity, openness and education. According to Goldman Sachs, an unstable macro environment can hamper growth by distorting prices and incentives. Russia's inflation rate has been unexpectedly high in early 2006, so the government prepared a package of anti-inflationary measures in the context of proposals that included price controls, restricting wage growth in state-owned companies, restricting borrowing by state-owned companies, and reducing state expenditures. Although, according to expert assessments, the use of price controls as a means of reducing moderate inflation is not the best policy choice, the central bank's conduct of anti-inflationary monetary policy will be considerably strengthened when a larger internal bond market finally develops in Russia.

In 2003, the year Goldman Sachs first issued theit BRICs report, Foreign Direct Investment (FDI) reached nearly $4.3 billion in India, $10.1 billion in Brazil, and $53.5 billion in China. Russia took in just over $1.1 billion. However, given the active changes made, the situation has considerably improved. The Kremlin gradually loosens a grip on natural resources in favour of other promising economy sectors, including IT.

It is, however, noteworthy, that political conditions and relationships with the countries in the target markets might provide some limitations to Russia's IT services industry. E.g. political competition with the US might limit access to the US market for IT companies from Russia.

Another important growth-supporting factor – according to the BRICs research – is the state of the education system. As economies grow rapidly, they may face shortages of skilled workers, meaning that more years of schooling are a prerequisite for the next stage of economic development. The education in Russia, and former USSR region as a whole, is one of the strongest growth-supporting elements. The Soviet Union bequeathed to Russia a world-class education system with a strong emphasis on science and mathematics. This generates a large pool of engineering and mathematics graduates, which has traditionally been a good source of high-calibre software programmers. According to Microsoft Research, Russia's colleges and universities produce around 190,000 graduates a year capable of directly entering the IT sector, four times the figure for India.

Although I endorse the opinion that the Russian IT development model will never copy and should not copy that of India's, however, to win customer credibility and get noticed among the host of seemingly similar IT service providers, the IT companies from Eastern Europe, and Russia in particular, need to grow in headcount to meet the demand for reliability and scalability. Whether Russian companies will be able to meet this requirement depends on the country's demographic situation and the education system's ability to provide the industry with the specialists in future. Naturally, I cannot predict what the situation will be like in this respect. I can only hope for the best!

So the window of opportunity for the Russian IT industry remains open. I think that building up expertise in well defined areas of technical and business domains to be able to provide more science-intensive value-added and less human resource intensive services is the only way for Russian companies to remain competitive in the offshore software outsourcing market.

To my mind, Russia can become an IT service hub for Europe if the level and unique character of Russian expertise makes the customer choose their services irrespective of other factors. Despite the consolidation trend, the Russian offshore IT vendors will never beat such an IT monster like India by trying to override it in size. Not that they really need to make this competitive parameter a priority. As I see it, Russian companies have good chances to succeed at the market as high-end service providers by focusing on specialisation and services quality, not sheer size. The strong Russian educational system is one of the preconditions for this, and I hope that it will remain so. Russia holds the third position in the world on skills certification, only with the US and India ahead, and is listed among the top five countries for C#, Java 2, .NET Framework, C++ certifications, according to the 2006 BrainBench Global Skills Report. Russian software engineers are widely known for their high level skills and a creative approach to work, which makes them a suitable option for companies seeking to implement complex projects requiring a special approach. Russian IT vendors are realising that specific skills can be seen as their main advantage in the market and are taking steps to improve their employees competence. The well beyond average education level of the Russians combined with natural savvy and good abstract thinking, in addition to very good problem solving skills, which are one of our biggest national assets, and the drive to explore new opportunities provide a good ground for that. Russia's talented pool of resources with an excellent technology oriented mindset has all the prospects to turn Russia into a partner for innovation.

Nevertheless, if the opportunity for this global role is lost then it just means that the Russian IT talent pool will have to play a much more local (from the market point of view) role and might shrink its numbers as well. As noted above, Russia's domestic demand for IT services is expanding fast.

If Goldman Sachs assumptions are correct and by 2050 the Russian economy overtakes that of Germany, France, Italy and the UK, it will mean that Russia itself will become a huge target market for IT services. While the majority of projects today are coming from the US or EU, in the future more and more IT services will be requested by Russian local clients.

The window of opportunity is not closed yet. Russia has good chances to become the IT hub to serve Western and Eastern Europe. This hub is not going to be as large as India or China could become, but it might still play a global role in international division of labour. But this depends on many factors (Russia's education systems, investment, government and legal support for the IT industry, demographics, etc.) and the window is not going to be open too long. India and China are developing very aggressively and might prevent Russia's significant growth and advancement to be the global IT power. Now, even more so than ever, Russian software engineering companies have to find their focus and make their own brand, distinguishing them from others. Today is the time to find it and build their expertise.

I want to add that although long-term predictions and forecasts like the future of BRICs analysis by Goldman Sachs is based on facts and built with the help of logical extrapolations and careful calculations, these are still estimates that should be taken with a pinch of salt. Logic gets interfered with by the unpredictability of reality, and some seemingly insignificant factors that will turn out to be crucial later on, may escape the analyst's eye at present. However, I don't wish to derogate the importance of such far-reaching projections. Even if the future numbers fail it still allows us a better understanding of the present.

# Outsourcing as a Strategic Business Model for "Futurised" Organizations

*Dmitry Loschinin*
*President and CEO, Luxoft, Moscow, Russia*

## Introduction

Once relegated to simpler commodity work, outsourcing has become more mainstream since the dawn of the 21$^{st}$ century. Early experiments with outsourcing created a bumpy road for companies looking to reduce their overall costs and stay true to their core business functions. The fearful started their engines, stalled, and hit reverse. The fearless raced their engines and took each bump as part of the learning curve, each pit stop as an opportunity to sharpen their knowledge and skills as they integrated and revved outsourcing to its maximum horsepower.

The chase is on for companies driving towards a winning and sustainable future. These winning organisations know that outsourcing has proven itself to be a viable business model to speed time to market, attain leadership and competitive advantage, complement existing in-house resources, save money and ultimately, grow and thrive.

The outsourcing market is maturing at a rapid pace; in addition to India, the contenders from China, Russian and Brazil are gaining speed. In just a few short years they will move front and centre on the global track and create niche outsourcing market opportunities that will leverage their resources and strengths. There will be road hazards along the way – for these players as well as for the companies that do business with them. But make no mistake: Outsourcing is not a trend or test drive, it is on the fast lane of the future.

# The Outsourcing SuperHighway

Outsourcing is big business. By the year 2009, International Data Corporation (IDC) predicts that the global outsourcing market will reach $641.2 billion.[1]

A large portion of that business already flows into BRIC countries – Brazil, Russia, India and China, with the latter two taking in the majority of work. A recent survey by the Outsourcing Institute of 138 outsourcing decision-makers indicated that 41 per cent already outsourced to China as an alternative to India, and 13.6 per cent already outsourced to Russia. More importantly, these respondents expected their outsourcing work to these countries to continue in the coming years, with outsourcing to China increasing to 44.3 per cent and outsourcing to Russia increasing to 15.7 per cent. Outsourcing work to other countries was expected to remain the same or decline.[2]

Other studies have indicated that increasingly work is being assigned to Russia, particularly work from the U.S. and Europe, and outsourcing to Brazil is a small but growing trend. Brazil has the advantage of being in a similar time zone so it might seem an attractive choice for some.

## Outsourcing as a Strategic Business Practice and the BRICs

Early adopters saw outsourcing solely as a means to cut costs by farming out non-critical work to lower waged workers in other countries. Industry analysts recommended India as the destination of choice for outsourcing work, and India rose to prominence with its large labour pool, growing economy and skilled workforce. Today many organisations rely on outsourcing vendors to continue with this commodity-type work, and the BRICs as well as countries such as Mexico, Malaysia and the Philippines have benefited. But we also see a trend emerging of simple outsourcing functions moving back "home" – away from the offshore markets in India and either integrated back into organisations or located conveniently and cheaply near-shore.

According to Phil Hatch who heads consulting firm Ventoro, Western Europe, for example, is increasingly looking at Scotland and Ireland for call centre work closer to home, and Canada is home to the world's largest call

---

[1] Strategy and Business Magazine, „How to Be an Outsourcing Virtuoso," by Vinay Couto and Ashok Divakaran, 9/14/06.

[2] Outsourcing Institute, „Offshore Outsourcing and Risk Diversification," 11/06.

centre. That is not to say that all of this commodity type work is cycling back inside or nearby. This area still presents opportunity for the BRICs, particularly for those countries that don't have long technical histories or experience in taking on more sophisticated outsourcing assignments.

For mature companies with complex outsourcing needs, outsourcing will move well beyond the trend or commodity stage and emerge as a major strategic practice. Just as Six Sigma has been integrated throughout many a corporation, outsourcing will become part of the core business model under which many companies operate. To borrow a phrase from my friends at consultancy neoIT, these mature companies are "futurised" organisations.[3] They not only have thought seriously about the future, but also they have put that vision into action with the right blend of structure and systems, resources and geographies to seize every possible opportunity to deliver on its strategic mission. Futurised organisations are more adaptive to change moving forward, especially as the dynamics of competitive advantage change. Futurised organisations recognise that they can't always do it alone, and look at new markets as well as the way they outsource to stay on track against their overall business goals.

In the business practice model of outsourcing, companies will be challenged to find the right vendor for the right job. While India is booming and continues to be the first choice for many, companies recognise that a single source country can't keep up with anticipated demand or guarantee the best developers for each and every assignment – or even guarantee attention for small clients because vendors may be focused on larger projects. Major outsourcing players in India had some challenges over the past year keeping up with orders as their new business accounts soared. Companies that want to reduce their risks will migrate some of their outsourcing work to other geographies and to other outsourcing players. Companies want to feel that their work matters to their outsourcing vendors and that they, as customers, are important to their vendors.

There is an opportunity for multisourcing products, people and services that frees up internal resources for core business functions, leverages the culture and talent and resources of multiple geographies and provides a range of options for customers on the outsourcing track. This portfolio approach maximises the potential of outsourcing in all possible ways: By geography, by engagement model, by talent, by risk potential via working with multiple vendors and leveraging local economies. These factors present enormous opportunities for BRICs; Russia and China are especially suited for these tasks.

---

[3] Eugene Kublanov, neoIT, 10/06.

China is growing, and currently is the lead alternative to India. When it catches up and outpaces India – and it will, probably in less than 10 years – the country will be a formidable competitor for outsourcing needs.

Russia is stepping up as a leading player for complex outsourcing projects, leveraging the world-class talent pool that exists throughout the former Soviet Union. Overall, companies see Eastern Europe as the destination of choice for projects such as quality assurance (QA) and software support and look to Russia in particular for sophisticated product development, high-end consulting and mission-critical application development.

We have been talking here about basically two concepts of outsourcing – the simple and the complex – and how there will always be a need for both and where some of the BRICs generally will respond to those concepts. Let's focus now more specifically on Russia and the opportunities that emerge where Russian strengths and customer needs intersect.

## To Russia, with Love

Analysts and industry experts such as Esther Dyson, editor at large at CNET Networks, have said that the Russians are the absolute tops when it comes to complex programming such as mainframe programming, application development, web application/design, and content management skills. Russian legacy programming expertise is vast and deep; custom R&D and design work, embedded systems development, and specialised testing are all other hallmarks of Russia's quality work.

Gartner and Datamonitor, among others, estimate that Russian outsourcers will capture between a five to eight per cent share of the North American offshore services revenue by 2007. Already, the Russian outsourcing sector exceeds $1 billion. Luxoft has opened an office in Canada to augment the work done in its New York and Seattle locations and to serve as both near-shore convenience for North American customers and a feeder pipeline for projects going to Russia.

Russia will also become a major go-to nearshore vendor for European vendors due to its physical proximity. Look for close integration with customers and a lot of sophistication in projects in such areas as financial services, for example, where equity trading requires a lot of modelling and complex, analytical work. This is where core business functions are integrated with service performance. Very few companies outsource this area because it requires high-end support.

## But Why Russia?

So why is this happening in the first place? In addition to the qualities cited by analysts above, the interest in Russia is due to a variety of broader environmental, economic and human resource reasons, such as a good technology infrastructure, stable wages that are competitive with India, and perhaps most importantly, Russia's highly educated workforce with strong abstract thinking skills and creative problem-solving approaches.

## IT Focus

At the time of writing this chapter, the Russia-based offshore software development sector is comprised of 300 companies employing more than 250,000 IT professionals, and a total market size of $2.5 billion. Some of those companies include IBM, Dell, Intel, and Sun, who have R&D centres in Russia. In fact, Boeing's Moscow development centre is its largest outside the United States.

The outsourcing segment is smaller, with more than 80 companies employing an estimated 30,000 programmers. Outsourcing companies tend to be small, with Luxoft one of the largest at more than $65 million in 2005, but the entire market is growing. Outsourcing companies in Russia have bench strength in a range of industries such as financial services, technology, embedded systems, engineering, and manufacturing for larger companies. For example, Luxoft's clients include IBM, Boeing, Dell, T-Mobile, Deutsche Bank, Caterpillar and Citibank, and smaller software companies such as Ping Identity Corporation, Jabber, AirData and others.

Smaller software and product companies have tremendous success outsourcing to Russia because leading vendors have already demonstrated that Russia can play at the high end. The *Agile* software development methodology is an increasingly popular approach that shifts the traditional focus away from documenting and planning to communication and continual change. Product companies appreciate the proprietary client-centric engagement model Luxoft has developed, for example, to identify whether Agile will work for them. If Agile does make sense for the client, our process maps out the development and project management process every step of the way, ensures every single change is addressed, and mitigates any hidden risks.

They also appreciate the technology expertise that Russia brings to the table. Platforms such as Java and Microsoft .NET are second nature to

Russian developers. This familiarity with the development platforms makes it easier for product companies to outsource to Russia.

The whole notion of Agile, the facility with common development platforms and ongoing changes in development style will shape the outsourcing market in the future. Traditional methods will not go away; but collaboration methods such as Agile will enable people to work together better – whether they are 1,000 miles apart or even in the next cubicle.

## Economic Flexibility

There is more economic flexibility in Russia than in many of its outsourcing counterparts. In July 2006, the Russian government loosened restrictions on the rouble and how it flows in and out of the country; a step in the direction of a free market economy. In a September 2006 story that appeared on cnn.com, Steve Hanke, a Professor of Applied Economics and Co-Director of the Institute for Applied Economics and the Study of Business Enterprise at The Johns Hopkins University in Baltimore, said, "Russia's fledgling capital markets stand to become deeper, more efficient and more fully integrated with international markets. In short, convertibility will push Russia further along the globalist path…"

A stable economy makes customers feel comfortable doing business in Russia and attracts venture capital both from within the country and across its borders. According to Editor Svetlana Vronskaya in the October edition of the Russian IT Quarterly, "this summer … tremendous activity … went on in the governmental bodies of Russia, all of it being geared towards shaping the new line of legislative and administrative support to Russian IT exporters."[4]

State-owned funds, which will transition to private funding over the next several years, along with new agencies to provide tools for marketing and lead generation for Russian companies wishing to export their products, were established to spark additional growth in the IT sector. Thousands of Russian companies have already submitted applications for the new funding stream, and the numbers are expected to grow. These are just some of the economic drivers that spell visibility for all of Russia and help put it on the global outsourcing map.

---

[4] Russian IT Quarterly, 10/06.

## Outstanding Talent

The Outsourcing Institute's recent survey on the opportunities and risks of outsourcing, the talent available in Russia is a prime decision factor in choosing an outsourcing partner. "Of those research respondents whose organisation is currently offshoring work to Russia or planning to in the future, two-thirds said they consider the size and quality of the labour pool to be the most important attribute of that country."[5]

Russia's workforce is comprised of skilled and highly experienced high tech and engineering talent with creative minds and good communication abilities. Russia was ranked third by UNESCO in the number of scientists and engineers per capita worldwide. The country has a talent pool of over 4.7 million students, 50 per cent of which are majoring in science, math, and computer sciences.

Further, these students regularly win international programming contests. In the world's most prestigious competition, the Association of Computing Machinery (ACM) International Collegiate Programming Contest, Russia has won four gold medals in the last six years. Russia has a steady pipeline of brilliant engineers and developers coming out of its education system for years to come.

Dr. Deborah A. Palmieri, president of the Russian American Chamber of Commerce headquartered in Denver, Colorado, agrees, particularly when talking about technology. As she told me last year, "Russia is of great interest to the American high tech industry because of the superiority of its software engineers and their exceptional theoretical ability."

## Faster Time to Market

Furthermore, by using Russian talent for complex outsourcing tasks, Western firms can bring products to market far faster. How? Russian talent can be used for important, creative and innovative outsourcing work that normally would compete with other priorities that in-house talent focuses on. With a Russian outsourcer on board, companies can empower in-house talent to focus on their core competencies and still get the other priority assignments accomplished via leveraging the education, talent and valuable coding and product experience of the Russians.

---

[5] Outsourcing Institute, „Offshore Outsourcing and Risk Diversification," 11/06.

Dan Marovitz, chief operating officer for technology at Deutsche Bank's global banking unit told *Business Week* in 2006, "We wanted to accelerate what we were doing developmentally and couldn't afford to do it onshore." Responding to a question about the difference between Russian and India programmers, Marovitz replied, in part, "There is a real history of technical innovation in Russia, and there is almost a demand by the Russians we work with to be innovative and creative."

It seems that others concur. After a visit to Russia, *eWeek's* executive editor, Stan Gibson wrote, "Russian providers bring valuable qualities to the table: high-level thinking, strong English skills among executives and key staff, and a desire to break new ground on leading-edge projects."[6]

This has truly been our experience. Our clients often tell us that our people are our "secret sauce." Seventy per cent of Luxoft's employees bring more than seven years of IT background to every assignment and all experience wonderful challenges, growth opportunities and professional training in industries, technology and English right on our Luxoft campuses. They stay with us – an outsourcing industry astounding 94 per cent of the time. Clients see that and like that – and stay with us as well. Our commitment to quality and over delivering to our customers translates each year to an impressive 90 per cent client retention rate.

For Denver-based Ping Identity Corporation, an identity management company, Luxoft's commitment to people and training has paid off. "The success with Agile starts with really great people and that means the engineers and others in Luxoft," Bill Wood, Ping's vice president of engineering, told me at our most recent customer advisory board.

## Futurised Outsourcing Firms Map to Futurised Companies

Just as companies are maturing in the outsourcing process, vendors are, too. Futurised outsourcing providers – in India and Russia for example – will look to move up the value chain in the professional service arena. They'll try to be the next McKinsey – true high-end management consultants. They'll look at centres of excellence concepts for management services, and move away from head count billing and time/materials pricing. They'll start to pitch higher value and integrated service offerings that map to the evolving needs of their customer base.

---

[6] eWeek Magazine, „The Russians are Coming," by Stan Gibson, 6/12/06

Futurised outsourcing providers understand they have to demonstrate to their clients that they can handle a mission-critical function and build trust. Once they do that, the outsourcing provider gains permission from the client to talk about further innovation and more critical work that moves it further up the value chain. This trusted advisor role takes years to create and shape – it does not happen overnight and it won't be for every vendor in the outsourcing space.

Andre Durand, the CEO of Ping Identity, recently told an audience gathered at the prestigious think-tank DaVinci Institute that it can take upwards of 18 months or more to develop a solid, trustworthy, reciprocal partnership with the right outsourcing provider, one that has built its competency area over years, not months, that has a great engineering leader and relationship manager, that truly integrates with the customer as one team. Each side needs to commit 100 per cent and deliver/communicate 110 per cent of the time to truly make a relationship stronger and better.

Futurised outsourcing providers recognise that current delivery models will evolve and the lines will blur. In addition to pure nearshore and offshore models, we'll see the emergence of blended models. One scenario that is emerging occurs when a customer places the majority of its work nearshore, with auxiliary functions handled offshore, often times by the same vendor. Another potential scenario on the horizon is when just key design functions are delivered via nearshore centres while the bulk of the work is handled offshore.

## Building an Industry BRIC by BRIC

So what are the industries that present huge opportunities for BRIC countries and their outsourcing leaders? An interesting outsourcing scenario to watch will deal with the intersection of tech domains and front-office industry functions. Packaged services packed with value added components will be de rigueur for outsourcing companies maintaining global brands. Here are my predictions:

**Financial services** will continue to be a huge growth area, not only for India and Russia but also China and Brazil, too. Russia will remain an attractive destination because of its long history with huge legacy applications and will leverage this experience into more front-office, core applications. Select Indian players that have been in the outsourcing business for a long time are also poised for this growth area.

**Engineering** will be a huge opportunity for BRIC countries. Outsource vendors who already have domain experience doing engineering work, such as modifications to traditional machine building or test engineering, and have the right tools will be front and centre of the next wave of projects being outsourced.

**Software and technology** will continue to be in high demand, particularly in the U.S. and in Europe. There is a lot of work and not a lot of the right people to do the job, so there is tremendous potential here for BRIC outsourcers.

Deeper into technology are **embedded systems**, which again will be a major outsourcing play in the years to come and an opportunity for BRICs to put their pedal to the metal. This area requires tremendous software skills and electronics experience and will see non-BRIC outsourcing vendors playing to their electronics strengths.

- **Internet-related technologies** such as search engines or medical records will remain hot opportunities. As the size of information grows on the Internet, there will be a need for new and better methods of searching through all of the data.
- **Telecommunications** will continue being hot, both in hardware and in software. There are new developments in this industry daily and companies are looking aggressively at ways to maintain their competitive edge. Staying integrated and on top of all the aggressively evolving changes will be a welcome challenge for outsourcing vendors.
- **Healthcare** will remain an interesting industry from an outsourcing perspective. There is an ongoing need for electronic data capture balanced by compliance regulations such as HIPAA.
- As **manufacturing** becomes even more automated and shipping costs escalate, there appears to be a trend to bring manufacturing back home, onshore or nearshore. So BRICs considering beachhead offices closer to the U.S. and Europe may find some opportunities here.

These opportunities will translate into an overall sharpening of skills and more sophistication on the vendor side, regardless of whether they deliver the simple or the complex solutions of outsourcing. Major outsource vendors in BRIC countries will fuel growth in their local industries, their local communities and in turn their geographies. As a result, these companies and countries will mature to the point of offering next generation products and services that futuristic companies will demand, wherever they reside.

As a high-end outsourcing supplier, Luxoft recognises that embracing resources in other countries that strategically map to its vision is a critical step. Luxoft bridged in late 2006 to Vancouver to take on even more complex assignments from North America that require lots of iterations, sophisticated skills such as systems architecture and performance testing, and when needed, limited proximity to the client. In the first half of 2006, Luxoft acquired IT Consulting International, with a 12-year track record of successfully providing IT outsourcing, on-site staffing and project management services for Fortune 500 and middle market businesses. In 2007, Luxoft will open an office in Poland to provide new fronts of support in Europe that complement Luxoft development centres in Moscow, St. Petersburg, Dubna and Omsk, as well as in Kiev and Odessa, Ukraine. These moves are in direct response to the needs of our customer base: futurist organisations that want to save on cost but more importantly want their outsourcing efforts to tie directly into their strategic business practice. For them, and for us, Luxoft is a long-term partner in their success.

## Caution: Changing Road Conditions Ahead

As you can see, a variety of industry opportunities exist for BRIC outsourcing vendors to move into the fast lane. Their customers – whether they be "futurist" organisations or those that simply aspire to be – also have the potential to experience the thrill of helping to drive the BRIC outsourcing roadmap. As with any driving adventure, there is the thrill of the chase and well as the potential road hazards up ahead beyond the curve. Here are some trends to watch, things to think about and areas in which to act quickly in the big outsourcing race.

- **Think value, not just cost.**
  Companies who think only about cost savings may not even make it to the chase. This is particularly true when dealing with complex outsourcing projects such as product development. Companies should look for partners who can provide maximum agility and flexibility to be able to quickly shift priorities brought on by new or changed product features.

- **Outsourcing will be as commonplace as Six Sigma.**
  Companies will equate outsourcing to competitive advantage and embrace it as a strategic business function. It will be a natural extension of the self-audits they undertake to keep their competitive advantage, such as the review and globalisation of functions and the evaluation and restructuring of resources. Outsourcing is a perfect example of where strategic ROI and financial ROI not only intersect but also create positive momentum for the company.

- **Choose a trusted partner, not just a vendor.**
  Customers should also look for outsourcing partners whose engineers operate as a completely integrated team with the customer so that everyone – no matter where or for which company they work – operates as a single entity, as a crew bound by a singular purpose, values and goals.

- **Fluency is your fuel.**

  Fluency and competency – in English, in technology, in specific industries – need to guide a company's decision making. Companies should look for outsourcers that provide their employees with ongoing training – so that the team is expert in their business and is motivated to stay on and complete the work. Who wants to lose precious development time training new hires if workforce attrition is high?

- **Cultural diversity is your innovation starter kit.**
  If innovation is your business, you need to embrace cultural diversity. Like- minded people on a project may foster repetitive thinking, while the various thinking styles of those from different cultures will spark new, fresh thinking and approaches.

- **It's always about the customer. Period.**

  A customer-centric approach is at the heart of most successful companies, and the smart ones take that a step further to ensure their outsourcing partners feel and act the same way. Look for an outsourcing partner that can not only promise but also deliver real value, in the way of robust product or service offerings, clear economic or leadership advantage and/or operational or infrastructure benefits that impact the bottom line. The more mature outsourcing partners are already doing this.

- **A Balanced Portfolio Takes on New Meaning.**
  Companies need to understand and embrace the BRIC geographies and leverage the resources within them. A portfolio approach leverages the strengths of all the geographies a company chooses to work in – the challenge is effectively integrating the portfolio. Companies need to ensure they put the right links in place so that all parties know their role and are working off synchronised project plan, and have the best resources in tools in place.

Outsourcing is entering an exciting stage of growth and the BRIC countries are going to be directly in the midst of all the opportunities and challenges. Companies who fail to get into the race, fail. In fact, Forrester Research expects the total value of outsourced information-technology services by companies in North America alone to cross $100 billion by the end of 2006. Expect that to grow even more significantly once the BRICs play front and centre on the global stage.

The key is to find quality, trustworthy outsourcing vendors, whose work, business style, culture and ethics are synergistic. From there set tangible and clear collective goals, and apply appropriate and reasonable client resources to help drive program results and remain committed to a long-term and successful partnership. In sum, leverage outsource partners and their integrated service offerings, flexible methodology and top resources to create competitive advantage and significant ROI. Outsourcing is one core business practice model that is here to stay.

## Acknowledgements

Developing a chapter for a major book such as this involves the contributions of many people. Luxoft wishes to thank the following people who helped inform content, share stories and willingly contribute their ideas and support: Eugene M. Kublanov, Managing Director and Chief Operating Officer at services globalisation firm neoIT; Phil Hatch, head of the offshore outsourcing consulting firm Ventoro; as well as senior executives of the Luxoft management team.

# Eastern Europe as Most Promising Market

*Alexander Egorov*
*CEO, Reksoft, St. Petersburg, Russia*

*"Nobody knows exactly what Russia's future is. But there is only one way to bring the parameters of our lives – first of all, labour productivity and then net income, level of education and science, and live duration – closer to those of our more successful neighbors in the world.*

*It is necessary to develop legal and moral conditions for consistent, fair and exciting competitiveness in all spheres of human life, in business and politics. It is only fair and honest competition that helps successful countries grow richer launching new products and services everyday. It is only competition that makes it possible for intellectual elite to reach management positions in the society and closes the entrance door for tramps.*

*Aforementioned legal and moral conditions are the base for modern successful liberal democracies in the West. The substitution of fair talents' competition with struggle of administrative resources as well as all-powerfulness of the government constitutes the gap between us and civilised countries. If we, in our country, don't create the base for liberal society we will perhaps avoid crisis, but will stay poor..."*

Dmitry Zimin
Honorary President of OAO "Vympelkom",
founder of "Dynasty" investment fund
1992 – 2001: President and CEO of OAO "Vympelkom"

*"The tendency of the international media to highlight bad news rather than good can lead to perceptions of risk among foreign companies that outstrip the reality...Yet many investors have decided the rewards outweigh the risks"*

*Financial Times* Special Report "Investing in Russia", November 2005

The Russian Federation is commonly accepted as the most promising market in Eastern Europe. The reality of Russia's steady economic growth is recognised by such credible sources as the World Bank, UNESCO and the Economist, indicating that the country's macroeconomic climate has surely reached the threshold of fertility.

However, the global positioning of Russia has little changed since the 1850s. So far our country is best described as a raw materials economy – as no other industry can compete with oil and gas exports in terms of revenue, which comprised just a little below $164bn in 2005. The export of oil and gas makes up to 67 per cent of all export volume from Russia, which indicates the dependence of the country on the world prices of energy resources. Such a state of affairs cannot be viewed as normal and Russia needs some serious measures to diversify its export portfolio.

However there are a number of industries in the Russian economy that can bring substantial export volumes if they are properly handled. One such industry is the Russian IT services industry.

I would like to comment on the common perceptions of the Russian software industry and the way changes have been introduced. I will also elaborate more on the macroeconomic developments as well as the government support, which are two critical factors for the success of the industry internationally. In conclusion I will point out the pathway to success, which I personally think of as the only viable way for the Russian software sector.

## New Old Opportunity

The global market for offshore IT services continues to grow at a remarkable rate, driven primarily by U.S. customer demand, according to IDC. McKinsey predicts global offshore outsourcing spend to hit $110 billion by 2010. The main customers of offshore outsourcing service will still be North American enterprises (44 per cent of the world offshore outsourcing consumption) The active growth of IT outsourcing services consumption can be however seen in other developed countries as IT outsourcing becomes a standard cost optimisation practice in the leading global companies.

India dominates as a country fully exploiting its first mover advantage gained in the 1970-80s where body-shopping arrangements were followed by the first offshore jobs from the USA and UK. China is investing a lot in increasing the market share. Russia still thinks of the game as worth playing and has all the necessary prerequisites to play a much more important role in the global IT sourcing market.

By 1989 the Indian government was already actively involved in subsidising and promoting the offshore IT outsourcing industry. At the same time in the Soviet Union, a real software and service industry was only beginning to emerge. The situation in the 1990s in Russia was not favourable for the development of IT services exports. Despite a large number of highly qualified IT specialists who could be used in international projects, the most serious hindrance was a lack of any entrepreneurial culture as well as management and marketing human resources. This is easily explained by the fact that such an industry sector as industrial software development for export did not exist in the USSR.

The negative image of the country was also a significant weakness as it pictured an unstable country with high levels of corruption, crime and bureaucracy. As a result despite some initial positive results, Russian companies did not succeed in benefiting from the Y2K problem, nor from high demand during the Internet bubble of the late 1990s. Whilst by the end of the decade, the revenues of Indian companies were billions, Russians could only count their first millions.

The weakness of young companies and lack of awareness of the IT exports opportunity by the Russian government led to the current situation where the market volume of the more than a decade-old IT industry in Russia is still insignificant compared with other industries. According to a number of sources, in 2005 the software exports from the country was $1bn. Just compare this figure with the volume of export from India – in financial year 2005 it exceeded $23bn.

An "accepted wisdom" about the Russian offshore industry, based on market research studies and industry surveys and on other publications, laid out arguments for and against outsourcing to Russia. A limited number of the academic literature is exclusively devoted to assessing the successes and shortcomings of this industry so far. The "accepted wisdom" is frequently repeated and elaborated in different reports, as presented in "The maturation of the Russian Offshore Software Industry" research paper by William McHenry and Stephen Hawk.

### *Positives*

- Excellence of Russia's IT Human resources, e.g. in-depth technical skills, R&D experience, experience with complex projects
- Excellent education system
- European / Western Culture

- Location (close to Europe and the U.S. east coast)
- Low Labour Costs

*Negatives*

- Inexperience in offshore software development; poor understanding of business practices and project management on the part of Russian software firms
- Poor English skills
- Difficulty of visiting Russia due to visa requirements
- Bandwidth costs; deficient telephone and data communications infrastructure
- Lack of certification organisations (and CMM certified IT firms)
- Offerings too narrow; too little forward-looking strategic planning
- Poor marketing capabilities; lack of a campaign; poor foreign representation
- Poor business environment (intellectual property protection, tax and labour laws, perceptions of corruption and instability)
- Lack of meaningful support by the Federal government for the offshore industry
- Lack of world track record; perceptions of software piracy

It is obvious to every industry insider that the situation in the Russian IT export sector has improved dramatically over the past four years. However, these changes are often not obvious to the outside observer. Russian companies have to communicate with the market in a more professional manner to avoid old prejudices and eliminate the negative effects, which may arise from them in sales channels.

Russian pioneer companies achieved some results in creating a totally new sector of Russian exports, but they could not demonstrate the growth achieved by the world market of IT services so far. However, the appearance of Russian suppliers in the reports of the leading analytical houses in 2002-2005 gives them a chance to play big.

According to Gartner Group, Russia has all the prerequisites to gain 5-6 per cent of the world market of IT outsourcing. In 2007 that could mean an additional export volume of US$ 5bn for the country, which – for example – is more than Russia's weapons exports (which was as high as $4.3bn in 2003).

Still, the overall impression about Russian IT by Gartner Group – one of the most influential analyst companies in the IT world – is as follows: "Lacking government support, Russia is facing the threat of a rapidly closing 'window of opportunity' for establishing a credible offshore services industry."

I assume that this window of opportunity will not close and that Russian companies will eliminate their weaknesses quite fast, taking into consideration the dynamic of changes in 2003-2005.

Over the past two years a lot of different research has been published by some well-known Western and Russian institutions such as Gartner Group, IDC, Forrester Research, META Group (later acquired by Gartner), CNews, Expert RA, etc. According to their data and based on my own observations of the market, I can assess the pluses and minuses of the Russian offshore software industry in a different, more favourable way.

The most important improvements of the past two years can be summarised as:

| Prior Assessments | Current Assessment (September, 2006) |
|---|---|
| Poor marketing capabilities; lack of a campaign; poor foreign representation | Representation improved greatly; marketing capabilities improving; global campaign is set to come in a few months (see below the part on the government support) |
| Difficulty of visiting Russia due to visa requirements | Still a large difficulty for both inward and outward travel |
| Lack of world track record; perceptions of software piracy | Piracy perception no longer a problem; still need better track record, although greatly improving with new MNC coming to work with Russian software vendors |
| Inexperience in offshore software development; poor understanding of business practices and project management on the part of Russian software firms | Very considerable improvement with quality certifications (ISO, CMM/CMMi) rapidly acquired both by large and smaller players. |

| | |
|---|---|
| Lack of certification organizations (and CMM certified IT firms) | More than a dozen of CMM/CMMi certified ESPs, creation of government-supported fund for certification. |
| Offerings too narrow; too little forward-looking strategic planning | Remains a problem area. Historically, Russian vendors offered services covering the entire range of the market, without any particular vertical specialization. |
| Excellence of Russia's IT Human resources, e.g. in-depth technical skills, R&D experience, experience with complex projects | Still a major plus being a heritage from the Soviet times. |
| Excellent education system | Still a major plus with 225 thousand students in IT-related areas graduating annually and the large companies in IT investing heavily in additional education programs together with state universities. |
| European / Western Culture | Still a plus always mentioned by existing European customers in customer satisfaction surveys. |
| Location (close to Europe and the U.S. east coast) | Still a plus saving traveling time and not overlapping much working hours. |
| Low Labor Costs | Competition on cost alone becoming harder, but large savings still possible |
| Poor English skills | Considerable improvement with more than 50 % of all employees in the Russian software sector speaking English on advanced level |
| Bandwidth costs; deficient telephone and data communications infrastructure | The infrastructure in Russia is considered being up to Western level. As reported by AT&T "mobile phone penetration is higher than in major U.S. cities: 70% in Moscow compared to 54% in New York City; VoIP is growing in Russia: The largest market in Europe, 6th largest in the world; Broadband is widespread: Over 1,250,000 active xDSL lines" |

| | |
|---|---|
| Lack of industry associations as effective as NASSCOM | Russoft IT Services association (http://www.russoft.org) is gradually emerging as the premier industry group for promoting country's software sector. |
| Lack of meaningful support by the Federal government for the offshore industry | The government started to pay attention to the industry since 2004. See the part on the government support below. |
| Poor business environment (intellectual property protection, tax and labour laws, perceptions of corruption and instability) | Overall business environment is improving; specific law reform and enforcement are being introduced. |

Although there is a long way to go, the improvements at the industry level are obvious. It is however important not to forget the crucial external factors that influence the performance of the Russian software sector in general – which are the economics of the country and measures that the government has been undertaking to reinforce the developments in the IT sector.

## Russian Federation Economic Overview

The economic performance of the Russian Federation over the last five years is more than impressive. According to the estimates of the World Bank Economic Unit, in the time span between 1998 and 2005, Russian GDP grew by an estimated 48 percent, while the real income of population went up by 46 percent. The country achieved an unprecedented macroeconomic stability along with strong budgetary and current account surpluses.

2004 was Russia's sixth straight year of growth, with the average of 6.5 per cent annual growth rate. The Russian State Statistics Service indicated that the GDP grew by an estimated 5.7 percent in the first half of 2005, as compared to 7.4 percent growth during the same period of 2004. It estimated the GDP in the first quarter of 2006 to have grown by 5.5 per cent year-on-year to 5.72 trillion roubles ($212 billion). Russia's Ministry of Economic Development and Trade forecasted the GDP growth to be 6.4-6.5 per cent by the end of 2006.

Undoubtedly, rising oil prices and a relatively cheap rouble rate are important drivers of the country's economic rebound. However investment and consumer-driven demand have played a noticeably increasing role, too.

The present state of affairs in the Russian economy is best conveyed by the following World Bank quote: "Russian economic growth in 2005 has been influenced by three primary factors: a continuing rapid expansion of domestic incomes and demand, improvements in the expectations of investors, and growing competitive pressures from the real appreciation of the rouble. In this context, Russian economic growth remains strong".

Personal incomes and wages also grew quite rapidly over the last year, with this growth continuing into 2006. According to data from the Ministry of Economic Development and Trade the growth in Russia's household incomes hit a record in the last two years in June 2006, increasing by 15.2 per cent year-on-year. Household income had increased in the first half of 2006 by 11.1 per cent against the same period last year, and personal salaries increased by 12.1 per cent.

Investment growth in all sectors of the Russian economy has been picking up with the significant investments having accelerated across the board. Inflows of foreign direct investment increased by around 30 percent in the first half of 2005, according to a number of sources. Investment activity, including Foreign Direct Investment (FDI), appears to be currently soaring. It reached 15 billion USD by the end of 2005 and stood at 8.8 billion USD in the first quarter of 2006 according to the Federal State Statistics Service.

The reforms in taxation, budgetary institutions, and the removal of administrative barriers to business facilitated the rapid development of market institutions in many areas. Besides, the government has taken a number of initiatives to reassure private investors of a political commitment to improving the investment climate. There could be a genuine investment boom in Russia in the near future.

Russia has also dramatically improved its international financial position since the 1998 financial crisis, with its foreign debt declining from 90 per cent of GDP to around 28 per cent. Strong oil export earnings have allowed Russia to increase its foreign reserves from only $12 billion to some $120 billion at year end 2004. These achievements have raised business and investor confidence in Russia's economic prospects. This fact was confirmed by the international credit rating upgrades that Russia gained in 2005 and 2006. January and October last year have seen Standard and Poor's and Moody's correspondingly awarding Russia an upgraded investment rating. Ratings agency Moody's Investors Service is quoted as saying "Russia's liquidity and debt ratios have improved dramatically in a relatively short time period. The outlook for the rating is now stable". Its rival Fitch upgraded Russia's sovereign rating in August

2006 to 'A-' from 'BBB+'. Standard and Poor's has placed Russian debt the equivalent of one level higher in its 'BBB-' category.

In its annual foreign direct investment rating in 2005, A.T.Kearney moved Russia from the 11th to the 6th place in their index of the most attractive countries for investment. According to A.T.Kearney consultants, because of growing consumption, Russia is becoming increasingly attractive for carmakers, retailers and telecommunications companies.

2005 has also witnessed some progress in the business-government relations in Russia. The new concessions law, priorities for the development of private government partnerships (PPPs), and special economic zones for joint state private projects are all part of this initiative.

Looking back, the last two years were years of aggressive economic growth. Russia's macroeconomic accounts all remained in surplus: with 34 billion USD in the Stabilisation Fund there was a substantial growth in almost all regions and sectors. High commodity prices boosted Russia's economic prospects – not only for short-term growth. Most international investors have revised upward their expectations and therefore increased the perceived attractiveness of Russia's resources. Foreign direct investments are pouring into the country and the real appreciation of the rouble is carrying on.

## Russia in the Global Economy

*The Economist* puts it straightforwardly: "The emerging markets are the future". And Russia presents the best example of a rapidly emerging market that is set to become the most attractive place for near future investments. The booming domestic demand and consumer spending (expected to raise up to $500bn in 2008), driven by soaring personal incomes and an expanding middle class, all make the market outlook excellent for years to come.

Cost efficiency rules today's world, and so it is no surprise that Russian companies can offer a good opportunity for cost cutting initiatives. The main reason for this fact is that those who survived the 1998 economic crisis in Russia became very "lean and mean" in their own cost structure and can offer the same model for their partners.

Russia has already become the key EMEA market for most international companies with growth rates ranging from 15 to 45 per cent in all industry sectors. A survey of Vienna in the Economist magazine rates Russia as the best market for all of CEEMEA. It will come as no surprise when – finally – Russia is identified as the exports launch pad for all European countries.

Notwithstanding, some moderate risks apply. The issue of corruption is mentioned above all else. However the recent surveys among the executives of the MNCs show that most concerns come from those who have not yet started operations in Russia, while there is a significantly lower level of worry from companies that are already on Russian ground. This means that an outdated perception of the country's economic topology still plays a role in the decision-making process of those considering working in Russia, whereas the Russian reality is really very different.

## Living Standards in Russia

The standard of living in modern Russia is best described in the recent article by Dmitri Trenin in "Carnegie Moscow Centre" – "Reading Russia Right":

"Muscovites' average incomes are superior to those in many capitals of the new EU entrants. All Russia (144 million people) is not Moscow or St. Petersburg (10 and 5 million people, respectively), but each provincial capital in the country is a Moscow of sorts to its neighbourhood. All are ringed by thousands of newly built, expensive dachas (summerhouses), all have traffic jams, ... and all have stores open around the clock selling goods for which there is a market.

Moreover, this market is expanding. Freedom House's index ranks Russia very low on the democracy scale, but the "IKEA" index (named after the Swedish furniture and home accessories company) reveals a different dimension. Giant IKEA stores are fanning out from Moscow to nearly all the major cities in the country. Russia is unlikely to go through a political revolution anytime soon, but it is in the midst of a revolution in retail trade. Although this development promises no triumph of democracy, it does give many a very real right of choice. Millions of ordinary Russians exercise their right to choose in this expanding market. For example, planeloads of business travellers converge on London, Zurich, and Frankfurt daily; hundreds of thousands of Russians, thinking they have lost the Crimea as a vacation destination, are rediscovering the Mediterranean or, for those living in Siberia and the Far East, the Yellow Sea. Of the 6.5 million Russians who travelled abroad in 2004, 1.5 million went to Turkey, and around 1 million each to Egypt and China.

## Business Culture in Russia

Although it is often treated as a separate course in cross-cultural classes, Russian business culture shares common values with its European counterparts. Realising a customer-centric corporate culture has become the mission for a growing number of Russian companies. Russian businesses realised that acting responsibly toward its own employees and society in general can enhance the long-term economic performance of the enterprise.

In view of the expressed desire by many Russian companies to become members of the global business community such values as customer satisfaction, integrity, social responsibility, and innovation are perceived to be crucial for sustainable success.

## Government Support for Software Exports

I have made this part separate to emphasise the importance of the attention that the Russian state has recently paid to the software exports industry. Along with the overall favourable initiatives brought up by the government for the whole high-tech sector (which include the development of a number of technoparks around the country, the federal law "On Special Economic Zones in the Russian Federation"), the achievements so far include one of the most useful and fast-paying laws on the industrial VAT exemption for IT services companies (effective from January, 2006).

On August 11, 2006, Russian Prime Minister Mikhail Fradkov signed a law that will launch a *venture fund with a special focus on ICT industry*. The fund would obtain financing of around $52mn and initially be 100 per cent-owned by the state. By the end of the first year of operations, the government stake will be decreased to 49 per cent and after the third year of operations, the fund should be entirely private. The Ministry of IT and Telecommunications lobbied for the IT fund to be created to ensure that the sector does not remain underfinanced compared to other high-tech sectors.

The State Duma of the Russian Federation has finally passed the long-awaited *law on tax incentives for export software development companies* based in Russia. The law was prepared by the Ministry of Information Technologies and Communications and has already passed the third and final hearing in the Duma. According to the new legislation, companies engaged in software outsourcing activities will get a major tax relief due to the reduced unified social tax paid per employee. To be able to act under this new legislation, a company needs to generate more than 70 per cent of its revenue from IT consulting, software export or other IT outsourcing services and have not fewer than 50 employees on its payroll.

And on top of that, less than a month after the President Putin had signed the law on tax incentives for Russian software outsourcing companies and just a few days since a new state-funded venture capital body with a special focus on IT sector had been launched, the Russian government stepped forward with a new initiative to support the ever growing IT exports industry. The Ministry of IT and Communications announced in August 2006 that it created *the Federal Agency of Software Exports support*. The main goal of this entity will be the promotion of software outsourcing sector in the global marketplace through the support of special events in the target markets as well as raising the public awareness of the opportunities which the cooperation with Russian ESPs provide.

Among other tasks of the Federal Agency will be the accreditation of individual companies to become eligible for the tax breaks as stated in the recent legislation. The Minister Leonid Reyman stressed that firms established in the Russian Federation as well as foreign companies with Russia legal entity are eligible both for tax incentives and the state support.

## Maturing Trends

I see plenty of evidence of the maturation of the Russian IT outsourcing industry. First of all, the top Russian players (10-12 companies) are maturing their offering, thus widening the gap between themselves and the rest of the domestic competitors. There is a clear sense of differentiation in the leaders' strategic positioning. Staying competitive in the long run calls for above-average growth rates, which organic growth cannot secure. With this in mind, there is an M&A mood in the air with more Ms than As expected. At the same time, the market stays fragmented with a multitude of providers having 10 to 40 headcount. They look for larger players to team up with, and the most plausible scenario of development for the next two-three years, is that we will be seeing a lesser number of ESPs active in the Russian software outsourcing industry.

Another trend of the past year that is worth mentioning is the occurrence of FDIs into Russia-based IT services companies. We have witnessed the Nordic investment into St.Petersburg-based Reksoft in November, funds coming to EPAM Systems in February and acquisition of Nizhny Novgorod's Telma by a Swedish system integration house. The Nordic Venture Network visit to Russia in April and the creation of a state-managed investment fund with a special focus on IT are all evidence to the rising attractiveness of investing into Hi-Tech Russia.

Another remarkable tendency in the market is the appearance of European system integrators on Russian ground, either through building their own captive centres or by planting development centres at third-party provider sites. Although the government support was not as active as the Russian IT community had hoped, there is still plenty of IT favouring legislation being passed.

The year gone has left a strong sense of the fact that Russian vendors are leading in Eastern Europe, both in terms of size and capabilities. With the outsourcing market of one billion USD in volume for 2005, Russia is expected to grow at the rate of 30 per cent in the next three years and thus surpass the whole of Eastern European.

As Pascal Matzke of Forrester Research pointed out, Central and Eastern Europe is getting stronger, but advantages will be short-lived due to a number of risk factors such as the lack of national champions, absorption of the local talent by global providers and wage inflation which has already hit the large metropolitan areas. This gives the Russian players a chance to take over Eastern Europe in the global outsourcing marketplace. The clients that already chose Russia as an outsourcing destination over closer Eastern European regions are the best proof: Deutsche Bank, Fujitsu Siemens Computers, Nokia, Siemens, TietoEnator, T-Mobile and T-Systems.

There is an excellent passage in the Forrester Research paper titled "Debunking Russian Offshore Myths". It was written with respect to the Russian information technology market, but could speak for industry across the entire country: "Give up using myths as decision tools. Some of the myths about Russia and its offshore software developers hold at least a measure of truth. But others fall down on close inspection – and may not have been really founded in fact in the past. IT execs looking for sound offshore software development skills should use a more fact-based platform to evaluate their Russian opportunity".

## Conclusion

I believe that there are two ways that the Russian offshore software industry can follow. The first way is to emphasise the uniqueness of Russian technology firms as the only ones to be able to carry out high-end innovative work for western customers that draws on the strong science/technical orientation of the top layer of Russian programmers. Although this strategy is well suited to the somewhat limited resources available in most firms for rapid growth, it is difficult to expect great demand for such sophisticated work. Of course, it will also be an attractive niche in the software market, but I do not think that the Russian companies should seriously rely on a substantial number of Western companies coming to Russia for innovative solutions rather than for reducing costs and/or diversifying their provider portfolio.

The second way to develop the Russian software industry is to offer experienced software developers who are now becoming fully proficient domestically in modern business systems and business system programming. The leading companies in the market are getting large enough and have obtained the needed quality certifications to make the Russian outsourcing industry increasingly capable of competing closely with Asian firms in developing business systems and business system programming.

And I hold a firm belief that Russian IT will miss its historical chance if it continues positioning itself as a premium-level world product (the first way) while not being one. The "new wave" of Russian IT will come from the IT service market sector, based on companies that have been built from scratch within the past decade. These companies went back to their roots and began to exploit some fundamental advantages of the Russian IT workforce, which are:

- Well-educated, scalable resource pool with high cultural proximity to the target markets;
- Economy cost level (also in the long run);
- Large domestic market, which could help building up efficient IT solutions suitable for world market, at a later stage.

Such companies already started to climb up the value chain. Therefore, today's most important task for the Russian IT industry is to integrate itself into the global IT service market as broad and deeply as possible. Only at this frontline I can see people developing themselves personally to the level required for real competition. The worst thing could be to shorten the frontline by positioning ourselves as a boutique just because we do not have a clue how to compete in the mass markets or try to hide within the domestic market where competition is largely substituted by "administrative networking."

Without the creation of a mature national IT ecosystem nothing positive will happen – in services or the product sectors. The foundation, the base of this ecosystem is the service/systems export market, and the larger it will be, the better will be the result for Russia in the long run.

# Dreaming with BRICs

*Dmitry Ponomarev*
*President and Chairman, Mera Networks, Nizhny Novgorod, Russia*

The BRICs dream is here. How overstated and unbelievable it might seem, it is slowly but steadily becoming a reality. Although sceptics would argue that dreaming as far as more than 40 years into the future is a debatable point, the BRICs economies are definitely following the track to achieve the 2050 landmark that Goldman Sachs have projected for them.

The Goldman Sachs predictions set challenging objectives for the Russian government and economy. The country has already achieved notable progress in economic and social development; however further advances will present challenges to overcome. Russia has all the potential necessary to cope with the problems it faces today and there is not a single reason why Russia should not keep pace with the BRICs projections.

In this chapter, I will give an overview of the BRICs projections with regard to the general economic and social situation in Russia, review the Russian IT service industry's present standing, apply the BRICs projections to the IT industry including both its domestic and export-oriented components, and elaborate on potential scenarios and changes we shall expect to come in the future.

## Review of the BRICs Economic Predictions

The economic report "Dreaming with BRICs: The path to 2050" by Goldman Sachs released in October 2003 examines the future economic trends of the BRICs economies based on a solid and profound economic model simulating temporal dynamics of various economic parameters such as GDP, GDP per capita and currency appreciation. The overall results of economic analysis are mind-boggling and can be briefly summarised as follows:

- Over the next 50 years, the world economy could undergo drastic changes and the BRICs economies could evolve to become a much larger force in the world economic landscape: while currently they are worth less than 15 per cent. If things go right, by 2025 the BRICs economies could account for over half the size of the G6 and in less than 40 years, they could jointly outsize the G6 in US dollar terms. Moreover, out of the current G6, only the US and Japan might retain their standing among the six largest economies in 2050. The signs of significant impact of the BRICs economies as a source of new demand and spending could start showing even earlier: as early as 2009, the annual increase in US dollar spending from BRICs could be greater than that from the G6 and more than twice as much as it is now. By 2025, the annual increase in US dollar spending from BRICs could be twice that of the G6, and four times higher by 2050.

- About two-thirds of the increase in US dollar GDP from the BRICs economies should come from a higher real growth, with the balance through currency appreciation. The BRICs real exchange rates could appreciate by up to 300 per cent over the next 50 years (an average of 2.5 per cent a year).

- Individuals in BRICs are still likely to be poorer on average than individuals in the G6 economies, with the exception of Russia. By 2050 the projected GDP per capita for Russia (about US$50,000) could match or exceed that of major European economies (Germany, France, Italy) while remaining lower than that of Japan (about US$67,000), UK (about US$59,000), and the US (about US$84,000). By 2050 India could have the lowest GDP per capita (US$17,000) among largest economies including both G6 and BRICs (Russia – US$50,000, Brazil – US$27,000, and China – US$31,000), while China and Brazil could be roughly what the developed economies are now.

The further publication "The BRICs and Global Markets: Crude, Cars and Capital" by Goldman Sachs released a year later, expands the previous economic analysis and focuses in detail on what such intensive BRICs growth could mean for the three major areas of global market development: demand for major commodities (e.g. energy and oil) and consumer goods (e.g. cars) as well as for growth of capital market. The analysis shows that continued growth in BRICs could push the near-term world growth rate above 4 per cent and produce an impact with most visible and broadest global consequences – increasing demand and corresponding price pressures in commodity markets in general and energy, oil and metal markets in particular. The BRICs contribution to global oil demand is set to increase further, with the BRICs share rising from 17 per cent now to some 30 per cent in 2025.

The key assumption of the BRICs projections is firmly based on the premise that the BRICs nations follow policies and develop institutions that are supportive of growth. Yet another important factor that might prevent the BRICs dream from becoming a reality and whose influence could not be undermined is whether the advanced economies actually 'allow' the BRICs to develop along the above lines.

## Why BRICs?

If Brazil, Russia, India and China follow the BRICs projections they are going to change the earth's economic landscape dramatically. However, what are the reasons for bunching these highly heterogeneous economies into one group? Why do Goldman Sachs assign BRICs the role of the future key players of the world economy?

The reasons are obvious. The four giants differ very much, however they perfectly complement each other. The first two BRICs – Brazil and Russia – are huge countries exceedingly rich in natural resources; hence it is logical that these economies will further enforce their positions in a world short of commodities and energy. Accordingly, they are likely to gain greater geopolitical influence in the American and Eurasian regions respectively by providing other world's largest commodities consumers and diversifying their own economies based on the global commodities boom.

India and China – the other two giants – have tremendous human resources. The populations of India and China combined together account for 2.3bn, which makes 35 per cent of the world's total population of 6.5 bn. Whereas in terms of production, currently India and China yield a mere 4 per cent of global GDP. Nonetheless India and China are going through rapid urbanisation and industrialisation which in combination with their vast human resources will most likely allow such countries to outperform the present global economy leaders.

Obviously it is not the current economic standing of the BRICs but rather the changing economic landscape and the growth rates within these countries that gives food for Goldman Sachs' reflections. Hence, the BRICs taken as a whole possess ample human power and abundant natural resources, which will enable them to fuel each other's growth and thus follow the Goldman Sachs challenging projections.

When one speculates on the future of ICT services and how the emerging BRICs economies will affect the global ICT market it is absolutely a must to consider where BRICs countries start with relation to their respective IT capabilities.

**Table 1.** BRICs: Population vs. national GDP vs. total national IT revenues vs. total IT & software exports for 2005

|  | Pop. (m) | GDP, $ bn | Total national IT Revenues, $ bn | National IT Revenues, per capita, $ | Total Outsourcing Services Exports, $ bn |
|---|---|---|---|---|---|
| **Brazil** | 188 | 619.7 | 17.20 | 91.5 | 0.3 |
| **Russia** | 143 | 740.7 | 11.00 | 76.9 | 1.0 |
| **India** | 1,095 | 719.8 | 28.40 | 25.9 | 13.5 |
| **China** | 1,314 | 2,225 | 48.75 | 37.1 | 3.6 |

*Data sources: Wikipedia; Brazil-IT; Russoft; the Russian State Statistics Service; NASSCOM.org; China.org.cn*

At the moment Brazil demonstrates fairly modest figures for outsourcing exports volumes. At the same time, the national IT GDP per capita – measure of nationwide penetration of various IT technologies – is the biggest of all the BRICs. The standings of other BRICs countries in terms of national IT GDP per capita do not come as a surprise: Russia slightly lags behind Brazil; while China's and India's national GDPs per capita are twofold and threefold lower than that of Russia respectively.

The Indian IT industry is very export-oriented and holds the biggest share in the international outsourcing market. However, it demonstrates the lowest indices for IT products and services consumption per capita within the country.

With the biggest national GDP per capita, Russia comes second with just a little lag after Brazil in terms of domestic IT products and services consumption. Obviously among the four BRICs, Brazil and Russia stand out as the most IT-enabled nations whose presence in the offshore outsourcing market is well below their real potential.

## The Russian IT Industry in Numbers

According to the Russian ICT Ministry, the Russian IT and software services market totalled USD 11 billion in revenue in 2005. The annual growth averaged 20 per cent over the recent five years, which exceed the average Russian GDP growth rates by a factor of 3. The revenue of the IT exports industry reached a total of $1bn in 2005. In 2006, the national IT revenue is predicted to exceed $13bn, whereas IT exports are expected to total in between $1.4bn (RUSSOFT estimates) and $1.8bn (Russian ICT Ministry estimates).

The total IT revenue accounted for a tiny 1.5 per cent share of the Russian GDP in 2005, which does not reflect the real IT potential of the country. Partly, the lag can be attributed to the fact that the industry took a long time to get established – only after Russia began to recover from the geopolitical catastrophe of recent years. Thus, the industry has plenty of room for growth and will follow the trend with about 19 per cent annual growth rate (IDC estimates).

A strong demand for IT services from domestic consumers – corporate sector and state agencies – has laid a solid base for such a rapid growth. The major domestic IT consumers are the machine building industry, oil extraction and refinery enterprises, metal, chemical, and electric power industries.

Remarkably, the Russian state agencies IT spending is also on the up due to a steady inflow of petrodollars that enables them to expand their IT budgets tremendously. The administrative reform that has touched all national and local government agencies and the State "Electronic Russia" Program are currently well advanced and already have converted the Russian State into the biggest national consumer of IT services. Today, the Russian government institutions invest heavily in their IT infrastructure and implement large scale management systems, ERP, CRM, database management and storage solutions, etc. with an aim to boost public management effectiveness and provide Russian citizens with ready and unhampered access to critical social and public information.

The long expected move toward Russian IT industry consolidation has already begun. The Russian IT and software development services market is rapidly maturing and gaining broader service capacity. There are many factors that determine this evolution. Among those, the emerging industry leaders already play an important role in boosting the national IT industry development. Jointly, the top 100 Russian IT companies earned 96 per cent of total Russian IT industry revenues in 2005. Whereas the top 10 largest IT businesses accounted for over half of the top 100 companies joint

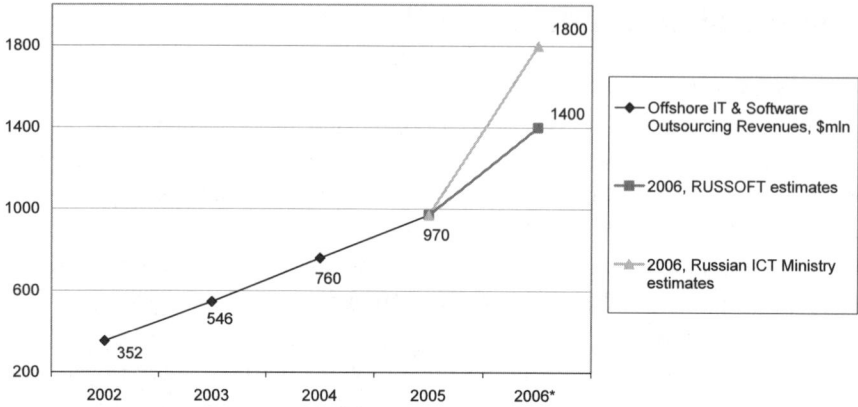

**Fig. 1.** The Russian software outsourcing industry growth dynamics and forecasts; Source: RUSSOFT, Russian ICT Ministry data

revenues in 2005 with a slight increase in the share over recent years – from 49 per cent in 2003 to 57 per cent in 2005. (CNews Analytics Data)

Largely, the sustained upswing of the domestic IT market has resulted from the high oil and gas profits pouring into the country, which boosted IT spending across all sectors – not only the oil and gas industries and state agencies. This leaves the Russian domestic corporate and state IT budgets dependent on the highly volatile world oil and gas prices. The IT services export revenues, on the contrary, are free of such dependence. It is worth noting that 5-6 years ago the Russian export IT industry demonstrated average annual growth of 40-50 per cent – which was, more than double the rate of the overall domestic IT industry. Nonetheless over last two years the growth rate started showing a decline towards more moderate numbers – though still in the range of 30-35 per cent.

From the historical point of view the Russian capitals – Moscow and Saint Petersburg – had a head start over the rest of the Russian IT export industry. Originally, in the early 90s the two cities evolved as the prime destinations for software outsourcing due to a number of objective factors such as:

- Telecommunication infrastructure – historically, Moscow and Saint Petersburg pioneered deployment of Internet in Russia (early 1990s).

- Social and business infrastructure – Moscow and Saint Petersburg are the two centres of Russian political, governmental and economic infrastructure;

- Transport infrastructure: Moscow and Saint Petersburg enjoyed better international transport communications ensuring convenience of business trips.

However what originally appeared as a blessing for IT export industry located at capitals in terms of availability of all sorts of infrastructure turned out to be its curse. After the severe economic set back of 1998 the country has been growing rapidly. As economic and business centres, Moscow and Saint Petersburg enjoyed a tremendous business boom and attracted the majority of Russian enterprises – establishing their headquarters, representative offices and operations there. International business also kept pace with Russia's enterprises and got established in the capitals. As political centres, the cities as well enjoyed rapid development of the Russian government infrastructure. All the above processes fuelled extensive IT infrastructure development and determined strong demand for the IT labour force.

Back in the early 90s offshore outsourcing businesses would compete with each other only due to lack of demand for IT talent from international corporations and other Russian domestic IT players. Currently the competition pattern has changed tremendously – the capitals experience considerable pressure for human resources from other emerged IT industry players. In Moscow, offshore software outsourcing businesses face tough competition from the domestic IT companies and various non-IT businesses including government agencies that also lure IT talent to support their IT-enabled operations. Saint Petersburg has become an R&D hub for several global IT giants – Alcatel, Borland, Intel, Motorola, Siemens, Sun Microsystems – that have established their R&D operations there, which further aggravated the local IT labour market situation. While the competition patterns in the capitals differ in terms of competing players the effect is fairly the same – a shortage of IT labour force resulting in ever-increasing wages and high attrition rates. Importantly, job-hopping and the resulting high attrition rates in the capitals impede effective accumulation of the most vital asset for the IT business – technological expertise and process maturity. Moreover, the infrastructure costs (office space, utilities, etc) are also higher in the capitals than in the regions. Hence, the overall costs of software R&D services in the capitals are considerably higher than those in the regions thus lowering competitiveness against the regions considerably.

Therefore, based on the above facts we uphold a different vision of the Russian offshore outsourcing industry's present status and future. The regions are set to play a major role in the further development of the Russian IT export industry. The process of migration of the Russian IT export industry from 1st tier cities into the regions is well under way. In the near term we expect that the growth of the Russian IT export industry will come solely from the regions. Successful expansion into those regions will allow scaling up of the industry in terms of human resources – thus sustaining the current high growth rates. In the long run we believe that the Russian IT export industry will leave 1st tier cities completely and reside in the regions.

As opposed to capitals, regions definitely do not represent centres of political and economic life thus both competition for IT labour and costs of infrastructure support in the regions are significantly lower. Moreover the regions offer ample human resources featuring R&D strength with a unique, almost genetic, background in science and technology.

Put together Moscow and Saint Petersburg account for one-tenth of the total Russian population; the other nine tenths reside in the regions. Now let us see what Russian regions are able to put on the table for the software outsourcing industry. The overall Russian annual supply of graduates is summarised in the graph below.

As of the year 2005, out of the just over a million graduates in Russia 260,000 of them were from the capitals. The other 800,000 graduates came from regions, namely, 2nd tier cities – and to name just a few:

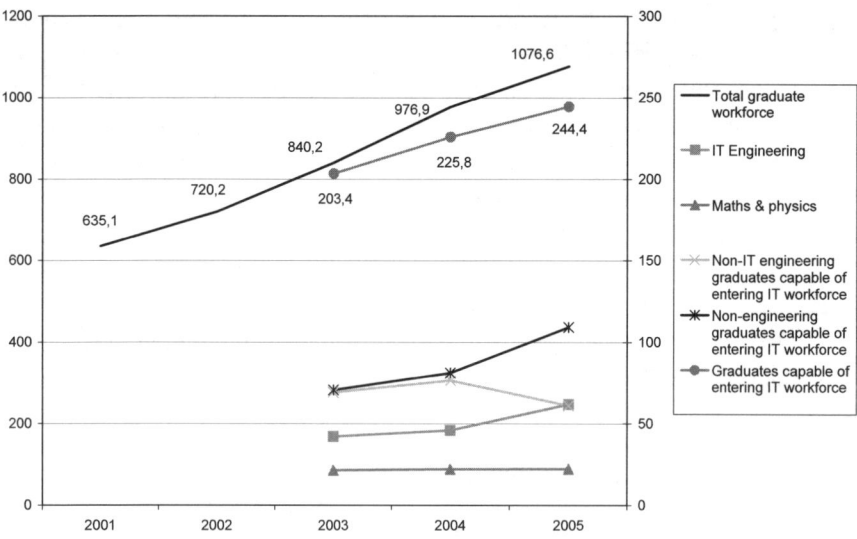

**Fig. 2.** Annual supply of graduate labor force (in Thousands). Source: StatEdu.ru, Russoft

- **Chelyabinsk**: 24,700 graduates annually, Chelyabinsk ranks among Russia's ten nuclear cities, it is the biggest educational, industrial and scientific centre of the Southern Urals, key industries: heavy machinery, tube rolling, metal production, the city is conveniently located on a major traffic junction.

- **Krasnoyarsk**: the industrial, educational and scientific heart of South-East Siberia; 20,000 university graduates annually from above 30 local universities, the Akademgorodok scientific and research district similar to that of Novosibirsk with scientific R&D centres focused on biophysics, thermophysics, computer simulation, chemical technology, industrial construction, and more.

- **Nizhny Novgorod**: 25,000 graduates in 2005, 33 higher educational institutions, 25 scientific R&D institutions focusing on telecommunications, radio technology, theoretical and applied physics, and more; leadership in automotive, aircraft, avionics, semiconductor, nuclear, chemical industries;

- **Novosibirsk**: 27,000 graduates as of 2005, strong universities and research institutions centred in the famous Akademgorodok, leading industries include electronics, instrumentation, machine building, aviation and more.

- **Omsk**: 15,000 graduates from over 20 local universities annually, leading industries – metal production, oil refining and petrochemicals, forestry, nuclear power engineering etc,

- **Perm**: 15,000 university graduates, strong engineering industries: machinery, defense, oil refinery, chemistry and petroleum chemistry with a network of special and general design offices and research institutes embracing a wide array of technical knowledge fields;

- **Samara**: 26,000 graduates in 2005, over 30 universities, key R&D-intensive industries include aerospace, aircraft, automotive, chemical and petrochemical, mechanical engineering.

- **Tatarstan** (including Kazan, Naberezhnye Chelny, etc): 29,500 graduates annually, above 60 higher educational institutions; 100+ scientific and research institutions; leading industries profile: production of crude oil, petrochemicals processing, mechanical engineering, aircraft, automotive, hi-tech electric and radio devices production.

- **Tomsk**: 16,000 graduates annually, more than 60 scientific R&D institutions, major industries: gas and oil production and machine building.
- **Ufa**: 27,000 university graduates annually; industries include electrical and mining machine building, oil refinery, petroleum chemistry, and other.
- **Volgograd**: 17,000 graduates, major industries include shipbuilding, oil refinery, metal production, heavy machinery and machine tools building, chemical production, agriculture.
- **Voronezh**: 19,000 university graduates annually; regional industries: aircraft, aerospace, machinery production, radio electronics, agriculture etc.;
- **Yekaterinburg**: 34,000 graduates, a big industrial centre with above 200 large and medium enterprises producing manufacturing equipment, electronics, radio equipment, steel and more; 30 universities, 120 scientific research institutions.

Importantly, a few large 2nd tier cities such as Nizhny Novgorod, Kazan, Samara, Naberezhnye Chelny, Voronezh etc are located in the European part of Russia and thus have an additional competitive advantage over other regions as they can be considered as nearshore to Western Europe.

In terms of quality Russian education in exact sciences (math, computer science, physics, engineering...) is widely acknowledged to be one of the best in the world. It is important to stress that the Russian educational system features quite a specific approach to education, which has proved to be extremely effective. The university curricula are focused not only on training in current industry-specific technologies/best practices but also on developing and nurturing a special analytical mindset and ability to learn. This is exactly what Russian engineers are well known for – ability to adopt and learn quickly in the fast paced and rapidly evolving technological world.

In the Russian IT export industry, on average, software engineers hold the Russian type of university engineering diploma equivalent to a master's degree (5.5 years of studies). In addition to professional courses, university curricula for engineering and IT students also include a heavy English component thus resulting in fluency of most graduate techies in English.

A number of international businesses already use this huge potential and leverage from rich R&D expertise offered by the Russian regions. For instance Intel have chosen the captive business model and have already established captive R&D centres at $2^{nd}$ tier cities – Nizhny Novgorod and Novosibirsk. Others giants like Nortel and Motorola to name just a few followed the vendor business model in the Russian regions and outsourced their R&D operations to prominent regional leaders of the offshore outsourcing industry.

The major Russian software outsourcing industry players have also followed the general move to regions through expanding their R&D operations in the regional cities trying to bring down development costs and flee away from pressing competition for qualified IT labour and high infrastructure costs, with a final goal to sustain labour force growth and secure major outsourcing contracts.

## Russian IT Export Industry Expansion to the Regions

The following section provides a mix of comparative analysis and opinion of potential near- and long-term trends and scenarios for development of the Russian IT export industry. The trends/scenarios are correlated with and mapped upon the overall economic BRICs predictions for Russia, which provide an invaluable basis and a roadmap for the analysis.

There is a common view actively broadcasted by western analysts that the Russia's offshore outsourcing service offering – application development and maintenance (ADM) or software R&D for a number of verticals – is rather narrow if compared to that of India. Indeed, presently the Russian IT export industry offers little if any ITO and BPO in the structure of its revenues. It is important to note that Russia joined the global offshore outsourcing game almost a decade later than India and its chances of joining and growing on ITO and BPO markets are fairly weak. The global ITO market is rather mature and heavily dominated by a few large players thus setting the entry level to the broader ITO market beyond Russia's reach. The BPO market is less mature and consolidated, which leaves a chance for Russia to tap into it; however overall low English proficiency in Russia as compared to that of India would definitely impede Russia's growth in the BPO market.

The global software R&D services market as contrasted to ITO and BPO is rather young and currently is at early stages of its development. This market allows Russia to capitalise on its most prominent competitive advantage of talent and technology expertise rather than cost reduction. Note that Russia has been penetrating this global market quite rapidly with growth rates exceeding such for the global software R&D services industry by a factor of 3-4.

In terms of revenues, Russia with its $1bn dollars is not that far off from India which reported software R&D services revenue of $2.3bn for the same year. Hence Russia already presents a strong competitor to India on the global market of software R&D services. Admittedly, Russia has an edge over India in terms of software R&D labour quality; Russia also enjoys cultural affinity and geographic proximity to Europe as compared to both India and China. Hence there are no external objective reasons for Russia not to grow on the global market of software R&D services.

The Russian IT export industry leaders keep questioning the world-recognised offshore outsourcing experts and gurus if Russia needs to expand its offering and what domains it needs to expand its offering into. The answer to this question lays right in the BRICs projections. According to BRICs analysis Russia would most likely drop out of low-cost destinations for offshore outsourcing within next 15-20 years. Therefore, it is not advisable for Russia to consider expanding into IT services such as ITO and BPO which clearly fall into category of non-core activities for which low-cost will always be one of the top decisive factors. The BRICs projections hence reinforce the importance for the Russian IT export industry to keep its current focus on R&D intensive IT industry niches such as cutting-edge software R&D services. In contrast to ITO and BPO, software R&D services could be attributed to core activities such as creation of innovation. The latter is the key to staying competitive in today's fast paced IT business environment. It is availability of brilliant and ample labour force capable of thinking outside of the box rather than low cost that drives the decision to offshore outsource software R&D services. Hence, the current industry's focus on software R&D services is well justified and BRICs projections imply that it will be a viable choice throughout years to come.

As it is stated above, the major move of the Russian IT export industry from the Russian capitals to other regions is well under way. The reasons for expansion of software R&D operations are quite objective – severe competition for the IT labour force and booming infrastructure costs at the capitals as compared to the regions. The expansion to $2^{nd}$ tier cities obviously presents a great opportunity for scaling up the industry and thus sustaining the current growth rates.

We believe that software R&D operations are most likely to expand into $2^{nd}$ tier cities via a combination of evolutionary and revolutionary scenarios. In the evolutionary scenario, expansion to $2^{nd}$ tier cities would be realised through evolutionary growth of regional industry leaders, small local companies, and established representative offices of major players from the 1st tier cities. The evolutionary scenario presents a slow process and thus it is unlikely to sustain current high growth rates of the Russian software R&D export industry. The expansion of R&D operations into 2nd tier cities could be boosted via a revolutionary scenario, namely industry consolidation through mergers/acquisitions of secondary regional players by industry leaders. Obviously, this scenario could provide the most favorable conditions for sustaining the current growth rates and help the export industry scale up rapidly.

Importantly, the Russian IT export industry has already reached the critical mass that most likely would intensify its growth by significantly increasing the share of the revolutionary scenario in the overall expansion pattern. Prominent industry leaders from both 1st and 2nd tier cities could potentially play a major role in sustaining the growth rates by serving as drivers and centres of further industry consolidation. Moreover, consolidation could also produce an overall positive impact on the industry through propagation of best business practices and maturity of processes from industry leaders to other industry players. Note that a share of a revolutionary scenario in the overall pattern of R&D operations expansion would be mostly limited by the availability of investment capital.

The BRICs projections underlie the importance of not only expanding but also rather moving the focus of the Russian R&D services export industry from 1st tier cities to the regions. If Russia follows the projected BRICs lines then its GDP per capita will match or exceed that of major European economies by 2050 while remaining lower than that of Japan, UK, and the US. While GDP per capita does not directly translate into wages it can be used as a relative measure of people wealth. Therefore, according to the BRICs projections, the Russian IT export industry could gradually lose its low-cost advantage. Due to a significant gradient in GDP per capita between 1st tier cities and the Russian provinces, the 1st tier cities will obviously lead the trend and most likely lose their current low-cost advantage over Europe within 15-20 years while retaining a marginal low-cost advantage over the US – one of its target R&D services export markets. Russian regions would follow the trend with some lag behind. And eventually, the Russian R&D services export industry could hit the BRICs projections for 2050 and completely lose its low-cost advantage over Europe while retaining a marginal low-cost advantage over Japan and the US. The BRICs projections suggest though that out of all four BRICs countries, India alone would enjoy its low-cost advantage throughout the period to 2050.

The current growth of the Russian IT industry oriented at the Russian domestic market is energised mostly by the world high prices for commodities. According to the BRICs projections, the continued growth in the BRICs would most likely result in increased demand for commodities and excessive price pressures in corresponding commodity markets such as energy, oil and metal – where Russia currently has most of its exports. Thus the BRICs projections imply that most likely the domestic Russian IT industry would continue its growth and it is highly unlikely that competition between domestic and export-oriented Russian IT industries for IT talent will get weaker in the near future. This point also reinforces the importance of not only expanding but also moving R&D operations from $1^{st}$ tier cities into regions.

An important factor which could play a positive role in boosting the expansion of the Russian IT export industry into the regions and thus sustaining current growth rates is government support. According to the approved Russian Federation government programme the regions of Moscow, Novosibirsk, Nizhny Novgorod, Tyumen and Kaluga as well as Saint Petersburg and the Republic of Tatarstan were chosen to host high-tech technoparks. The technoparks – modern spacious offices featuring state-of-the-art ICT and physical infrastructure – will be made available to Russian companies at moderate rent prices. Such a form of government support will definitely ensure a "soft landing" for the Russian IT export industry in the regions and facilitate its rapid expansion from $1^{st}$ tier cities to the latter.

The Russian Federation government has also announced plans to establish a Federal agency for IT Exports Development. The new agency's scope of reference will include analysis of export potential, marketing and PR support to the national IT export industry. To facilitate development of the Russian IT innovation ecosystem the federal government founded a dedicated Russian Investment Fund for Technologies and Innovations. Other Russian government initiatives include the introduction of tax incentives and special customs regimes for IT export companies. The first edition of tax code amendments to the Tax Code of Russia for export IT companies fell short of the industry's expectations; currently another taxation scheme for IT companies is under development by the Russian Ministry of Information Technologies and Communications.

Nonetheless, there are a few factors that could potentially limit Russian IT export industry growth. One of these factors – the Russian educational system – has been given a lot of attention lately. The fast-paced business environment indeed sets challenging goals for the Russian educational system in terms of adaptation to and evolution along the rapidly changing

IT industry needs. Trying to respond to these challenges proactively, the Russian government developed and launched in 2005 a comprehensive reform of education within the framework of the "Education and Development" national project. In the near future, the educational system is expected to further increase government sponsored quotas for engineering and other IT related specialties to match the ever increasing IT labour demand and thus redress the current situation.

In the long run, the reform is aimed at turning the educational system into a highly adaptive system of replenishing and managing the Russian intellectual resources. Meanwhile in addition to government-sponsored education in IT, Russia features a number of private computer science and IT academies and institutions providing various IT-related training in specific or proprietary industry technologies, project management methodologies, best practice, and more. Typically created alongside the large IT companies, such educational institutions ensure a smooth transition of fresh graduates from the university bench into real IT business and provide a means for knowledge (technology, best practice, management methodologies, etc) build-up and retention.

Another negative factor, which has been debated all around the world, is the declining quality of Russian education. We strongly disagree with this point. The approaches for assessing the quality of education are extremely subjective and biased therefore we can only leave it for the future to judge.

And finally – needless to say – that by far the most important limiting factor of the Russian IT export industry growth is presented by the notorious long-lived misperceptions of Russia and the lack of a coherent PR and marketing campaign at the country level aimed at promoting Russia as a place of choice for outsourcing software R&D services.

## Conclusion

To summarise, the Russian IT export industry has all the prerequisites to sustain its current rapid growth and in the near future Russia could potentially evolve as the number one global destination of choice for offshore outsourcing software R&D services.

The BRICs analysis forecasts a rosy future for Russia with regard to GDP per capita. While this is overall a positive for the country, it would mean a loss of a low-cost competitive advantage for the Russian IT export industry. Hence it is highly advisable for the Russian IT export industry to keep its current focus on software R&D services – core IT services delivering *innovation* – instead of diversifying its offering into non-core service areas such as ITO and BPO.

The current rapid growth of the Russian IT export industry can only be sustained by scaling up the resources through intensive expansion of software R&D operations from the capitals to other Russian regions – $2^{nd}$ tier cities. Importantly the latter offer ample and brilliant IT talent, relatively weak competition for IT labour force as well as low cost of infrastructure support.

If the Russian IT export industry follows mainly the revolutionary pathway – further industry consolidation through mergers and acquisitions of secondary regional players by industry leaders – then most likely the current growth rate will be sustained. Such a scenario would have an overall positive impact on the industry due to the propagation of best business practices and mature software R&D processes from industry leaders to other industry players. Otherwise, should the industry choose to grow via an evolutionary path, the growth rate will most likely level off. No matter what scenario becomes a reality, the industry will follow the ongoing government support in the form of IT technoparks as well as tax and customs incentives – clearly these initiatives will be invaluable in ensuring a "soft landing" of the industry in the regions.

A close look at other internal country-wide limiting factors such as Russian demography and education revealed that they will not have any effect on industry growth in the near future and most likely will have little or no effect in the long run.

The internal factors which might limit development of the Russian IT export industry are objective and can be dealt with. The subjective external factor such as the long-lived misperceptions of Russia are harder to resolve – here Russia should concentrate on promoting itself as a destination of choice for outsourcing software R&D services. Only by properly addressing the internal issues and fighting subjective misperceptions will Russia win in the competition with India and China and get the standing it deserves in the arena of global ICT services.

#  Part III: India

# Globalisation – There Is Much to Gain

*Shiv Nadar*
*Founder of HCL, Chairman and CEO, HCL Technologies, Noida, India*

The term "globalisation" has acquired considerable emotive force. Some view it as a process that is beneficial – a key to future world economic development – and also inevitable and irreversible. Others regard it with hostility, even fear, believing that it increases inequality within and between nations, threatens employment and living standards and thwarts social progress. This write-up is an attempt to offer an overview of some aspects of globalisation and identify ways in which countries can tap the gains of this process, while remaining realistic about its potential and risks.

Globalisation offers extensive opportunities for truly worldwide development, but it is not progressing evenly. Some countries are becoming integrated into the global economy quicker than others. Countries that have been able to integrate are seeing faster growth and reduced poverty. Outward-oriented policies have brought in dynamism and greater prosperity to much of East Asia, transforming it from one of the poorest areas of the world 40 years ago. And as living standards have risen, it has become possible to make progress on democracy and economic issues such as the environment and work standards.

By contrast, in the 1970s and 1980s – when many countries in Latin America and Africa pursued inward-oriented policies – their economies stagnated or declined, poverty increased and high inflation became the norm. In many cases, especially Africa, adverse external developments made the problem worse. As these regions changed their policies, their incomes have begun to rise. An important transformation is underway. Encouraging this trend, not reversing it, is the best course for promoting growth, development and poverty reduction.

The crises in the emerging markets in the 1990s made it quite evident that the opportunities of globalisation do not come without risks – risks arising from volatile capital movements and the risks of social, economic and environmental degradation created by poverty. This is not a reason to reverse direction, but for all concerned – in developing countries, in the advanced countries, and of course investors – to embrace policy changes to build strong economies and a stronger world financial system that will produce more rapid growth and ensure that poverty is reduced.

How can developing countries, especially the poorest, be helped to catch up? Does globalisation exacerbate inequality or can it help reduce poverty? And are countries that integrate with the global economy inevitably vulnerable to instability? These are some of the issues that I hope to answer in the following pages...

## Globalisation: What Does It Mean for You?

Economic "globalisation" is a historical process, the result of human innovation and technological progress. It refers to the increasing integration of economies around the world, particularly through trade and financial flows. The term sometimes also refers to the movement of people (labour) and knowledge (technology) across international borders. There are also broader cultural, political and environmental dimensions of globalisation that are not covered here.

At its most basic, there is nothing mysterious about globalisation. The term has come into common usage since the 1980s, reflecting technological advances that have made it easier and quicker to complete international transactions – both trade and financial flows. It refers to an extension beyond national borders of the same market forces that have operated for centuries at all levels of human economic activity – village markets, urban industries, or financial centres.

Markets promote efficiency through competition and the division of labour – the specialisation that allows people and economies to focus on what they do best. Global markets offer greater opportunity for people to tap into more and larger markets around the world. It means that they can have access to more capital flows, technology, cheaper imports, and larger export markets. But markets do not necessarily ensure that the benefits of increased efficiency are shared by all. Countries must be prepared to embrace the policies needed, and in the case of the poorest countries may need the support of the international community as they do so.

## Unparalleled Growth, Increased Inequality

Globalisation is not just a recent phenomenon. Some analysts have argued that the world economy was just as globalised 100 years ago as it is today. But today commerce and financial services are far more developed and deeply integrated than they were at that time. The most striking aspect of this has been the integration of financial markets made possible by modern electronic communication.

The 20$^{th}$ century saw unparalleled economic growth, with global per capita GDP increasing almost five-fold. But this growth was not steady – the strongest expansion came during the second half of the century, a period of rapid trade expansion accompanied by trade – and typically somewhat later, financial – liberalisation. In the inter-war era, the world turned its back on internationalism – or globalisation as we now call it – and countries retreated into closed economies, protectionism and pervasive capital controls.

## How Deeply Is the World Integrated?

Globalisation means that world trade and financial markets are becoming more integrated. But just how far have developing countries been involved in this integration? Their experience in catching up with the advanced economies has been mixed. In some countries, especially in Asia, per capita incomes have been moving quickly toward levels in the industrial countries since 1970. A larger number of developing countries have made only slow progress or have lost ground. In particular, per capita incomes in Africa have declined relative to the industrial countries and in some countries have declined in absolute terms. Part of the explanation – the countries catching up are those where trade has grown strongly.

Consider four aspects of globalisation:

- **Trade**: Developing countries as a whole have increased their share of world trade–from 19 percent in 1971 to nearly 32 per cent in 2005. But there is a great variation among the major regions.

- **Capital movements**: The pinnacle of what many people associate with globalisation – sharply increased private capital flows to developing countries during much of the 1990s. It also shows that... the increase followed a particularly "dry" period in the 1980s; net official flows of "aid" or development assistance have fallen significantly since the early 1980s; and the composition of private flows has changed dramatically.

- **Movement of people**: Workers move from one country to another partly to find better employment opportunities. The numbers involved are still quite small, but till 1990, the proportion of labor forces round the world that was foreign born increased by about one-half. Most migration occurs between developing countries. But the flow of migrants to advanced economies is likely to provide a means through which global wages converge.

- **Spread of knowledge (and technology)**: Information exchange is an integral, often overlooked, aspect of globalisation. For instance, direct foreign investment brings not only an expansion of the physical capital stock, but also technical innovation. More generally, knowledge about production methods, management techniques, export markets and economic policies is available at very low cost, and represents a highly valuable resource for developing countries.

The special case of the economies in transition from planned to market economies – they too are becoming more integrated with the global economy – is not explored in much depth here. In fact, the term "transition economy" is losing its usefulness. Some countries (e.g. Poland, Hungary) are converging quite rapidly toward the structure and performance of advanced economies. Others (such as most countries of the former Soviet Union) face long-term structural and institutional issues similar to those faced by developing countries.

## Advanced Economies Can Help

- By promoting trade – One proposal on the table is to provide unrestricted market access for all exports from the poorest countries. This should help them move beyond specialisation on primary commodities to producing processed goods for export

- By encouraging flows of private capital to the lower-income countries, particularly foreign direct investment, with its twin benefits of steady financial flows and technology transfer

- By supplementing more rapid debt relief with an increased level of new financial support. Official development assistance has fallen to 0.24 per cent of GDP in advanced countries (compared with a UN target of 0.7 per cent).

## Promote Globalisation, Promote Peace

As globalisation has progressed, living conditions (particularly when measured by broader indicators of well being) have improved significantly in virtually all countries. However, the strongest gains have been made by the advanced countries and only some of the developing countries.

Critics of globalisation forget that free trade fosters prosperity and know almost nothing about its most important benefit – its tendency to prevent war. Quantitative studies have shown that trade fosters peace both directly, by reducing the risk of military conflict, and indirectly, by promoting prosperity and democracy.

Quantitative research has established the viability and prospect of a capitalist peace based on the following causal links between free trade and the avoidance of war – first, there is an indirect link running from free trade or economic openness to prosperity and democracy and ultimately to the democratic peace; second, trade and economic interdependence by themselves reduce the risk of military conflict. By promoting capitalism, economic freedom, trade, and prosperity, we simultaneously promote peace.

## India Can Make the Difference

No essay on globalisation can be deemed to be complete without mention of the new pioneers that are stepping in to bridge the gulf between the haves and the have-nots, between demand and supply, between the developed, the developing, and the under-developed.

Similarly, no eulogy on the developing and fast-emerging economies in the world today can be complete without a close look at India – and particularly the country's benchmark information technology sector, which has proved to be the country's fastest-growing, even in a globally-challenging economic environment. The software and services industry – a major component of India's IT sector – showed significant momentum, higher than that of any other industry space in the country.

As for the hardware space, that should be the next big wave to sweep India on to firmer footing on the global economic map. Clearly, the Indian economy is poised to take even ever-stronger steps toward a greater presence on the global economic stage. Why?

- India boasts a large pool of skilled manpower across all levels and all functions
- Infrastructure in India is improving year on year
- Low cost of capital due to increasing availability of private equity and VCs
- Capable construction industry with ability to put up plants and facilities in just months
- Ability to reduce capital equipment costs, by local fabrication of bulky equipment

Admittedly, India has its weaknesses too – on the infrastructure side, particularly on the roads and electrical power fronts. But problems are there to be solved and many of the companies here have found their way around and solved problems – either hand in hand with the State, or on their own.

Having commented on Indian infrastructure, here's where it is growing …

- The Golden Quadrilateral Project (including the North-South Corridor) is well under way and, when completed, India will have six-lane superhighways connecting the four metros in north, south, east and west, extending over 10,000 miles. Just this one project is more than the motorable road in most central and east European countries
- Every month, there is an addition of 2.5 million cellphone subscribers. By December 2006, the total number is expected to reach 120 million (a 100% growth over the last two years)
- India has a strong and transparent legal and accounting system, plus offers legal protection for intellectual property rights
- The Indian consumer market is over 1-billion-people strong, of which 150 million are what we call "world-class middle-class" consumers – buying the same goods as anyone else in any affluent part of the world
- India is the second-fastest growing economy of the world

- The foreign exchange reserves have reached a record level of over $150 billion. India is the fifth-largest foreign exchange holder in the world. Remarkable, considering that Forex reserves went under $1 billion in 1991, when the economic reforms program was kicked off
- International trade of $175 million, and growing – 15% every year
- The Government has decided to (i) discontinue receiving aid from other countries except the following five: Japan, UK, Germany, USA, EU, and the Russian Federation and (ii) to make pre-payment of all bilateral debt owed to all the countries except the five mentioned above.
- The inflation rate has been contained to near 4% levels...

India and Indians have undergone a paradigm shift. There have been fundamental and irreversible changes in the economy, government policies, outlook of business and industry, and in the mindset of the Indians in general.

- From a shortage economy of food and foreign exchange, India has now become a surplus one
- From an agro based economy it has emerged as a service oriented one
- From the low-growth of the past, the economy has become a high-growth one in the long-term
- After having been an aid recipient, India is now joining the aid givers club
- Although India was late and slow in modernisation of industry in general in the past, it is now a front-runner in the emerging Knowledge based New Economy
- The Government is continuing its reform and liberalisation not out of compulsion but out of conviction
- Indian companies are no longer afraid of Multinational Companies. They have become globally competitive and some of them have started becoming MNCs themselves
- Fatalism and contentment of the Indian mindset have given way to optimism and ambition

- Introvert and defensive approach have been replaced by outward-looking and confident attitude
- Graduates no longer queue up for safe government jobs. They prefer and enjoy the challenges and risks of becoming entrepreneurs and global players

In its 2003 report, 'Dreaming with BRICs: The Path to 2050', Goldman Sachs says the following about the future of the Indian economy

- India's GDP will reach $ 1 trillion by 2011, $ 2 trillion by 2020, $ 3 trillion by 2025, $ 6 trillion by 2032, $ 10 trillion by 2038, and $ 27 trillion by 2050, becoming the third largest economy after USA and China
- In terms of GDP, India will overtake Italy by the year 2016, France by 2019, UK by 2022, Germany by 2023,and Japan by 2032. Chinese GDP could overtake Germany by 2007, Japan by 2016, and the US by 2041
- Among the BRIC group India alone has the potential to show the highest growth (over 5 percent) over the next 50 years. The Chinese growth rate is likely to reduce to 5% by 2020, 4% by 2029, and 3% by 2046

## India and HCL: Having Run the Marathon, Now Ready to Sprint

Clearly, India has reached a veritable crossroads and gone beyond it, marching strong along the path to being counted among the global economic giants. And leading this march have been companies from all walks of industry, with the HCL Group being among the frontrunners in that list.

As India's original "garage start-up", HCL has been hardwired into India's digital multiplier right from the start. It was HCL that spawned the concept of computer literacy and education way back in 1981, identifying a yawning gap between the growth in technology and education at the user level. NIIT was born out of the drive to plug this need gap, and has become the leader in IT education by empowering millions of people not just in India but parts of Asia too.

Many more technology penetration initiatives from HCL are empowering individuals and industries. It is HCL that pioneered the sub-Rs 10,000 PC and has taken connectivity to remotest parts of India by setting up the country's largest Vsat network. India's banking network has virtually been set up by HCL. HCL has built networks for over 6,500 branches and more than 5000 ATMs across the country. The financial markets too are powered by HCL's IT infrastructure. Traders in any part of the country enjoy real time connectivity to country's leading stock exchange. HCL is also developing a comprehensive solution to help the market regulator monitor the market.

Indian corporations are bridging the digital divide internationally too. HCL is engaged in mission-critical work on next generation aircraft, implantable pain relieving medical devices and remote monitoring of complex IT infrastructure. Such high-end work is being carried out of design and development centers based in India.

## Leadership Through Value-Centricity

Today's successful businesses have set themselves a clear goal – that of emerging as 'value leaders'. The sheer implication – they focus incessantly on creating and delivering value to their customers. When we talk 'value', we shouldn't get confused with 'volumes'. Value is something that needs to be measured only in terms of any company's strategic relevance to its customers – regardless of the size of the relationship.

For any company, being perceived as a 'strategic' partner by customers is the only proof of its offering value – and over the longer run, only this form of delivery, in any field or business sphere, will lead to sustainability and longevity. Today, the Indian information technology industry finds itself at crossroads where it has to take a call on 'size' – sheer size of an engagement or order is of little significance now, and even large engagements will die down or become irreversibly unsustainable if they offer low or no value creation.

The lesson to be learnt here is a simple yet critical one – it is better that industry works proactively towards moving relationships up the value chain, from *tactical* to *strategic*, engaging deeper with the customer. Only this will demonstrate to enterprises worldwide that they can leverage the service capabilities and competence of Indian IT companies to create significant competitive differentiators for themselves.

## Beyond the Numbers

If we look closely at the fine print, and beyond the heady growth numbers that the IT industry has been witnessing again after suffering some nervous hiccups between 2000 and 2002, the industry stands at an inflection point. Sure, India and Indian firms are ready to leapfrog into the big league, particularly so as they hold out the potential of transforming not only the global IT landscape but also the very roots of businesses worldwide. For that, however, some serious thought needs to go into delivery, product offerings, and the very way in which we operate.

IT offshoring is today a strategic imperative for global firms. It is not only an integral part of their strategy, but in many ways defines the way a firm works. It is no longer about low-end work, and all about 'embedded' – both in terms of our software and the criticality of our service offerings to our customers. The data on outsourcing by *Fortune 1000* firms, visits from CXOs to India, and the IT-led services boom are clear manifestations of this fact. If Indian IT and outsourcing are not the flavor of the month, then CXOs must ensure that they are at least on their menu cards!

The last financial year saw the Indian software, services and infrastructure sectors build on solid momentum and consolidate. The industry is now well on its way up a serious growth curve. A simple extrapolation – if Indian IT maintains a growth rate of around 35% YoY for the next two-to-three years, the $50-billion exports revenue mark set out in the Nasscom-McKinsey Report a few years back would be very achievable. And at that point, Indian IT would be contributing to a heady 5% of the country's gross domestic product.

Over the last couple of years, there has been a discernible shift in the strategy of Indian IT companies as they have begun to focus more on the higher end of the services spectrum. Increasingly, Indian IT majors are offering services in IT consulting, systems integration, remote infrastructure management, network consulting, KPO (not to be read as BPO) and integration processing services. Simultaneously, the Indian software and service industry is gaining access into newer markets – Europe and the Asia-Pacific region stand out in particular – thereby reducing dependency on any single market.

Overall, it is fair to say that India has made far more progress in the spread and diffusion of ICT than traditional notions of the digital divide suggest. What we need today is not radical new policy initiatives but much more of the same opportunistic creativity and enlightened policy that has already put India on the digital map. Ten years from now, I can confidently predict that this momentum will place India high among the world's digitally empowered nations.

As an addition to this essay, I would like to also examine two very specific and related matters.

## Does Globalisation Reduce National Sovereignty?

Does increased integration, particularly in the financial sphere make it more difficult for governments to manage economic activity, for instance by limiting governments' choices of tax rates and tax systems, or their freedom of action on monetary or exchange rate policies? If it is assumed that countries aim to achieve sustainable growth, low inflation and social progress, then the evidence of the past 50 years is that globalisation contributes to these objectives in the long term.

In the short-term, as we have seen in the past few years, volatile short-term capital flows can threaten macroeconomic stability. Thus in a world of integrated financial markets, countries will find it increasingly risky to follow policies that do not promote financial stability. This discipline also applies to the private sector, which will find it more difficult to implement wage increases and price markups that would make the country concerned become uncompetitive.

But there is another kind of risk. Sometimes investors – particularly short-term investors – take too sanguine a view of a country's prospects and capital inflows may continue even when economic policies have become too relaxed. This exposes the country to the risk that when perceptions change, there may be a sudden brutal withdrawal of capital from the country.

In short, globalisation does not reduce national sovereignty. It does create a strong incentive for governments to pursue sound economic policies. It should create incentives for the private sector to undertake careful analysis of risk. However, short-term investment flows may be excessively volatile.

Efforts to increase the stability of international capital flows are central to the ongoing work on strengthening the international financial architecture. In this regard, some are concerned that globalisation leads to the abolition of rules or constraints on business activities. To the contrary – one of the key goals of the work on the international financial architecture is to develop standards and codes that are based on internationally accepted principles that can be implemented in many different national settings.

Clearly the crises would not have developed as they did without exposure to global capital markets. But nor could these countries have achieved their impressive growth records without those financial flows...

## Hardware Outsourcing: The Next Wave

After IT services and BPM, it is hardware manufacturing that is fast emerging as the next big thing shaking up the global infotech market. Apart from the domestic players already in the market (HCL is the #1 player in the PC space in India), there are global MNCs who have joined the manufacturing bandwagon in India – Samsung, IBM, and contract manufacturing giant Flextronics.

This wave is being driven by several macro and micro forces that have been unleashed in India, e.g.

- India's strong hardware, engineering services, and design capabilities are now integrating with the local manufacturing capabilities
- The talent pool of engineers in this area is continuing to grow, albeit within the ambit of constrained supply
- The SEZ scheme being rolled across India can be a powerful answer to China's extremely successful SEZ programs pursued over the last several decades.

India has so far been at the forefront of the IT/ITES services wave while China has clearly led the manufacturing one. Today China seeks to challenge India in the IT/ITES space where as India has begun to make its presence felt in the traditionally Chinese domain of manufacturing.

The possibilities this throws up in terms of global impact will be a key trend to watch in the future and the emerging giants begin to impact the global economy in their uniquely creative ways.

# Sourcing Without Borders – Sourcing in a Flattening World

*Nandan M. Nilekani*
*Co-Chairman of the Board of Directors, Infosys, Bengaluru, India*

Over the next 10 years, the IT and business process service industries are set to change dramatically. At Infosys, we foresee acceleration and expansion of the economic, technological, demographic and regulatory forces that have shaped these industries in the past decade. Concurrently, these forces are altering the shape of the global economy, causing it to become flatter – to paraphrase Thomas Friedman's bestselling book *The World is Flat*.

What does this augur for businesses? For IT and business process services vendors, in particular, it means that traditional economic barriers are collapsing. Organisational hierarchies are dissolving into distributed workforces and increasingly global supply chains are being linked through horizontal information flows. With the rise of emerging economies and the ubiquity of technology, the competitive playing field is being levelled.

These changes have already left their mark on the services market, as illustrated by the disruptive impact of offshore outsourcing over the past decade. Its evolution from labour arbitrage to strategic global sourcing has not only changed the cost-and-quality equation of service delivery, it has fundamentally altered the competitive landscape.

The flattening of the world and the services industry has fostered a close relationship between the two. As one changes, it drives the other, producing an expanding cycle of opportunities and challenges, each with a profound effect on demand and supply activities. The globalisation of services contributes to the flattening of the world.

Business and IT leaders are now compelled to think about global sourcing in new ways. The outcomes: new thinking about core versus non-core, closer alignment of business and sourcing strategies, the adoption of new sourcing models, and closer yet more flexible client/vendor relationships.

On the supply side, the principal factors that influenced global sourcing decisions during the past decade – cost, quality, and cultural compatibility – are becoming the norm. Experienced sourcing practitioners are expecting more from service providers – deeper industry expertise, flexible contracts, and expanded geographic delivery options.

As companies respond to, and seek, ways to leverage these disruptive, flattening forces, the demand for services that can address them will increase. Similarly, the variety of ways in which those demands can be met will increase, shaping the supply and demand cycle of global sourcing.

## From Offshore Outsourcing to Strategic Global Sourcing

In the infancy of offshore outsourcing, most companies followed a tactical approach focussed on cost reduction. Individual groups within IT departments – among the first organisations to move work offshore – contracted independently with vendors. Others chose to work with specific vendors but in an *ad hoc*, opportunistic fashion.

The lack of a strategic approach, coupled with internal resistance, led some companies to outsource too little to take full advantage of offshore skills and costs. Others yielded too much responsibility, losing vital internal knowledge and expertise. Both approaches often led to inefficiencies, limiting the benefits of moving work to low-cost locations.

For some companies, the path to maturity started with the recognition that sourcing is a strategic activity. In most cases, however, it has been the result of experience gained over time. No matter how maturity is achieved, it is being transmitted throughout and across businesses in every industry sector, providing organisational models and best practices for other companies to follow.

For example, among many of Infosys' largest clients, we witness the emergence of sourcing management as a specialized discipline, one dedicated to developing processes and metrics for making and executing strategic sourcing decisions. The result: lower sourcing management costs and increased productivity.

Companies that once engaged in sole-source contracts are now moving toward strategic partnerships with selected best-of-breed vendors. Those that contracted with multiple vendors are consolidating their relationships and partnering with selected vendors.

This trend, known as multi-sourcing, stems partly from dissatisfaction with traditional outsourcing models. Equally, if not more important, is a growth in the size and scope of client/vendor global sourcing relationships. Increasing brand preference for Infosys and other leading service providers from India has created opportunities to expand client relationships, even as large outsourcing contracts come up for renewal.

Multi-sourcing has changed the nature of client/vendor relationships. Instead of sourcing projects piecemeal, companies are assessing and optimising their application portfolios and assigning vendors greater responsibility for "bundles" of work based on common requirements, technology platforms and business alignment. The result is a shift to service-level agreements based on deliverables, not day-to-day activities, allowing vendors greater flexibility to design, staff and execute for results.

This approach has seen mature practitioners achieve process uniformity and optimise internal/external resource mixes and skills ratios. By aligning sourcing with business strategy they are also realising operational efficiencies, staffing flexibility, better understanding of internal costs, and the ability to focus on core competencies.

A key element in multi-sourcing is modularisation – a concept derived from manufacturing – which Infosys refined and articulated as Modular Global Sourcing (MGS) in 2004. It involves deconstructing complex business processes and their supporting applications and IT infrastructures, enabling them to be examined and analysed individually and in terms of their relationships and interdependencies.

An alternative to traditional "mega-deal" outsourcing, MGS defines a way of thinking about sourcing at an enterprise level. It provides a mechanism for organising business and IT assets and their associated functions and activities to achieve sourcing flexibility and ensure predictable costs, quality, risks and resource utilisation.

Meanwhile, as attitudes toward global sourcing and its adoption as a strategic activity have evolved, so have roles and responsibilities within client organisations. For example, the CIO's role is being transformed from a primarily technical function focused on delivering operations excellence to one that emphasises the alignment of IT investments with business objectives.

This trend is leading to the management of IT as a business – one measured, if not strictly by profit and loss, at least by its impact on the company's bottom line. In light of these changes the CIO's role has become increasingly focussed on procuring the right services for the company – internal or external, local or global.

Decision criteria are thus shifting from what IT functions and business processes can be outsourced to how best to access the capabilities for delivering on business goals. Consequently, businesses are shifting their focus from cost reduction and operational efficiency to increased competitiveness, productivity and innovation.

This, in turn, has led to rising expectations and demands for more advanced capabilities from vendors. The same shift is being applied to the sourcing of business processes. Here, too, there is a movement toward transferring higher value activities offshore to achieve business results beyond cost reduction.

In addition, modularisation and multi-sourcing have enabled the alignment and bundling of business processes and the applications and IT infrastructures that support them. This has created new opportunities to leverage global sourcing for business benefits by consolidating activities and functions and delivering shared services across lines of business.

Although these trends point to the growing importance of global sourcing and its continued evolution, its applicability to changing economic, demographic, technological and regulatory forces are just beginning to be recognised.

To reach the next level, Infosys believes that business and IT executives must think more globally and holistically, shift operational priorities, and leverage the disruptive forces driving the flattening world. Service providers must also take on a flat world mindset, adopting a broader, less country-centric approach and shifting operational priorities to meet the changing needs of clients while augmenting the global delivery model.

## Sourcing to Compete in the Flat World

It is widely accepted that fundamental changes will continue to take place in the global economy. There is also broad agreement on the forces propelling these changes, validated by academic and market research, including a survey conducted in late 2006 by Infosys in collaboration with the Economist Intelligence Unit, a global research and business advisory firm.

In the survey, 500 Fortune 2000 business and technology executives from around the world – including 200 C-Level executives – were asked to gauge the impact of economic, demographic, technological, regulatory, and business cycle changes on their respective industries.

To each question, over 60% of the respondents stated that the impact of these forces on their industries would be significant to very significant.

Among the most interesting findings were the responses to the question about the impact of expanding role of technology and information: 38% of the respondents stated that it would be significant and 37% selected 'very significant', for a total of 75%.

The survey also examined executive attitudes toward a number of operational shifts for responding to and leveraging flat world forces. These shifts comprise activities and capabilities for achieving customer loyalty through innovation, globally competitive cost structures, monetising information, and strategies and processes for enabling rapid responses to changing business cycles.

As expected, the responses to these shifts vary by industry and geography. Nevertheless, the survey found that the majority of respondents' companies had begun or were on the threshold of enacting the most basic of them. In other areas, however, the findings show that the majority of respondents have yet to undertake or consider many of the shifts linked to flat world forces, including strategic sourcing.

Not surprisingly, Infosys believes that companies that do not strategically leverage global sourcing will be at a competitive disadvantage in the flat world. On the other hand, those that follow the path to a higher level global of sourcing maturity will be better positioned to adapt and succeed.

## Sourcing for Globally Competitive Cost Structures

Large, established companies are often blinded by the desire to cater to their most sophisticated customers. They add features, functions and advanced capabilities to products – thus raising their price.

Meanwhile, upstarts can produce simple products with 80% of the functionality of large companies, and steal market-share. These new competitors may come from emerging economies, catering to price-conscious consumers as sophisticated as any. They are also making their presence felt in developed countries.

Ranbaxy Laboratories in India sells a generic version of the antibiotic Cipro for 63 cents. The same generic sells in the US for $51 a dose. A premier supplier in Europe, it has 58 generics pending approval by the US FDA. Huawei, the Chinese communications technology company, sells VOIP equipment for 20%-50% less than Cisco.

To counter these threats, leading companies in developed economies are looking to overhaul their cost structures and invest the savings to reduce prices, invest in R&D, and create a level playing field to compete in new markets with low-cost rivals.

Already a proven mechanism for reducing IT and business process operations costs, global sourcing is a means to these ends. One that has been shown to improve, rather than diminish quality, as illustrated by Infosys' and other global delivery service providers' leadership in the adoption of SEI CMM standards and other process and quality improvement innovations.

Building a globally competitive cost structure through sourcing requires more than engaging in opportunistic labour arbitrage. It takes new ways of thinking about what is core and what is not. It means raising the bar by fully outsourcing bundled functions and services to increase utilisation of offshore resources and take fuller advantage of cost advantages and vendor thought leadership.

## Sourcing for Innovation

Everybody is talking about innovation as the key to winning customer loyalty. Good service is no longer enough to differentiate one company from the next. Competition today is global, powered by the Internet, fast and fierce. Today's technology-savvy consumers can access information not only about prices but also about the latest products, and they are making their wants and desires known.

Creating channels to enable customers to interact with products, offering unique experiences in accessing products and services, and understanding what motivates them are essential to gaining and keeping their loyalty. This calls for speeding up and institutionalising innovation and looking beyond organisational boundaries for new ideas.

One example of this non-traditional approach to innovation is Eli Lilly and Company, which launched a new company "InnoCentive" to access global talent pool. Applying what essentially is an open source model, Lilly and other pharmaceutical and chemicals companies can "post" R&D problems with an award amount, which can be solved by any of the over 80K scientists around the globe.

In the flat world, seeking innovation beyond company boundaries means reaching out past geographic and cultural ones as well. Human ingenuity exists everywhere and demographic change and technology are making it available to those willing to search for it. Increasingly, it is being found in India, China and other emerging economies. Leading companies are looking to these countries as sources of innovation.

Telecommunications OEMs, software vendors and other technology companies, as well as automotive and other traditional manufacturers, already source R&D and product designs from around the world. Current trends point to substantial increases in these activities. In addition, offshore call centres, once the realm of customer service and support, are not only expanding into revenue generating sales and marketing activities, they are becoming centres of customer research and intelligence.

Used to support emerging economy market strategies, these centres provide in-depth knowledge of local requirements and the ability to create culturally appropriate price-competitive products. Companies are also applying offshore market research to identify new or under-served sectors in existing markets to create new products or variants at lower price points.

Meanwhile, global service providers are gaining deep knowledge and understanding of client applications and process by virtue of long experience in maintaining and executing, and increasingly, by helping create them. Knowledge transfer, once a one-way process from clients to vendor partners, is becoming a two-way exchange with the former increasingly looking to the latter to contribute ideas for improvements and innovations.

### Sourcing to Monetise Information

Winning in a flattening world requires harvesting information for profit – using it to work effectively across the globe, continuously improving efficiency, and proactively identifying new revenue opportunities.

After years of investing in information gathering and management systems, however, many companies have accumulated reams of data but little knowledge. They struggle to give stakeholders the information they need to meet regulatory requirements or capture those pieces required to solve pressing business problems.

Winning the loyalty of customers through innovation and personalisation will happen only when companies learn more about them. Efficient, cost-effective supply chain and inventory management will occur only when data from different touch-points can be gathered and analysed quickly and inexpensively.

The problem is not with technology but the cost of implementing it. RFID, CRM, executive dashboards and other technology solutions have enabled companies to move toward these goals, but often at a high price.

Instead of investing more, companies should leverage global sourcing to invest smarter in low-cost, highly skilled resources to create the tools to gather, manage and analyze information. Information can thus be a tool to solve current problems and quickly spot and respond to unanticipated ones.

## Sourcing for Adaptability

Business cycles often change in ways that no one can predict. Surviving and benefiting from these changes means preparing for them, however uncertain they might be. This requires the ability to track and monitor trends and adopt new operating models for adaptability and flexibility.

Xilinx, a US chip manufacturer, showed its adaptability in 2001 during the IT industry downturn. It offered employees sabbaticals, forced vacations and pay cuts rather than laying them off. Company executives realised that the cost of hiring and training one new engineer would cost the company a quarter of a million dollars. They also wanted to prevent competitors from tapping Xilinx employees to learn valuable company secrets.

Ultimately, the company saved more than $35 million in labour costs, and as the chip sector recovered, Xilinx rolled out several innovative new products, capturing market share from competitors in the process.

During the same downturn, when many US companies were slashing IT spending, Infosys organised a series of internal workshops to focus managers on ways to best take advantage of the downturn. One outcome was a recruiting campaign to find and hire consulting and service delivery talent in the US. We significantly deepened our skills base in our most important market.

Creating flexible and proactive human resources practices is one way for companies to alter operating models to compete in the flat world. Companies can also adapt their operating models in a number of ways, in particular through global sourcing.

Among our more mature clients we are seeing the outsourcing of fixed costs such as talent, real estate and procurement with the goal of making them variable. We are also witnessing the modularisation of global processes for scalability and, in offshore back offices, a noticeable increase in forecasting and planning activities.

As global sourcing evolves and new services and delivery models emerge, they establish the foundation from which companies can adapt to, and succeed in the flattening world. As sourcing strategies, organisational approaches and governance models mature, the stage is set for further growth. The onus is on service providers to do their part.

## Becoming a Flat World Service Provider

The success of the global delivery model can be seen not only in the spectacular growth of Infosys and other leading Indian companies but also in that most sincere form of flattery, imitation. Hardly a month goes by without a business magazine or technology journal article on the subject of which country "will be the next India." Meanwhile, service providers across the globe have emerged to fulfil the growing demand for skilled low-cost labour.

This proliferation is already resulting in mergers and acquisitions or, in the case of Infosys, organic growth as vendors seek to acquire in-demand talent, branch out into new service sectors, and capture market share. Some are taking the path toward becoming full-service providers. Others are carving out specialised niches. How it will all play out, no one can be certain.

One thing is certain – that the boom cycle in global sourcing will end some day. To flourish in this time of change and remain successful, service providers must become flat world companies in their own right.

This means taking advantage of demographic change and leveraging global talent. It requires competing not only on price but on innovation against established and emerging competitors. It means understanding the impact of privacy and regulations and other business risks and helping clients overcome them.

Being a flat world service provider also means aligning technology and business strategies and acquiring and managing information to build knowledge on behalf of clients as well as for competitive advantage. Finally, success in the flattening world demands depth and breadth of technical and business expertise, process excellence, and the ability to identify and proactively respond to changing business cycles.

## Shifting Focus – From Country to Company

In the early years of offshore outsourcing, Infosys and other Indian service providers collaborated to build a country brand image while still competing with one another. Combining entrepreneurial drive, technology expertise, a large pool of skilled labour, and the disruptive force of global delivery, this effort resulted in India being synonymous with IT and business process service excellence.

Today, Infosys is a recognised brand and India is the world's largest IT and business process global sourcing destination. However, in a flattening world, the role of countries is becoming less important than the client/vendor relationship. Companies are looking beyond India, China and other established locations and seeking trusted service partners to aid their quests.

Becoming a flat world service provider means expanding beyond the boundaries of primary locations to acquire and apply the skills of a worldwide talent pool. Although this may sound like the standard definition of a multinational business, it is significantly different from a flat world company.

The former implies maintaining operations in different countries, serving local clients independent of other locations. The latter involves building and managing globally connected operations based on a delivery model focused on providing the right skills at the right cost at the right level of risk to the client. It means hiring locally and training globally to acquire and deliver industry, process and technical expertise where required and blending it with local business culture knowledge where appropriate.

Being a flat world service provider is also about leveraging multiple locations to support client business interests and avoid the risk of being overly invested in one country. For example, cultural compatibility and avoiding perceived global risks are among the reasons why some European companies favour Eastern European countries as sourcing destinations over India, the Philippines, etc.

Serving Japanese, Korean, Taiwanese, and other East Asian companies from China makes good cultural *and* good business sense. So does supporting clients' in-country activities, as well as directly participating in China's growing services market.

It is for these reasons that Infosys has development centres in China, a large multi-lingual near-shore European workforce in the Czech Republic, and onshore delivery capabilities close to client locations in the US, Canada, Germany and the UK, and is continually looking to other geographies.

However, not all facets of service delivery require high cultural compatibility or proximity to clients. Rather, the key to delivering services in the flat world is having a global delivery network comprised of the right locations, hiring and developing the right skill sets, balancing service activities to apply them cost-effectively, understanding and mitigating risks, and having everything work together.

Mature company sourcing practitioners recognise this. Their interest in leveraging different countries is balanced by an understanding of the complexities involved. They look to vendor-partners who have the willingness and capability to seamlessly operate from multiple locations.

The keyword is 'transparency' – unburdening clients from having to work with multiple vendors in multiple countries representing different cultures and ways of doing business.

## Demographics and the Competition for Talent

One of the most important questions about the current and future status of IT and business process sourcing from the standpoints of client demand and service delivery supply is centred on the availability and cost of skilled workers. Changing global demographics clearly point to developing countries as the chief source for such talent.

However, there are important questions to be answered – especially about the impact of economic development and competition for skills going forward. This topic was the basis of a comprehensive report by the McKinsey Global Institute, *Emerging Global Labour Market*, in June 2005. Studying employment categories across a range of industries, the researchers focused on the percentage of those jobs that could potentially be moved offshore.

A key focus of the study was the "suitability" of workers in low-wage countries, by which the authors meant the ability to work for multinational companies. Citing relatively low experience levels, wide dispersion of workers, domestic competition and other factors, they predicted that the number of suitable workers was far lower than raw population numbers suggest.

Noting that although current supply exceeds present demand across all job categories, the report authors predict that the situation will soon change for certain high-demand skills. Illustrating this point they note that together the projected US and UK demand for suitable young engineers will absorb the projected supply available in China, India and the Philippines by 2011.

Competition for the best and the brightest is not limited to multinational companies and developed countries. Infosys selects a small percentage of candidates from the top universities and technical schools – both in India and abroad – competing with other vendors and multinationals in the process. Taking into account that economic growth in China, India and other current sourcing destinations is increasing and will increase domestic demand in these countries, the competition will only grow.

The pressures of rising salaries on global delivery service vendors' cost competitiveness will be offset to some extent by equivalent increases fuelled by rising demand across locations. However, in the flat world, it is not enough for global service providers to rely on rising labour costs to remain competitive. They must help increase the labour supply and raise skill levels.

This means working with government education bureaucracies and reaching out beyond top-tier schools, as Infosys is doing in India, to help raise standards and make curricula more relevant to the real-world needs of businesses. It also means investing heavily in in-house training, for new hires and existing employees. Further, to ensure consistency and excellence, such training must be provided to all employees across all locations.

Ironically, it wasn't long ago that the populations of India, China and other developing economies were seen as burdens. Today, they represent a potential benefit, one that with a mix of public and private investment can serve as a major source of skills in the flat world. Beyond education, however, the realisation of this potential also rests on improving worker productivity and effectiveness through technology and innovation.

## Technology Impact on Service Delivery

The global service delivery model could not exist without high-speed digital communications, distributed computing platforms, and collaboration tools. Needless to say, advances in such technologies will have a profound effect on the future of IT and business process services.

One sector where this effect is being felt is in infrastructure management, which accounts for over half of all IT services spending. Long the domain of traditional data centre outsourcing, it is being transformed by a combination of reliable high-speed communications in low-cost locations, automated tools, and increasingly effective processes. The advent of remotely manageable network devices, servers and other platforms are also driving the globalisation of this service.

The trend toward modularisation provides a means to couple IT infrastructure outsourcing with processes and supporting applications in an incremental approach. It could start with transferring discrete processes to offshore locations to reduce costs. Server migration and consolidation might follow, financed by labour savings, as well as application support and maintenance.

With experience gained from working the links between processes, applications and hardware, vendor staff can identify areas of improvement and additional cost savings, not to mention process transformation.

In a June 2006 report, *Moving IT infrastructure* labour *offshore*, McKinsey and Company noted that many companies maintain distributed infrastructures, resulting in operations being scattered around the world. This has enabled companies to consolidate labour in low-cost offshore centres, creating an opportunity to raise application and user service levels.

The report also points out that since many companies have already moved application development and maintenance functions offshore, related activities such as internal help desk and server support represent a logical next step. As examples, it cites the ability to provide affordable 24/7 support. The authors also note that early adopters that made this move two to three years ago have by now achieved savings of up to 60%.

Beyond its transformative effect on current service offerings and solutions, technology change, coupled new business models are creating opportunities for global sourcing vendors. Software as a Service or SaaS is one example. Actually an old model, one that started with service bureaus and morphed into the ASP model, SaaS offers the potential of turning software from a capital expense to an operating expense.

Given the right SaaS business model and risk profile, independent software vendors could partner with service providers who would either work with hardware OEMs to create, or invest in delivery centres located in favourable locations as defined by the availability skills, communications infrastructure, and cost-versus-risk conditions. In this scenario, service providers' value-add would start with existing services such as systems integration, implementation and ongoing maintenance and support.

Although this model is typically associated with small and medium-size businesses, it has potential for large enterprises. In addition to packaged software, service providers could partner with clients, taking ownership of legacy applications and delivering through some variant of SaaS.

Also on the horizon is the potential impact of Service Oriented Architectures (SOA). Infosys' R&D and training investments have led to consulting, architecture design and implementation and integration engagements with early adopters, delivering cost savings, enabling agility, and creating revenue opportunities through the ability to leverage technology to adopt new business models.

Where this will lead in terms of new delivery models and services, including variations on SaaS, is an open question. One that will be answered by service providers willing to invest in people and technology, innovate, and partner with clients open to new ideas.

## External Forces for Good or III

Economics, demographics, and technology have a direct impact on the future of the IT and business process services industries that vendors can leverage to chart their destinies. However, other forces that exercise an equally powerful, although unpredictable indirect influence on the global services market include regulation and economic nationalism.

Regulations have the potential for levelling the competitive playing field and for lessening the negative environmental and social effects of globalisation. At the same time the complexity of privacy, accounting, and other regulations and their impact on businesses are growing exponentially.

Adding to this complexity is the fact that regulations vary from country to country. Today's companies operate at a level of global integration unmatched by law. Often, the only way to conform to every nation's laws is to set a standard that exceeds all others.

As a publicly traded company in the US, Infosys is required to be SOX-compliant, and has adopted the necessary security standards and governance practices. However, it is incumbent on us to help clients mitigate regulatory and other risks using the highest levels of security and disaster recovery technologies, standards and practices.

Going a step further, it is to the benefit of the global services industry that service providers work with domestic regulatory agencies to promote standards consistent with those in other parts of the world, while simultaneously promoting good corporate governance locally. The flip side: in addition to protecting the health, safety, financial security and privacy of citizens, regulations also facilitate protectionism, which runs counter to the better aims of globalisation. This applies equally to developed and developing countries.

On the positive side, we see a growing realisation that global sourcing can bring benefits to domestic economies, and not only by helping local businesses become competitive. Just as states that once saw Japanese auto companies as threats now compete for their US manufacturing jobs, countries around the world – including developed ones – will soon seek the employment and tax revenue opportunities that come from having Indian or other vendors build and staff local service centres.

## The Next Level of Global Sourcing

Taking responsibility for developing and maintaining applications and managing back-office functions gives global service providers knowledge and insight into how these technologies and processes support and advance company business strategies. This presents them with the opportunity to engage with clients at a higher level and deliver greater value.

In the early days of offshore outsourcing Indian companies, including Infosys, tended to shy away from presenting clients with options for project designs or proactively suggesting improvements to current applications and process. The focus then was on understanding the requirements and delivering on them with quality and timeliness.

Times have changed. We no longer hide our light under a bushel basket, as a major client once said. The depth and breadth of today's client relationships and the need for continuous improvement and innovation have reached a point where clients seek more, and global service providers can deliver more.

By building consulting, R&D, testing, product design and other capabilities, Infosys and others moved in that direction. Other steps include partnering with niche vendors when required skills are not available in-house or fall outside of standard service offerings. The increased use of collaboration tools to reduce client management overhead and service delivery costs allow the movement of more and higher value work to low-cost locations.

One thing is certain: vendors cannot continue to rely on cost alone for competitive advantage. For the global delivery model to remain a force for change in the flattening world, service providers and clients must look beyond cost savings to how they can be applied in different ways. It is through such changes that the future of the IT and business process services will be defined.

A picture of that future takes shape from our assumptions based on current trends and past experience. For example, the services industry, with its large and growing number of vendors, will no doubt undergo a period of consolidation. Hundreds of small companies in India, Russia, China and other emerging sourcing locations will be absorbed or disappear. At the same time there will always be a need for niche providers, and partnering will become more common.

Automated tools, reusable code and network services will reduce labour requirements in some disciplines, but the demand for skills will simply shift to newer, higher-value activities. Then, too, as emerging economies grow the demands of their domestic markets will ensure competition for resources.

Global competition will ensure that the demand for price value will continue to apply downward pressure on margins, forcing service providers to create ever more efficient delivery mechanisms while constantly watching quality.

Finally, relationships will firm up as companies become more closely linked internally as well as with their partners and customers. In this context, the need for efficient and transparent service delivery that transcends geographic, cultural, and other barriers will become ever more important. This, Infosys believes, is the future that will dawn on IT and business process services industries in a flattening world.

# The World's BPO Hub

*Ananda Mukerji*
*Managing Director and CEO, First Source, Mumbai, India*

## An Emerging Global Power

India has always been a country of radical thinkers and innovators. As the shackles of the country's history have been thrown off and India starts to take advantage of its wealth of resources, population growth and entrepreneurialism, it will increasingly be able to take a leading position in the global economy.

In recent years the growth in the Indian economy has outstripped most of the 'developed countries'. Admittedly, we have a lot to catch up, but the figures are impressive and there's a lot to be proud of: India's economy grew 6% a year from 1980 to 2002 and 7.5% a year from 2002 to 2006, making it one of the world's best performing economies for a quarter of a century. In the last 20 years, India's middle class has quadrupled (to almost 250 million people), and 1% of its poor have crossed the poverty line every year. India is now the world's fourth largest economy and is expected to overtake Japan as number three (in terms of purchasing power parity).

Government policy, particularly the series of reforms instigated in 1991 by the present Prime Minister Manmohan Singh, when he was Finance Minister, has been a key catalyst. Singh devalued the rupee, reduced business red tape, and encouraged foreign investment. Furthermore, India has a strong capital markets infrastructure and a modern stock market, western legal institutions, and a strong private sector, which generated a 16.7% return on capital for the average private company in 2004.

A measure of the strength of the Indian economy has been the confidence with which Indian companies have gone on the acquisition trail. Indian companies are storming ahead, with the number of cross-border mergers and acquisitions noticeably increasing in recent years. According to Deallogic, the data provider, in the first three quarters of 2006, Indian companies announced a record 112 foreign acquisitions, with a combined value of $7.2 billion. This compares with a value of $4.5 billion for 2005's deals, which was three times the figure for 2004.

This expansion is a trend that will continue and in the future there will be an increasing number of multinational 'superpower' companies based in the now emerging nations. Indian companies have a way to go before they rival the likes of global giants such as Walmart and General Motors, but the large Indian conglomerates are building up speed and establishing themselves as multinationals. If these companies continue to grow at their current rate, there will certainly be an Indian company in the Fortune top 10 global corporations within the next ten years.

This prediction is in line with forecasts that India's economy is likely to become the third largest in the world by 2030 after the US and China. Even now, India is the UK's second largest foreign investor, after the US, pushing Japan into third place, according to the Ernst & Young investment monitor. India is now a major player in the world economy, hosting an annual global economic summit in its own right, under the auspices of the World Economic Forum, to showcase the Indian economic triumph, address the challenges to economic prosperity and also to encourage inward investment and partnership.

In line with the growth in the economy, India's outsourcing industry has been a success story and is a major contributor to the country's economic success. The outsourcing industry is just one aspect of India's ' Knowledge Revolution', which started in the early 1990s and builds on the expansion of the IT and other service industries in India.

Those of us who operate in the services sector are familiar with the rise and rise of the outsourcing industry in India and the corporate rationales behind the trend to outsource non-core aspects of an organisation's activities, to enable a focus on core competences.

As organisations, both private and public sector, become more sophisticated in their sourcing strategies, two key trends emerge: Firstly, the location of the outsourced services becomes a more complex decision and secondly, the actual services that are outsourced are increasingly reduced to a basic process, enabling greater standardisation of service. These two trends are related. As business processes are increasingly standardised, it becomes easier to select the most appropriate location for each particular process.

## Rightshoring

As each business service is analysed down to its key components, it is possible to identify the optimum location for each process. The advisory firm Capgemini has even trademarked the term 'Rightshore' and defines it as a business model that 'cuts across geographies to access the right service, in the right place, at the right price.' The principle of rightshoring is now becoming accepted in all aspects of outsourcing, whether it be IT or business process outsourcing and according to Capgemini, offers 'the most advantageous mix of resources worldwide, lowers costs and boosts business performance.'

Rightshoring is also cited as enabling outsourcing organisations to spread their risk, and certainly there are merits in having multi locations for critical processes, even if they are only used as a backup as part of a disaster recovery platform. Given the number of countries that now claim to offer offshored services of various kinds, (The consulting and research firm Gartner identifies at least 59 challengers to India's pole position) rightshoring offers more than Capgemini's assertion of 'The best of both worlds', but rather truly can offer the best of ALL worlds.

Strategic rightshoring requires a more in depth analysis of the processes outsourced and a review of the services provided by the different outsourcing service providers. Selecting the most appropriate destination for service provision will depend on a complex variety of factors, including the nature of the service, expertise of the preferred service providers, the available skill sets in the potential locations, labour costs, infrastructure, time differences, customer and investor requirements, union attitudes, and the competition's outsourcing strategies.

There is no absolute right or wrong location for a process, but common sense needs to be applied when considering the most appropriate location. For example, a process that requires lots of voice communication and a strong cultural understanding, such as vehicle breakdown call-outs, may be best placed onshore nearest to the end consumer. Other, more structured information based voice interactions, such as bank balance information or transfers, can easily be carried out offshore. Email communications are geographically neutral and can be carried out in the most cost effective location.

Some organisations are implementing a 'follow the sun' outsourcing strategy to facilitate 24x7 services – i.e. the customer calls are directed to whichever location is operating within normal working hours – a policy that saves money through not having to pay premium wages for anti-social hours, and contributes to lower attrition rates for the same reason.

Non-voice work and back office processing can be carried out in the optimum location for the particular business service, and an offshore location is often the most appropriate solution, provided training programmes in language and application skills are put in place. And India has demonstrated its particular aptitude for back office processing.

Just as China has become the world's factory, India will become the global back office. China has shown that it can manufacture a wide variety of high quality products from small electronic consumer items to cars and computers at a much lower cost than its competitors. Fewer consumer goods suppliers are actually manufacturing their products themselves but are outsourcing to China and this is a trend that is being applied across the globe. For example, 50% of the world's cameras are made in China, which also accounts for 25% of the world's washing machines. Take a look at many of your branded household items from white goods to clothes and you will find they are made in China, despite bearing the name of a western brand or designer.

In the same way that manufacturing is outsourced, it is becoming less cost effective to carry out time consuming and labour intensive back office transactions in-house. And as business processes become more and more standardised, the argument for retaining back office functions in-house becomes less attractive. A focus on core competences will increasingly become the driving force in successful business, so companies will become more imaginative in their outsourcing strategies.

## Standardisation of Services

The maturing of the global outsourcing market will lead to a harmonisation of BPO service standards, particularly in back-office processes like accounts and mortgage processing, claims handling, policy administration, cards and payments processing. This trend will be driven by consolidation of the third party Indian providers, each processing greater volumes of work at lower margins. The consolidation process has already begun; the research group Evalueserve believes that of the 400 Indian BPO firms, the top 15 already have 60-70% of the market.

And as the Indian merger and acquisition fervour is likely to continue its relentless pace, there will be rationalisation of the outsourcing service providers, resulting in the BPO environment becoming dominated by 10 giant, global service providers, supported by a smattering of niche specialist operators.

As part of the standardisation of BPO services, long-term outsourcing contracts will no longer be the norm, as most outsourcing organisations will require shorter contracts for more specific activities, perhaps based around spikes in demand following marketing campaigns, for example. The industry will have developed to the point that organisations will be able to have 'just-in-time' services, delivered remotely, or locally, by a BPO provider.

In the future, hardly any back office processes will be carried out in house. Just as it has become natural to outsource catering and cleaning services, administrative processes that can be broken down into logical components will generally be outsourced. These standardised services will be provided in mass volume by a handful of global Indian operators with large hubs in India, but supported by their subsidiary delivery centres worldwide. Thus delivering the right outsourcing solution in the right location for the client's specific process requirements.

## Higher Value Outsourcing

There will also be enormous growth in higher value, more complex work going to India. This section of the outsourcing industry has come to be known as Knowledge Process Outsourcing (KPO). Research from Frost & Sullivan shows that the Indian KPO industry generated $405.2 million in 2005, representing a 59% increase on the previous year, and could be worth $5.5 billion by 2019. Retail banks and insurers are starting to offshore higher value work, including financial analysis, statutory and regulatory reporting, and risk assessment.

India is the natural home for knowledge process outsourcing due to its pool of highly educated graduates who can carry out complex analysis and reporting at a fraction of the cost of carrying out such processes in western countries. The banks are making huge savings in labour – Wall Street banks pay their Indian staff about $20 an hour, compared to about $100 an hour for juniors in the US.

There is also a recent trend for legal or paralegal work to be carried out in India. With its similar legal system, India is the natural home for processes such as patent applications, legal research, conveyancing and contract drafting, as well as litigation support. A fast growing area is 'e-discovery' where Indian lawyers analyse and audit electronic communications. As well as the major UK and US law firms outsourcing some of their support activities, there are also opportunities to develop legal processing work with the specialist international legal research houses and publishing firms.

Global spending on legal services is estimated to be around $250 billion, with the US accounting for more than two-thirds of the market. The breadth of the potential legal services that could be outsourced indicates that the market potential for the US alone is in the region of $3-4 billion.

The accounting sector is also starting to see the benefit of outsourcing to India, with a trickle of work moving there, and there are examples of other highly entrepreneurial KPO work that could have huge potential. Outsourced training is also a growth area, with Indian firms providing online tutoring for students in the US and the UK.

Medical outsourcing is another massive potential growth area, with estimates that subcontracting work from the British National Health Service could earn India's economy more than $1bn per year. Well-trained Indian surgeons, working in new highly equipped hospitals can carry out standard operations at a fraction of the UK cost. As a back office process, Indian specialists now frequently do medical imaging from major US and UK hospitals.

This model of global delivery of outsourced services will become the new norm for outsourcing and with its established lead in the world market for outsourced services, India will continue to dominate. However, with that global dominance, Indian companies must be wary of complacency.

## Challenges to India's Supremacy

There are three major potential challenges to Indian outsourcing predominance:

Firstly, the leader will always be challenged for market share and there are regular reports of new emerging princes competing for India's crown in the outsourcing market. There are countless countries that are vying to oust India from its throne. Chief among the contenders are the Philippines and China. Muscling in on the rightshoring argument for the UK are the Central European countries of the Czech Republic, Poland, Romania and Hungary, which all have burgeoning outsourcing industries, offering a nearshoring alternative to offshoring.

Having established their precedence and expertise in the global outsourcing market, servicing the UK and US economies, Indian outsourcers will use their prime position to consolidate their position. Indian outsourcers have carved out their position delivering what newcomers to outsourcing have not yet been able to do. Indian BPO providers have moved beyond the simple cost saving argument to justify outsourcing and deliver far higher value to their clients.

Companies that have outsourced to India are benefiting from the next generation of outsourced solutions, with improvements in productivity, efficiency and end user customer satisfaction. Indian BPOs have adopted continuous process improvement tools such as Six Sigma, COPC and Kaizen methodologies to deliver process efficiencies. These methodologies are not exclusive to India, but Indian outsourcers have adopted them enthusiastically and it is this leading edge that will maintain Indian companies' predominance in outsourcing, even if India's geographical market share is gradually eroded.

Equipped with these high standards, Indian BPO companies are expanding their geographical domain and setting up global subsidiaries and delivery centres across the world, taking advantage of the benefits of other countries' labour arbitrage, pool of educated English speakers and lower attrition rates, in the same way that UK and US companies originally came to India for outsourcing.

All of the leading Indian outsourcing companies have established delivery centres worldwide, either by acquisition or by investing in the chosen countries, to offer the rightshoring model to their client base.

## Reliance on Established Markets

Secondly, India must beware of too much reliance on the established western economies, which as has been pointed out earlier, are significantly declining in comparison to the emerging markets. The USA and UK are the two leaders in adoption of outsourcing but if India is continue its economic triumph, it needs to look beyond its traditional overseas markets. Weaknesses and uncertainties in these established economies could lead to a decline in consumer spending power with a consequent downturn in the demand for customer services, one of the cornerstones of the BPO sector.

For the medium term, the USA and UK will remain the principal outsourcing countries, but with increasing competition for these markets, India would do well to cast its net wider for new business. Continental Europe has been slow to seize the economic benefits of outsourcing. More rigid labour laws have been a major obstacle to European companies outsourcing and there also seems to be a cultural resistance to moving work overseas, even if it is non-core to the principal business. India, with its large English speaking population, has a more natural affinity with the US and UK and for similar reasons of language and heritage, Morocco seems the natural location for French outsourcing. However, India may not be overlooked by any French companies considering taking the BPO route. There is a significant French speaking population in the former French colony of Pondicherry, so India could take advantage of the predicted upsurge in outsourcing from France.

Despite the stagnating growth in developed economies, most analysts and economists agree that outsourcing offers benefits for western businesses, allowing them to save costs and improve productivity as well as focus on core activities. Most analysts put outsourcing into the context of inevitable globalisation and focus on the wealth creating benefits for the UK and US economies. Estimates are that for every £100 invested in India by UK companies, they receive back £141 and figures are similar for the US, with McKinsey's estimates indicating that for every $1 invested in India, the US receives back $1.12-$1.14.

A major opportunity for Indian BPO expansion lies on its own doorstep, with the expansion of the Indian domestic market. With the expanding middle class demanding consumer goods and financial services products, the Indian service sector is starting to follow the example of the developed economies. In 2006 alone, the domestic Indian BPO market is predicted to have grown by 60% to US $93.5 million. Most of this is phone-based customer enquiries and outbound sales. By 2009, India is expected to have nearly 100,000 contact centre workers, serving the domestic market, according to Datamonitor.

## India's Internal Challenges

The third challenge is India itself. Despite its impressive economic growth, India faces enormous challenges to sustain that level of expansion. Of its nearly 1 billion inhabitants, an estimated 350-400 million are still below the poverty line, We must strive to elevate the standard of living for all Indians because huge gaps between the haves and have-nots will hold us back, both in terms of dissatisfaction of those still below the poverty line, but will also affect the way India is perceived internationally. A successful international player must be seen to break down the barriers between rich and poor.

The infrastructure in India could also prove to be a significant obstacle to global success. Travel across the country is challenging, with ancient railways dating back to the era of the British Empire, (which ended in 1947), poor roads and horrific congestion in urban areas, and unreliable aircraft routes servicing the main cities. Electricity supply can still be intermittent, despite major investment and clean water is not universally available outside principal urban areas.

The Indian BPO industry must strive to ensure that it does not become a victim of its own success. Rising costs such as wage inflation and also high rates of staff attrition are often cited as key reasons why other countries are making inroads on India's supremacy in the outsourcing sector. With estimates of attrition in Indian BPOs varying wildly from 15-40%, depending on the process, this is seen as a fundamental weakness of the BPO sector. The National Association of Software and Service Companies (NASSCOM) predicts that the outsourcing industry as a whole will face a shortage of 262,000 professionals by 2012. In some of the main BPO hubs like Mumbai, Bangalore and Hyderabad, wage inflation and competition for experienced agents is driving labour costs up by around 20% per annum.

So will this upward trend continue until the salary differential between India and the developed world becomes eroded and other countries overtake India in the outsourcing league through undercutting on wage costs? Probably not. India's expanding population and increasing wealth will ensure that an increasing number of people enter the education market and join the potential catchment pool for new BPO recruits. Yes, there will always be a 'brain drain' of the brighter graduates who move on from the BPO to other more lucrative and prestigious businesses, but outsourcing will remain a great step onto the career ladder. We have many people at management level who have originally considered BPO to be a short term opportunity, but have discovered that due to the fast pace of the business, there are huge openings for upward progression and many BPOs prefer to promote from within.

## Overcoming Common Misconceptions and Attitudes

The Indian outsourcing industry has had a rough ride particularly in the western press, with journalists seizing the opportunity to paint a picture of offshoring companies as stealing local jobs and Indian contact centres selling off clients' bank details for £10 a go. Offshoring was singled out as a major issue in the 2004 US Presidential election, with calls for protectionism to face the challenge of the loss of American jobs overseas.

The UK government has been more open minded about the matter, with Prime Minister Tony Blair stating: "Companies are using relocation of call centres and outsourcing in order to build a more effective structure that benefits not just the places to which the work is outsourced but also the companies and people in the UK and Europe". Patricia Hewitt MP, when she was Trade & Industry Secretary, also welcomed offshoring as a mutual benefit, saying that if developing countries prosper, so will the UK. Regional development agencies in the UK openly court Indian companies and other offshore service providers, encouraging them to open contact centres in areas that need a boost to the local economy and helping the outsourcers to develop their global footprint.

There is always the potential for political backlash from western countries, based on the perceived loss of jobs to India, if the global economy sees a marked decline. Already, a number US states have passed laws restricting offshoring of state contracts, despite the increased costs, and some banks have taken very public stances about not offshoring their call centres to India. And there have been a few instances of US and UK companies, returning outsourced work back to home shores from India. Unions and the popular press have jumped on these isolated cases as indications of the demise of the Indian outsourcing fad.

However, this opposition is likely to wane. In the UK, some unions have already publicly recognised the inevitability of outsourcing and are working closely with outsourcing companies to bolster the job prospects of those affected by offshoring. Some UK organisations have made agreements with trade union Amicus, to invest some of the savings from offshoring into helping those whose jobs are threatened.

Secondly, the western world will come to the realisation that outsourcing jobs actually represents only a small proportion of normal job churn. Data from Forrester Research, for example, shows that by 2015 a total of 3.4 million jobs in services could have moved abroad, but that it is dwarfed by the 30 million jobs destroyed and created in the US every year. The west will also come to recognise that many of the media reports have been little more than scaremongering, without giving the full story. The call centre sector in the UK, for instance, is still thriving, with call centre employment expanding almost three times as fast as the UK national average in the past four years, and expected to employ more than one million people by the end of 2007.

Furthermore, negative emotions about outsourcing will be increasingly offset as the global expansion of Indian BPOs creates job opportunities for people in the US, UK and Europe. People are comfortable working for Japanese car manufacturers. Over time, the same will be true for Indian companies.

## Security

Security is seen as another big issue for Indian BPOs. Following a few incidents, unions, particularly in the UK, and the media, have jumped on the security of customers' information in Indian contact centres. But the reality is that there have been far fewer security breaches in India than in either the UK or the US. The UK's Financial Services Authority (FSA) recognised the country's security levels when it reported in 2005 that outsourcing to India's best contact centres carried no greater inherent risk than outsourcing in the UK.

Nevertheless, because Indian firms are extremely aware of their perceived lack of security, the leading players not only comply with international security standard, BS 7799, but also have in place 'Fort Knox-like' security measures to ensure that employees cannot access core data. Some of these systems imitate the security standards of many global banks. Airport style security checks take place for employees on entry and exit; it is the norm to ban mobile phones, CDs and sometimes stationery, and to block e-mail, the Internet and all forms of external disc drives; and shredding machines for customer conversation notes are common. Furthermore, 'thin-client' technology means that Indian workers never get to see the raw customer account data; it remains on secure servers domestically. Some Indian firms even employ teams focused entirely on trying to crack their own computer systems. NASSCOM also is working with the government to change India's Information Technology Act to improve data protection.

## The Future for Outsourcing

The days of tactical outsourcing are behind us. The issue of outsourcing is now viewed as a much more strategic focus for a successful company. The range of outsourcing options continues to expand and there will be an increasing number of high end complex processes that will be outsourced in specialist professions such as finance and accounting, legal, medical. We are continuing to see more outsourcing in horizontal applications such as procurement, design, HR and training. Publishing is another area where we are seeing growth as fewer organisations publish their own documents or research articles. The trend towards smaller print runs of niche topics and web-based publishing is also an opportunity for specialist outsourcers. The balance between front and back office outsourcing will be evened out, with

Datamonitor predicting that Indian BPO companies' share of front office vs. back office processes will be 50:50.

The thorny issue of 'cultural differences' will become less important as it will cease to matter whether a contact centre is in Belfast or Bangalore. What will matter in relation to customer service is delivery of excellent service that adds real value to the end customer's experience as well as to the bottom line of the company outsourcing the service. Outsourcers are becoming smarter and more scientific at measuring customer satisfaction levels, which are key to assessing the value of outsourced services.

There will be fewer questions raised about the security of offshore operations as the intensity of security measures become appreciated and any breaches come to be seen in the light of the global challenge of data and identity theft. Anyone who visits an offshore delivery centre will appreciate how much more stringent security often is compared to many onshore sites.

As part of the movement towards more the more strategic approach to outsourcing, there will be continue to be less emphasis on cost benefits and more focus on business transformation. This transformation can only happen if outsourcing companies view their relationship with their outsourcer as a partnership with joint ownership of the challenges. There will be less stick and more carrot in terms of the benefits to both parties.

There will be expansion at both ends of the contract spectrum with the 'mega-deals' of $100m plus, continuing to increase but at the other end of the scale, with more complex niche processes, calling for specialist service providers, there will also be an increase in the lower net worth contracts but these will continue for the longer term as the outsource company develops more expertise and becomes more attuned to the requirements of the client.

Ten years from now, we will be in a new era of globalisation. The global village will be smaller. It will include a handful of fully integrated, truly global Indian BPO companies, providing a comprehensive range of services, from the commoditised to the most complex, from a multitude of locations throughout the world. These companies will create thousands of jobs across the globe, and they will be an accepted part of commerce and employment.

For corporates, the competitive benefits to be gained from outsourcing will continue to grow: the range of services and countries from where to source them will continue to expand, and decisions about what functions must stay in-house and those that can be outsourced will become increasingly blurred. The flip side will be a commensurate potential rise in business and financial risk. Managing the global web of service providers will be a complex task, much as it is today for manufacturing companies. The result is that the future corporation will look very different. It's quite possible that within ten years, the Chief Business Process Outsourcing Officer will have emerged, to play a vital role in corporate decision-making.

# Indian Offshoring – Building Sustainable Excellence

*Rajendra S. Pawar*
*Chairman and co-founder, NIIT, Gurgaon, Haryana, India*

Global fora are alight with the matter of the BRICs – Brazil, Russia, India and China – that are expected to lead the next phase of international economic development and create new paradigms of growth for other developing nations. Tectonic shifts are redefining the world. From a time when the West – won by the low-labour cost model – offshored its entire manufacturing to hubs in the East, today, it is the turn of the services sector to witness the same movement. Increasingly, large companies are offshoring their non-core – and more recently – core processes to low-cost, high-quality foreign locations. This new wave, sweeping across the services economy, is expected to grow into a mammoth business opportunity for nations that are geared up with solutions for this space.

Countries such as India, in fact, have already emerged as major stakeholders in this rapidly growing marketplace. Over the past few decades, India has witnessed enormous social, cultural and economic upheaval and disruption – flux that has led to tremendous ideation, innovation and implementation, and enabled the country to build new and path-breaking differentiators for itself. It is these differentiators, in fact, that will enable India to emerge as a spearhead of the rapidly evolving global knowledge society, going forward.

It is clear then that within the elite BRICs group, India is the rising star. It has distinguished itself as the strongest name in the technology domain and the most likely to capitalise on the immense global opportunities being presented by the rapidly expanding offshoring industry. The balance is tipped in India's favour on account of the numerous strengths the country and its IT-BPO (Business Process Outsourcing) industry have built up, that give it a distinctive advantage.

Today, India is recognised for its vast pool of scientific, engineering and English-speaking talent, its significant cost advantage, process excellence and it's scaling up the value chain, where it brings advanced offerings to organisations across the world. India is being acknowledged as the playground for offshoring – the preferred destination where customers from mature economies are transferring their back-end and increasingly, crucial intellectual work, to gain significant competitive advantage.

By creating software solutions that manage knowledge and its transfer, India has kept itself on the innovation treadmill and ahead of contemporaries in the offshoring race. Take the instance of NIIT Technologies, a leading software exporter from India, and a company that has built an edge for itself by offering customers an unmatched value proposition. It has provided clients with the capability of transferring and hosting knowledge residing within their organisations into digital repositories through its Knowledge Portal technology, ensuring greater transparency and control for the offshore customers.

The company, which has taken the "Sliver-driven", "Focus and Differentiate" approach to IT solutions development, is positioning itself as a "Best and Big Enough" organisation within its chosen global verticals. In a landscape that also includes a number of "Big and Good Enough" options.

There is of course a larger picture, which suggests why India is best positioned to sustain its excellence and leadership within the offshoring sector. And a big factor has been the fact that the $21^{st}$ Century is the Century of the Mind.

## The Century of the Mind: India's Rich Heritage

It was in 1988, when addressing an audience comprising IT industry CEOs, academics and Government decision-makers in New Delhi, that I first spoke about how the $21^{st}$ century, was the "Century of the Mind," unlike the previous two hundred years that had been dedicated to the machine Gods. The dawning of the scientific revolution in the $17^{th}$ and $18^{th}$ centuries started transforming typically agrarian societies into ones where machines were the dominating force. The industrial revolution of the $19^{th}$ and $20^{th}$ centuries, where machines occupied pride of place, attempted to obliterate man from the development equation.

It was the transistor, perhaps the most important invention of the $20^{th}$ century – which represented changing information through zeros and ones – that sowed the first seeds of the Knowledge Society. The transistor marked the big leap from the Industrial to the Digital age. It kick-started the arrival of the post-industrial society, the service economy, and the knowledge era.

In a departure from the past, when man was taking a back seat and letting machines take over, the end of the $20^{th}$ century signalled the return of the Mind, as the centre-piece of the universe.

For two centuries, Man had been seen as an unnecessary appendage in the entire wealth creation process. One can recall the unsettling images of the "ghost factories," which became symbolic of the industrial age and conjured up bone-chilling visions of highly automated and mechanised facilities, where computers performed with clockwork precision, unmanned, unwatched and untouched by human hand.

With the arrival of the Knowledge Era, the balance is once again restored and Man has been placed back in the driving seat. From a time, when Man was an appendage to machines, we have moved into a phase where the computer, and more specifically information technology, has become a tool in the hands of Man.

The Century of the Mind has also been accompanied by other key developments, the most important among them the end of the cold war and the surge of democracy. The fall of the German wall, *Perestroika* in Russia, and the cry for more open and free governance by citizens, has led to democracy becoming the preferred political structure around the globe, a movement that is transforming the world.

Linked to a democratic framework have been the concepts of liberalisation, privatisation and globalisation, which have been adopted by countries such as India, as the new models for growth and economic development. In the late $20^{th}$ century, we have been hearing about free markets and entrepreneurship, which have emerged as the key drivers of the Indian economy. Democracy has liberated people and capital. It has moved capital from the state to the conglomerate to the entrepreneur. There has been an explosion of entrepreneurship in India in the $20^{th}$ century.

India has entered the Century of the Mind, riding on these fundamental forces of change. In the last few decades we have seen the world shrink, owing to internationalisation, a blurring of geographic boundaries and the metamorphosis of the world into a global village. As people travel, as societies communicate with each other and get closer and as cutting-edge telecom networks link lands, businesses and people, a whole new set of possibilities are opening up in the Century of the Mind.

It would of course be pertinent to mention the telecom revolution – centred around the arrival of the Internet and mobility – that has played a tremendous role in empowering enterprises and individuals and bridging the rural-urban, gender and digital divides in nations, especially India. In fact, it is the Century of the Mind that has enabled India, which missed the industrial revolution, to play catch-up with its more developed contemporaries.

## Mind Power, the New Reality

The India phenomenon and its surfacing into prominence as an important trading bloc, integrated with the rest of the world, rests to a large extent, on some of these developments. India has moved from the wings to take centre-stage, based on its "mind power", and its chief asset in the new society – its knowledge workers.

India's large number of English-speaking graduates represents a pool of raw talent that is being increasingly deployed by both MNC and Indian third-party service companies to move up the offshoring value chain. Today, the human minds in India are its strength and core competence, as is its population. A recent study by the All India Management Association (AIMA), has shown that India will have a significant edge over peer nations by 2020, owing to its potential surplus population in the working age group (15-59 years). Even as countries such as the US, UK, France, Germany, Italy, Russia, China, Japan and Australia, reel under major labour shortages owing to their ageing populations, India will have over 47 million surplus people in the working age group. The report also indicates that demand for outsourced services will increase due to ageing. In this scenario, India's people power could be its chief asset in capturing this opportunity, particularly in the area of knowledge-based services across various sectors. Of course, this vision and projection can become reality only if this workforce is built into a relevant, highly skilled, employable, specialised and readily available base of people.

Therefore, in order to ensure that the human minds within its realm become an asset, India must make sure that they are shaped, nurtured and made productive and proficient. If the population remains illiterate and untrained, it will prove to be a liability. If it is educated, it can change the complexion and fate of the country, sustaining its excellence and unassailable edge in the offshoring domain. India must make this choice. Does it want to harness its people power and move forward towards a better society and a better quality of life, or does it want to fall behind and lose the existing ground it has covered?

Clearly, the Government needs to intervene here and craft a National Policy that responds to this immense manpower need. Already, the foundational work has begun, with the first bricks being laid as far back as 1998, when the then Prime Minister, Atal Bihari Vajpayee declared that India should aspire for IT Superpower status by 2008. As someone who was part of the Prime Minister's IT Task Force at that time, I remember the importance the Group accorded to the issue of building technical resources, and the role these people would play in enabling India to achieve global IT leadership.

More recently, in 2005, the Indian Government announced the formation of the Knowledge Commission, headed by Sam Pitroda, one of India's earliest technology and telecom champions. The Commission has devoted itself to the task of making India the leader in the emerging global Knowledge Society.

## Education: Revolution Through Pioneering Partnerships

While India must understand that it has to leverage its relevant skilled manpower, it also has to grapple with a key challenge of creating an education ecosystem that nurtures such industry-relevant skill-sets within learners from an early age. India must begin then, from where it all starts. With possibly the most crucial element of any society – its education system.

It must understand the nature of education. Know how it is changing and organise itself to tap the opportunities that are being presented. Some successes have already been achieved in this direction, with the country taking its first steps towards ensuring that it gets "every child into the classroom." The Government's *Sarva Shiksha Abhiyan* (SSA) and midday meal schemes, which aim to universalise elementary education, and take it to the doorstep of every child, have crossed significant milestones. The initiatives have not only met their numbers targets, they have also been able to stem the flow of students dropping out of the system and led to a higher inclusion of the girl child into the process of education. The Special Innovation Fund available through the SSA has also enabled significant innovations to be implemented in the early education phase, particularly by private sector partners. NIIT, India's IT training leader for 25 years, has begun receiving support for its globally renowned, media-christened, Hole-in-the-Wall initiative, under the aegis of the SSA. The Government is beginning to buy into the Hole-in-the-Wall, a special experiment that draws from the expertise of its software business, NIIT Technologies and showcases the latter's immense software strengths and ability to provide highly ruggedised IT solutions, even in remote village environments.

The experiment, a foray into the realm of "minimally invasive education", indicates how a computer, placed inside a kiosk and made accessible to a group of children, can induce self learning, even in the absence of teachers. The software core in Hole-in-the-Wall and its Cognitive User Interface (CUI) helps resolve the complexities of reach, maintenance and remote monitoring and makes sure that the kiosks are up-and-running 24x7. Hole-in-the-Wall, the largest experiment in Primary Education in India, aims to lower the cost of imparting education, combat the paucity of teachers, and take learning to the maximum number of young people by harnessing technology. Using research funding from NIIT, the International Finance Corporation and the SSA Innovation Fund, the Hole-in-the-Wall project has been deployed in fourteen states in India.

## The Importance of the PPP Model

Whether it is school education, or college and higher learning, the Government will benefit by working closely with the private sector, gaining leverage from the eminently successful Public Private Partnership (PPP) model. The public and private sectors should marry their strengths – the public sector its vast infrastructure and financial resources and the private sector its explosive spirit of innovation and entrepreneurship – to better deal with the changing nature of education.

The involvement of the non-formal sector in the area of learning can help supplement the resources the Government currently has at its disposal. It can also bring in high quality, industry-endorsed curriculum, state-of-the-art learning methodologies and the best of the best faculty to improve the experience of learners.

Here, it would be pertinent to talk about the innovation NIIT has brought into the school education realm with its K-12 initiative, which touches the lives of 1.4 million students across India. By working with the country's state Governments to provide technology-assisted learning to children, NIIT is ensuring that not only is the K-12 segment literate in the traditional sense, it is also computer savvy and ready to join the ranks of the e-generation.

NIIT's foray into school education under the umbrella of its K-12 division has been powered by the system integration capabilities built up by its software business, NIIT Technologies. K-12 projects – that have undertaken the mammoth task of taking over 30,000 computers to 4,000 villages in India – involve the setting up of relevant IT and power infrastructure to provide technology-assisted learning in the unreached parts of the country. Overcoming challenges of distance, remoteness, absence of power and infrastructure with its software prowess, NIIT has made the K-12 dream of touching millions of school children, a reality.

The Post school education turf, particularly vocational training, (since it is far more "entrepreneurial" in nature and market driven), will also need higher private sector involvement. The PPP will be of tremendous value here too and India can harness it to build robust industry-academia interfaces and make education more relevant.

NIIT discovered the joys of PPP, when it launched its path-breaking GNIIT career program, with its 12 months Professional Practice to help the Indian IT sector plug the yawning demand-supply gap. As part of Professional Practice, which went on to become the world's largest industry-academia linkage, GNIITians were exposed to a live working environment, in a company for a year. By giving them an opportunity to gain first hand corporate experience, and giving the industry a chance to assess this talent, NIIT was able to bridge the world of learning and the world of work. Using the platform of the industry-endorsed GNIIT, NIIT has been able to build a high quality, process-driven IT workforce for the nation. One in every three IT professionals working in the IT and non-IT sectors has received some training at NIIT. The success of the GNIIT can be gauged by the fact that NIIT Technologies has been harnessing this ready pool of rightly skilled talent, and using it to stay ahead of competition. NIIT Technologies has also benefited from the exceptionally strong NIIT brand, which has enabled it to source and attract the best IT talent in India and across the globe.

In some of the most successful projects carried out by NIIT Technologies, a large number of GNIIT students, have played a crucial role. They have helped in delivering solutions for demanding global customers such as British Airways, ING, Generali, Deutsche Bahn, Toyota, SEI Investments and Sabre. This highly qualified talent, which is trained to work to zero defect standards, adheres to process discipline and conforms to the most stringent requirements of working within time and budget, has proved to be a great asset for NIIT Technologies – enabling the company to scale, while maintaining high standards of quality. The participation of the non-formal sector in the process of both primary and higher education therefore, will not only bring in fresh perspective and innovation in the way such learning can be improved, it will also help widen the pool of relevant skilled, employable people in the country.

## Work: Mentality of Service and Excellence

Having understood the nature of education in its entirety, India also needs to gain an understanding about the nature of work, which is gradually aligning itself to the altering profile of education. The changing nature of education is spawning a new workplace, which is expected to house a fresh breed of educated, highly skilled, learning-motivated workers that will usher in a learning society.

The enterprise of the future is one where the quest for excellence will become a way of life and an integral part of organisational DNA. Terms such as "zero defect", which first made an appearance on the lexicons of IT companies, are now getting accepted across India's industry sectors. Today, process excellence and the ability of a company to deliver high quality consistently, is a prerequisite, not a promise!

The world over, and especially in India, we have seen a host of global standards such as ISO 9000, SEI CMM Level 5, CMMi Level 5, BS7799, become the minimum requirement. Leading offshore service providers in India, have made sure that they set new quality benchmarks and routinely attain the certification of emerging standards.

NIIT's tryst with quality began in the 1980s, when it adopted quality models propounded by *gurus* such as Philip Crosby and made them a part of its process excellence strategy. NIIT Technologies' offshoring facilities have stayed at the leading edge of emerging quality standards such as SEI CMM Level 5, the People CMM, and CMMi. More recently, the company's IT facility in Thailand, for a global construction materials leader, became the first in Asia Pacific to get Certified to the BS 7799 standard. The quest for quality however, cannot stop at the certifications. The value of quality has to be lived in the truest sense of the word and result in a visibly superior and constantly improving output. A website created by NIIT Technologies for a leading retailer in the UK, recently became the number one web site in the retail industry.

## The Changing Customer Climate

With quality becoming an entry ticket, a given, in a highly competitive, "me too," scenario, organisations have to look for new differentiators that give them a unique edge and greater leverage over their competitors. As companies globalise and integrate into the international markets, they have to deal with demanding and discerning customers, with dynamically changing requirements. This rapidly altering customer climate and changing nature of work requires organisations to be nimble and proactive. No longer is it good enough to "respond" to client needs. Instead, organisations have to be proactive, anticipate emerging client requirements and trends and even guide them in the right direction.

In his popular book, *"The MicroMillennium,"* Christopher Evans defines Intelligence as the ability to adapt to a rapidly changing environment. What he is saying is that owing to the changing nature of work and the dynamic external environment organisations find themselves in, it is important to remain sprightly and adaptable. There is no room for the followers. Speed of action will ensure that companies remain in the race and not out of it. The changing nature of work is also demanding from organisations that they hone their service attitude. It is obvious that "Customerism" is the way to go forward for organisations. Here, I believe, India has an intrinsic advantage, owing to the fact that regard for the *"atithi,"* the visitor/client is almost a part of our DNA and culture.

Mahatma Gandhi, the Father of the Nation, who led India's struggle for independence, constantly emphasised the power of the customer. "A customer is the most important visitor on our premises. He is not dependent on us. We are dependent on him. He is not an interruption in our work. He is the purpose of it. He is not an outsider in our business. He is part of it. We are not doing him a favour by serving him. He is doing us a favour by giving us an opportunity to do so," he said, reflecting in a sense, India's deep-rooted commitment to this special entity.

This customer orientation is possibly what has given India an edge in the area of offshoring, where the country stands ahead of competitors in Asia, Eastern Europe and Latin America. Going forward, companies have to ensure that they build Best Practices and formal processes that place the customer at the centre of the planning and execution they do.

Besides focusing on the customer, organisations – both large and small – also need to create Thought Leadership. Companies, with distinctive ideas, path breaking, out-of-the-box products, processes, business and delivery models have a better chance of succeeding in today's environment. Innovation has to remain at the heart of the $21^{st}$ century enterprise.

A 2006 Study by NASSCOM, India's premier trade body and the chamber of commerce of the IT software and services industry, and McKinsey on sustaining India's leadership in the global markets, states that innovation will be the 'Next Big Thing' for the country's IT industry. Making a strong case for innovation, it suggests that the Indian IT-ITES sector can generate over US\$ 10-12 billion of additional revenues by 2010 – over and above its US$ 50 billion export target – provided it makes innovation its chief growth catalyst. A large number of Indian IT companies have launched initiatives that make innovation the cornerstone of their internal and external strategies. A good example of innovation is the Global Delivery Model – popularised by Indian IT-BPO companies – when they began emerging as MNCs. The recent move by the country's software and services companies to offer integrated solution – software development, managed infrastructure and BPO – is another innovation that has positioned Indian IT companies as end-to-end services suppliers, as opposed to firms taking the traditional, silo-based approach.

The effort, therefore, is to ensure that innovation assumes the form of a movement, which like quality, propels the ICT industry forward and assures it lasting success in the global market. At the end of the day, a blend of customerism, innovation and value-added services will enable companies to enhance client responsiveness and build their brand. Brand value, as we discovered with NIIT Technologies, is inextricably linked with customer intimacy. NIIT Technologies' motto – "Trust us to find the way – and its efforts to enhance customer responsiveness, have struck a chord with customers. This has found reflection in surveys conducted by the globally reputed Superbrands Council of the UK. The Council has accorded the Business Superbrand status to NIIT Technologies, placing it among the "Best and Big Enough" players in the world. The Superbrand status also validates and endorses NIIT Technologies' attempts to build Trust – the key value in the services industry today.

## Innovation: Leading the 21$^{st}$ Century Organisation

While recognising that the industry as a whole must innovate, gain greater customer insights and create higher value for clients, it must also be acknowledged that the revolution has to begin with the basic building block – the individual company. An industry is only as good as the various players it is made up of, which means that the greater the width and depth in the range of organisations, the greater the likelihood of the industry being more robust. The Indian IT industry is a classic example of great width and depth in its body. Take the instance of NASSCOM, a conglomeration of some exceptional companies operating within the IT services and BPO domain. The Chamber of Commerce – a platform for companies to work collaboratively – reflects the vibrancy, energy and thought and market leadership of each of its member organisations. NASSCOM's annually held "India Leadership Forum," the premier IT event to be held in the country, showcases the tremendous synergies achieved by individual companies, as they ideate together, deliberate and brainstorm together and partner to lift up the industry.

Of course, within this vast ocean, each company is a microcosm. The excellence achieved by the whole, is a sum of the initiatives undertaken by each of the parts. In their quest for excellence, these individual players are investing in organisation building – investing in their processes, technologies, customers and their people, they are taking the uncrowded path, and working with their heads and hearts, to create the vision and values that will keep them ahead.

I remember a rather memorable session at the World Economic Forum at Davos, where I had to share my thoughts on innovation in organisation building. This came close on the heels of an important recognition that came the way of NIIT Technologies, where it was ranked among India's "Best Places to Work."

I recall thinking about how we had done organisation building in NIIT, and how some other organisations I was acquainted with, had innovated in a similar fashion, to stay dynamic and vibrant. Successful organisations, it was becoming clear to me, were the ones that had embraced a business model based on four vital elements that I termed Inspiration, Aspiration, Respiration and Perspiration. Having made it work at NIIT, I can define Inspiration as the part that has to do with the vision of the organisation's leadership, the mission that guides the company and helps it put in place a value system and outline its future roadmap. It is this vision sharing between the leaders and followers that raises the Aspiration levels within the organisation.

In addition to setting ambitious growth and excellence goals, it is important to define for the organisation a larger purpose of societal value. I have seen the impact some of our key initiatives, such as Hole-in-the-Wall and K-12 – that attempt to improve the lives of the underprivileged – have had on NIITians. These programmes have inspired the people at NIIT to become socially conscious citizens and build a company centred on the philosophy of enlightened self-interest.

Once a level of energy is created by the interplay of Inspiration and Aspiration, leaders must create space for Respiration, which is essentially about energising minds through a "free" work environment, where people can speak their minds, share their ideas and challenge their seniors, without the fear of rebuke or ridicule. Respiration is about providing oxygen for the mind and encouraging employees to ideate in a completely open environment.

I have seen that organisations where there is abundant Respiration – interplay of ideas, team building, creativity, brainstorming – have teams that are high on performance. As the great Indian poet and Nobel laureate, Rabindranath Tagore said, "Where the mind is without fear and the head is held high... Into that heaven of freedom my father, let my country awake." Clearly, to Tagore, freedom of thought and actions was the first step towards building greatness – in individuals, organisations and nations.

In enterprises then, it should be the power of the idea, rather than the power of hierarchy that should reign supreme. It is here that structures should become subservient to the superiority of the idea. Modern organisations must attempt to build a environment of abundant Respiration if they have to nurture truly motivated teams that are high on Vision and passion and brimming with fresh, innovative ideas.

Finally, and the most crucial element of this logical progression is Perspiration, the blood, sweat and tears part of the story, which actually transforms the vision and dreams into reality, and the Inspiration and Aspiration

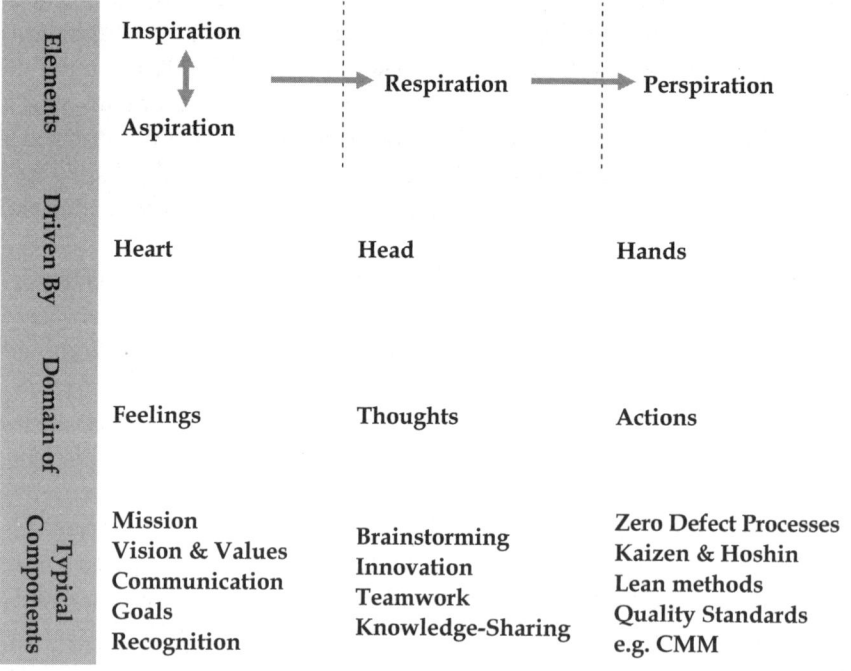

**Fig. 1.** Innovation in organization-building

elements into "on-the-ground" action. Having good ideas is not enough. Organisations have to implement them and put them into practice to realise a higher value for customers. This level is of course all about quality and processes, the nuts and bolts in the cycle of Inspiration, Aspiration, Respiration and Perspiration.

A vibrant interplay of these four elements is the hallmark of great organisations. At the end of the day, India – and by that I mean its offshoring industry, its government and academia – have to foster an ecosystem where excellence and innovation flourish. The country has to recognise the power of minds, the changing nature of education, work and organisation building and make sure the larger community understands these.

India has to ensure that companies that operate within its domain are keeping pace with these changes and remaining in step with this emerging world order. By doing so, the country will continue to hold its place as the key offshore outsourcing destination on the maps of global customers – not merely as the back office for global customers, but as a nation that has moved up the outsourcing ladder to offer a higher and bigger value proposition to the world.

# Part IV: China

# China – An Offshoring Leader?

*Remi D. Vespa*
*Vice President of Market Development, Venus Software Corporation, San Francisco CA, USA*

For the past 15 years, outsourcing applications to developing countries has been a major industry trend in the USA and Western Europe. Today, it is obvious to most companies and observers that outsourcing is here to stay. In the 1990s, TCS, Infosys, Wipro and the likes expanded rapidly to make India the world leader of IT offshoring.

Until now, India has set the pace for offshoring, and is still dominating this market segment. However, new countries are entering this profitable and fast growing arena, China being the most notable example. While there have been very little discussion in the past over the fact that India's domination was set for the long term, more and more voices now believe that China will dislodge India and take leadership by 2015.

"The Global Outsourcing Report 2005", a special issue of "CIO Insight" magazine, which ranks countries based on their opportunities, costs, and risks in relation to IT offshoring, predicts that in 2015, the top five outsourcing destinations will be China, India, the US, Brazil and Russia, in this order.

Is China going to become an IT offshoring leader? The answer is obviously yes, since China already is. Is China going to eventually take overall leadership over India? While we, at Venus Software Corporation (VSC), believe the answer is yes, we recognise this is a complex question; answering it requires a careful review of the macroeconomics and microeconomics trends.

Things do not happen by accident. Becoming the world leader requires a combination of many factors: a solid country infrastructure, an almost unlimited pool of talent, the willingness to succeed at the government and entrepreneurial levels, the access to finance, the ability to communicate properly at the international level, and of course the proper timing!

In the quest to make China the leading outsourcing destination, Chinese suppliers have to demonstrate a unique ability to expand rapidly in both the USA and the European Union, while keeping a strong identity and pursuing excellence, a great challenge, especially since the local Chinese IT outsourcing industry is still fragmented when compared to India.

Let's review the current situation from a VSC perspective and understand why we believe so strongly China in general – and VSC in particular – are en route toward world leadership.

## History of China

When talking about China, it is always important to first have a look at its history, since the country has important and long-lasting traditions deeply rooted in history.

China is one of the world's oldest civilisations. Its history can be reliably traced back to the 18th century BC, although evidence of former human settlements exists. For centuries, the "Central Kingdom" stood as a leading civilisation, often outpacing the rest of the world in the arts and sciences.

However, in the 19th century, the fortunes of China changed dramatically. Western powers forcibly occupied "concessions" gaining special commercial privileges, all symptomatic of the inability of the Chinese government to respond adequately to the challenging conditions facing China in the 19th century. Things only worsened in the early 20th century, when in 1931, Japan invaded Manchuria. In addition, during this period the country was beset by major famines and civil unrest.

In the early 20th century, two major political forces were fighting to reinstate sovereignty: the KMT (Kuo Min Tang) and the CPC (Chinese Communist Party) respectively led by Chiang Kai-shek and Mao Zedong. After World War II the tensions between these two groups resumed, ending in the victory of the Communist Party and the proclaiming of the People's Republic of China on October 1, 1949.

Mao Zedong believed that *"socialism was the only way out for China"*, as according to him the United States and other Western countries would not allow China to regain its dominant position. The country effectively regained full sovereignty and moved out of poverty but at the expense of millions of lives.

Shortly after the death of Mao Zedong in 1976, Chinese leader Deng Xiaoping put China on the road to market-oriented economy, declaring, "Science and technology is the primary instrument to create growth" and later "to get rich is glorious". In 1978, during the 11th National Party Congress, he announced the formal implementation of four modernisations:

- Agriculture
- Industry
- Science and Technology
- Military

Ever since this time, American and European companies have started to consider China as the fascinating potential business partner it was at the dawn of the nineteenth century. What does the history of China tell us regarding our purpose?

Compared to the other BRIC countries, China's history as a superpower, economically, culturally and politically is very long – something each of the 3 other countries lack to a certain degree. Chinese people in general have no doubt that their country will reclaim its leading position in the foreseeable future.

China has had a long tradition of centralised government and a strong civil service system. The directions given by the central government have a very strong impact, and receive little opposition, somewhat different to what happens in Western-style democracies.

From a Western standpoint, it is important to touch on democracy, since the current Chinese political system is often presented in the West as a major challenge to overcome. On the same note, a comment often heard when comparing China to India is that India is a democracy (often claimed to be the largest democracy in the world), a status yet to be achieved by China.

Assuming that to move forward China has to become a democracy is to ignore Chinese history. Confucianism has been at the core of Chinese culture for over 2,000 years. The Han Dynasty (206 BC-220 AD) was the first dynasty to embrace the philosophy of Confucianism, a philosophy that was already widely spread in China. Confucianism is a major pillar of Chinese life, even overcoming half a century of communism.

A culture based on Confucianism does not naturally lean toward a traditional Western style democracy, but rather toward a "benevolent despotism", a concept explored by many authors.

In China, a sudden move towards democracy – like in Russia – is highly unlikely. Moreover, should China face political and economical instability similar to what happened with Russia after the fall of the Soviet empire, it would come as a major blow to the world economy.

China is likely to take another route toward a more Singaporean-like society; a route much more adapted to its 4,000 years of civilisation.

Every political system has pros and cons, including the Chinese one, but also Western-style liberal democracy. A major advantage to a non bipartisan government is that the country does not live under the pressure of the next elections. Long-term plans can be executed at a rapid pace since there is little room for people and companies not to endorse a direction chosen by the central government. This is enabling the country to open up into a more economy-driven system at its own pace.

Moving at such a fast pace, it is also clear that China faces formidable challenges. The most often cited ones are air pollution, access to natural resources, and transformation of the rural population. While the country is sometimes put in an uncomfortable position over these issues on the international scene, there is certainly the highest level of willingness to tackle them. For instance China is among the countries that have signed and ratified the Kyoto protocol.

Lastly, a more interventionist government might be better adapted to tackling the challenges the country faces as consequences of its amazing development pace.

With so much being said on the challenges, let's conclude this section with a positive example: developed by the Shanghai Industrial investment Corp., Dongtan Eco City, roughly the size of Manhattan, will be the world's first fully sustainable urban centre when completed in 2040. Located on the Yangtze River, Dongtan is within close proximity to Shanghai. By the time the Shanghai Expo trade fair opens in 2010, the city's first phase should be completed, and 50,000 residents will call Dongtan home-sweet-*sustainable*-home.

## Economy

With a GDP growth close to 10 per cent in 2005 and an even higher potential moving forward, China is reclaiming its status of superpower and has become again a magnet to American and European businesspeople; no other country today, including India, compares to China in terms of attractiveness for foreign businesses. It is very visible in the Western media where China gets daily exposure at all levels. But where does China *really* rank today?

China's GDP measured in PPP (Purchasing Power Parity) is the second largest in the world after the USA. Measured in Official Exchange Rate, China's is the fifth largest economy after the USA, Japan, Germany and the United Kingdom.

Most analysts believe that China should overtake Japan by 2016 and ultimately the USA in 2020 to become the world's largest economy. In any case, China is in fact just reclaiming its dominant position, a position it held for centuries.

Comparing China to Brazil, India and Russia shows the obvious advantage and momentum the country currently has over them put together. China's GDP is larger than the sum total of India's, Russia's and Brazil's! Furthermore China is moving at a faster pace then the other BRIC countries, in almost every area.

Table 1. BRICs economies in comparison

|  | Brazil | Russia | India | China |
| --- | --- | --- | --- | --- |
| GDP (PPP) in trillion dollars | 1.536 | 1.584 | 3.666 | 8.883 |
| GDP (OER) in trillion dollars | 0.619 | 0.740 | 0.719 | 2.225 |
| Per capita in US dollars | 8,300 | 11,000 | 3,400 | 6,800 |
| Public debt (per cent of GDP) | 51.6 | 12.9 | 53.8 | 24.4 |
| Reserves of foreign exchanges and gold (in billion) | 53.8 | 182.2 | 136 | 825.6 |

Source: *CIA world fact book, Oct. 2006*

While Brazil and Russia stand really far behind China, let's have a closer look at India. According to an article written by Jehangir Pocha and published in Nov. 2006 in the San Francisco Chronicle, "both China and India were the dominant powers in Asia before the era of European colonisation, and close commercial ties between these rivals in the near term could create an economic power that could eclipse Japan and challenge the US influence in the world's fastest growing region."

At the time of writing, India runs a $2 billion trade deficit with China, although India has extremely stiff custom tariffs. In the same article, Pocha states that a reduction in these tariffs would cause the trade deficit to leap to almost $10 billion. The future of relations between India and China, including a possible free trade agreement between the two countries, is receiving considerable media exposure, even if both countries are moving these matters at a relatively slow pace. We use the word "relatively", because considering what is at stake here it might be very risky to move any faster.

It is also important to note that the Chinese reserves in gold and currencies are twice as big as India, Russia and Brazil combined! Even more impressive, both the USA and the European Community together have significantly less reserves! This is a huge point, since it demonstrates that China has the financial capability to tackle environmental issues, implement ambitious state plans, and better capitalise state-owned companies (like banks or car manufacturers for instance), preparing them to be more aggressive on the International scene.

Let's conclude this section with a recent interview (Nov. 2006) of Bill Gates, Microsoft's Chairman, which took place at Stanford University, during a technology event. Charlie Rose, the famous US interviewer, asked Gates whether he was worried about the mounting power of Asian nations, especially China.

Gates answered that "The USA have to get used to the fact that our relative share of everything, ability to make decisions, military power, economic power, or innovation, etc., will only be a portion of what it used to be, and certainly won't be as so out-of-line with our 5 per cent of the world population as it is today, and that is OK."

"China is the pace setter for a lot of things in this world". It is critical for Americans and Europeans to acknowledge that the power taken by China or India does not impoverish them. Gates added, "That may be an adjustment especially to those who think in terms of war type analogies with a winner and a loser in the relative position as opposed to the improvement of all". But this is not a "zero sum" – today the entire world benefits from inventions coming from other countries.

Gates concluded on this topic by saying: "Many reports say that if China would be made really poor, that would be good for the USA. The truth is the opposite", continued Gates. "If you believe in humanity, then of course China buying at our level is a good thing […] Even the USA, the world is much better off because of that, and we have to get used of that, because that is an unstoppable thing."

## Country Infrastructure

The general infrastructure of a country is a major key in enabling a country to become an IT outsourcing leader. The quality of the telecommunication infrastructure, the availability of high-speed Internet and the bandwidth available are paramount. However, there is more to attract foreign customers / investments: the banking system, the transportation capabilities, the number of Western-style hotel rooms available, the crime rate, etc. are also extremely important factors.

China suffered economically in the 19$^{th}$ and most of the 20$^{th}$ century, yielding until recently to a lagging modern infrastructure (rail, road, airports). The country is now catching up extremely rapidly at all levels, and has already outpaced its rivals in most areas.

**Table 2.** BRICs infrastructure comparison

|  | # of tel landlines (2005) | # of cell phones (2004) | Airports with paved runways (2006) | Railways (2004) | Roadways (2003) |
|---|---|---|---|---|---|
| USA | 268 (2003) | 195 | 5,119 | 226.6 | 4,164,964 |
| Brazil | 42.3 | 86.2 | 714 | 29.2 | 1,724,929 |
| Russia | 40 | 120 | 616 | 87.1 | 871,000 |
| India | 49.75 | 69 | 243 | 63.2 | 2,411,001 |
| China | 350.4 | 335 | 403 | 78.4 | 1,809,829 |

*Source: CIA world fact book, Oct. 2006*

The telecommunication industry provides perhaps the most successful example of how China's interventionist economic strategy has enabled the country to outpace its rivals. China has more cell phones than Russia, India and Brazil combined; the same remark applies to landlines.

The number of DSL (broadband Internet) connections in the BRIC countries clearly shows the advantage China has over the other BRIC countries. The latest statistics released by the DSL Forum show that by the end of June 2006 China was ranked # 1 in the world by the number of DSL connections with 33,305,000. Brazil was ranked 11$^{th}$ with 3,796,600, India a mere 15$^{th}$ with 1,537,000 while Russia did not rank in the Top 20. China has 5 times more high speed connections than the other BRIC countries together. Moreover the bandwidth generally available to Chinese consumers is usually between 264 Kbps and 1 Mps, which is more than India where the average bandwidth is of 64Kbps. In addition to the consumer market, Chinese businesses have access to very high-bandwidth leased lines. In addition, the Golden Projects or the more recent Government Online Project are evidence of the government's support for the Internet development in China.

But China is putting a major effort in creating a premier infrastructure at all levels, not only in ICT (Information & Communication Technologies). The many examples of recent achievements include the opening of the world's highest railway between Golmud and Lhasa, a route reputed as impossible to open because of the permafrost; visitors arriving at the Shanghai airport can take the train that connects to the city, whose speed culminates at almost 300 miles an hour. Moreover, and just to mention a few, China is building new architectural wonders that include the Central Chinese Television building in Beijing, the new Shanghai and Beijing aiports, the Olympic stadium in Beijing, the 20-mile long, 6-lane wide Donghai Bridge, the National Grand Theatre in Beijing, etc.

Visitors to any large Chinese city will use their debit card in most ATM machines (with a menu in English), pay their cab fare in cash, credit card, or using a local prepaid card, be able to use their cell phone, or buy a cheap GSM phone (around USD 50) with prepaid minutes and again a manual and software in English, pay their meal using any major credit card, etc.

## Population and Workforce

China has the largest population in the world followed by India. However, the Indian population grows at a faster pace, since China has enforced for years the one-child policy. The effects of this policy will start to be seen more than 40 years from now, and has therefore no impact on our subject. It is also important to note that China's current labour force in services (not only IT but all services in general) is twice as big as India's.

A qualified workforce is fundamental in the race to become a world leader in the IT outsourcing industry. Moving forward, Chinese companies need to be sure they can tap into a vast reservoir of qualified resources.

Today, China is the largest producer of engineering graduates in the world, with some 600,000 coming out of its colleges and universities in 2005. India follows with over 450,000 engineering graduates in 2005, of

**Table 3.** BRICs population comparison

|  | Brazil | Russia | India | China |
|---|---|---|---|---|
| Area (sq km) | 8,511,965 | 17,075,200 | 3,287,590 | 9,596,960 |
| Population | 188,078,227 | 142,893,540 | 1,095,351,995 | 1,313,973,713 |
| Median age | 28.2 | 38.4 | 24.9 | 32.7 |
| Population growth rate (per cent) | 1.04 | −0.37 | 1.38 | 0.59 |
| Labour force in services (in million) | 60 | 51 | 114 | 230 |

*Source: CIA world fact book, Oct. 2006*

which almost 30 per cent were computer engineers. Both India and China have over 2,000 colleges and Universities. Compared to India and China, the United States produces only 70,000 engineering graduates every year. All of Western Europe produces just over 100,000. Duke University in the USA recently released a report that looked specifically at all computer science and information technology degrees from four-year schools, Duke's initial study came up with 137,437 engineering graduates for the U.S., 112,000 for India and 351,537 for China. China is therefore the country that produces today the highest number of IT engineers, by far, more than India and the USA together!

While China produces the highest number of graduate students every year, there are also a fast growing number of Chinese students graduating from foreign universities. The Open-Door-policy in China had as one of its effects that hundreds of thousands of young Chinese got the opportunity to study abroad, mainly at American universities. For instance at Yale alone, the fall 2003 class had 297 Chinese students (and 23 Russians). Moreover, Chinese Americans represent a significant percentage of undergraduate and graduate students in the USA. Starting as a brain drain, the number of students leaving China that eventually came back to China is now turning into a brain gain and China is regaining much of the ground lost during the 1960s and 1970s, helping to train a new generation of scientists, engineers, and researchers to play a key role in China's scientific community.

Last, India is to become by 2010 the largest English speaking country in the world, and this is possibly the only area where China is seriously challenged by any of the BRIC countries. That said, young engineers graduating from Chinese universities all write and speak enough English to communicate efficiently. Moreover in China, the number of English-speaking graduates in the workforce – particularly crucial in software outsourcing – has doubled between 2000 and 2004 to more than 24 million.

## The Diaspora and Their Impact

An important element in bringing business to a country is the diaspora, i.e. the people living abroad. According to statistics provided by the Overseas Chinese Affairs Commission of Taiwan, the Chinese Diaspora (Chinese people leaving outside Mainland China and Taiwan) represents today 35 million of individuals – the largest in the world.

The Russian diaspora is probably the second largest one: about 20 million Russian people live in the CIS-countries (the former republics of the USSR), including 8 million in Ukraine, and another 10 million living in foreign countries. The third largest diaspora is from India with a little over 20 million individuals living abroad, according to the Indian Ministry of External Affairs. The U.N. Population Fund estimated that between 3 million and 4 million Brazilians live outside Brazil; 70 percent of them are in the United States, Paraguay and Japan.

If we exclude the Russian diaspora living in the CIS-countries, the Chinese Diaspora alone is larger than the combination of the Russian, Indian and Brazilian Diasporas! The *Huaren* (Chinese living outside China) are playing a key role in helping Chinese companies capture world leadership within the next 7-10 years. For instance in California, a state that has close economic ties to China and where the IT industry is dominant, hundreds of business associations exist that help American businesses smoothly outsource their IT to China.

## The IT Market in China

According to a report published in 2005 by Vinnova, the Swedish Agency for Innovation Systems, "the Information and Communication Technologies (ICT) industry is of special importance in China; it is considered a "pillar" industry in the national economy, a driving force for innovation and growth in other industry sectors, fundamental to national security, and a core industry for "informatisation" of the Chinese society."

During the 2000-2010 period, ICT is expected to grow at three times the GDP, which itself is growing at an impressive 9-10 per cent a year, a prediction that has already been outpaced for the first half of the 10-year period. In 2005, the value added of ICT accounted for more than 7 per cent of GDP. In the same year, ICT products accounted for 30 per cent of the Chinese export volume. By the end of 2006, ICT will have emerged as the largest industry in China.

According to the National Bureau of Statistics of China, the Chinese software industry (comprising software products, system integration and services) reached RMB 220 billion in 2004, 35 per cent higher than in 2003.

In 2004, China's industry exports reached RMB 21.8 billion, up from RMB 15.6 billion in 2003, a 34 per cent growth that followed a similar growth the previous year. Between 1999 and 2004 the export volume have been multiplied by 11!

Both domestic demand and a growing international reputation fuel the growth of the Chinese software industry. It has become abundantly clear that American and European corporations view China as the most attractive country today, and therefore they are likely to favour, when possible, business relationships with Chinese companies. For these companies, outsourcing their IT to China is part of a more global plan to establish strong business ties with China.

This spectacular growth has been possible thanks to a series of measures taken by the Central Government to effectively and aggressively stimulate the IT business. The major ones are:

- Tax incentives. They include rebates on VAT (Value Added Tax), waiving of tax for the first 2 years of operation, reduced tax rate for the next 3 years, income tax rebates, etc.

- Expedited visa procedures for foreign software experts entering the country, and special allowances in software import and export rules

- Preferential procurement to domestic companies for government projects, a critical decision to ensure that Chinese companies gain expertise on large, technologically advanced projects. To reinforce this decision, China's leaders have launched a series of online programs to accelerate the government's pace in implementing and using advanced solutions. These programs help promote the country's economic development, increase the government agencies efficiency and boost the local IT outsourcing companies overall capabilities.

But possibly the smartest measure taken by the Central Government was the establishment of over 50 national Science Parks throughout China. The purpose of these Science Parks is to create a stimulating and innovative infrastructure for companies in the high-tech sector, to attract talent, investment and companies from all over the world.

As mentioned before, the conditions are excellent and include seed-funding, affordable office lease, special support programs for students returning from overseas, tax deductions and a close proximity to R&D centres and universities. Most of the well-known universities have their own Science Park.

Intellectual Property (IP) protection is often mentioned as an issue in outsourcing to China. In fact, although the various countries do not publish any official statistics, the risks might not be higher in China than in the other BRIC countries. The same common-sense rule should apply everywhere, which is to work with a reputable local partner. At VSC for instance, we have implemented a whole set of robust rules to make sure the best protection surrounds the IP of our clients. More generally, a number of government agencies have jointly established an incentive mechanism aiming at promoting ICT innovations and thereby stimulating an increase in the number of patent applications.

This is no surprise that as a result of these measures aimed at beefing up innovation capabilities and technology infrastructure, giants like Intel, Google and Microsoft are favouring China more and more as a privileged place for their own offshore development centres. It gives them access to an immediate pool of best of breed talents. In exchange, the presence of these companies elevates tremendously the overall IT knowledge, and is an incentive for Chinese providers to adopt the highest industry standards.

## Panorama of Chinese Suppliers

By the end of 2003, there were approximately 8,700 registered software companies in China, of which 2,000 were new entrants. Private and foreign software companies dominate the market. For example, in Shenzhen, more than 95 per cent of the top 100 software companies are either private or foreign-invested companies. In order to gain more visibility on the international scene, a growing number of IT outsourcing companies are attempting to qualify for international standards, such as ISO9001:2000 or the CMM (Capability Maturity Model) certificate system, issued by the Software Engineering Institute, an internationally accepted evaluation of software firms. By March 2004, more than 100 software companies in China passed CMM2, 45 had passed CMM3, and 9 companies had passed CMM4 or CMM5.

Unlike India, where large Indian firms dominate the IT outsourcing market, foreign companies moving their own engineering operations to China are key drivers in China's outsourcing market. The growth of foreign development centres is important for at three major reasons:

- The influx of foreign expertise combined with the knowledge developed in the Science Parks is a formidable accelerator to the IT outsourcing industry. Expertise developed at these centres will ultimately diffuse into the Chinese market boosting the capabilities of Chinese software outsourcing firms, rendering them even more attractive on the International scene.

- Attracting foreign businesses to the country is a much smarter way to develop an industry than having individual local companies fight on their own to attract one foreign company at a time. By creating locally the conditions to attract foreign businesses, China is on a much faster track than any other BRIC country

- By creating strong and durable business ties with the USA and Western Europe, China becomes a strategic ally for these two other superpowers.

## Conclusion

With a better country infrastructure, more reserves, the biggest pool of graduate students, the highest attractiveness, an unbelievable momentum, better media coverage, etc., China seems to have it all.

The major strength of China in this race to leadership is that the focus of China is not on becoming the world leader, but in creating the conditions that make the country the privileged destination for IT outsourcing.

By providing a premier infrastructure, enabling local providers to equip the government with the most advanced technologies, making Intel, Microsoft, Google, and the likes call China their home when its comes to engineering, China is becoming the excellence centre of the world for IT outsourcing. Customers are flocking to China. Leadership will inevitably follow. In other words China has in fact created its own path to leadership. This is the route VSC has embarked on. Our focus is not our position relative to our competitors, but on providing our customers with excellence as a normal delivery. This is how our clients see us already, and we are working hard to make the entire market see us this way.

In seven years from the publication of this book, some individual leaders of IT outsourcing might still be Indian, but China will have become overall the world's number one destination for IT outsourcing, as it has become today the centre for goods manufacturing.

As a closing note, I would like to share this quote from Thomas Friedman's book "The World is Flat", a global best-seller: "If Americans and Europeans want to benefit from (…) the interconnecting of all the markets and knowledge centres, they will all have to run at least as fast as the fastest lion – and I suspect this lion will be China, and I suspect it will be darn fast."

# The Second Shift to China

*Jiren Liu*
*Chairman and CEO, Neusoft Group, Shenyang, China*

The shift of global manufacturing capacity to China has enabled rapid and sustainable economic growth in China over the past 20 years. Today, about half of the air-conditioners, one third of the TV sets, a quarter of washing machines, 40 per cent of the mobile phones and 80-90 per cent of all toys are made in China.

On January 1, 2005, the WTO lifted restrictions on textile quotas for China, contributing to its multiple increases in textile export. China has benefited again from the ongoing economic globalisation. China used to be a nation with a large population isolated from the world, but has since become a part of the global community. Over the past twenty years China has had a significant influence on the world's economy, which in turn has changed the life of its people. More than 420 million people are using mobile phones, the number of PC and Internet users has reached 111 million, and the ownership of private cars has also increased by five times. In 2006, the total retail sales of consumer goods is expected to be 1,000 billion US dollars. China has become the world's third largest trading power with the largest foreign reserves. These facts strongly indicate that the shift of manufacturing has changed China and China has changed the world.

## The Second Shift

The momentum behind the shift of manufacturing to China is that global enterprises are seeking new channels to enhance their productivity for greater profits – against a climate of economic globalisation. A total of 3 billion people in China, India, Eastern Europe and other developing countries used to be outside the market economy, but now make this system possible. Many multinational corporations have made international shifts for better survival and growth, causing a structural change to the market economy mechanism that in turn leads to significant changes to capital and goods flows, organisational systems, production modes, management, and strategy.

As the shift deepens and competition becomes fiercer, the rapid development of communications and Internet technologies makes the shift of services, R&D and office work a growing trend. For enterprises, their need to acquire improved competitiveness with better R&D and services at a lower cost has started the next round of economic competition and globalisation. Ever more services ranging from software development to Business Process Outsourcing (BPO) and R&D are shifting to those nations rich in intellectual talent. With the possibilities afforded by the Internet, everything becomes possible.

What distinguishes the second shift from the earlier wave of manufacturing processes moving to China? One can include the following factors: first, it depends more on well-educated talent and competitive costs – these people could only be available in a nation with a sound education system. Second, the target nation can offer attractive work and living conditions for that intellectual talent in addition to well-established infrastructure, especially advanced Internet and communications facilities. Third, the target nation has a stable social structure and an honest culture that will protect customer interests.

India is the first destination country where the United States has tended to shift its software development and BPO operations. Thanks to its great number of well-educated IT workers, who are also fluent in English, India has become a reliable IT service provider in a short period of time. It has demonstrated its capability and quality in the markets of the developed countries such as the United States. Nevertheless, the service that India offers has far exceeded its original coverage in software and IT. For the U.S. market, the major demands are shifting from integrated circuit designs and software development to some office operations such as financial and credit card processing – BPO – as well as customer services. The successive performance of many operations due to time differences has greatly enhanced efficiency. Also, the enthusiasm of local employees in India assures an improved quality of services. Last but not least, a huge low-cost pool of local human resources will help India keep a competitive advantage over a long period of time.

Over the past decade, Information Technology has been integrated closely within our society at an ever-higher speed. Corporations have increased their investment in information infrastructures. The wide application of digital products, such as mobile phones, music players, digital cameras, car navigation systems, generates more and more software and service based work. For instance, the rapid update and innovation in digital consumer products have created a shortage of 300,000 embedded software engineers in Japan. As a result, corporations have to search for more service providers worldwide. Among all the global candidates, China has the biggest potential in this arena – following the example created by India.

## Why China?

First of all, the rapid economic growth of the past couple of decades has helped China complete its education system and infrastructure. Currently, China has more than 2,000 colleges and universities with a total enrolment of 16 million students. It also has more than 500,000 students studying abroad. Over the past 10 years, the number of returned overseas students has been tripled. At present, there are 6 million people engaged in the IT industry, including 750,000 IT experts and 400,000 software engineers. Besides, 40,000 to 50,000 graduates with majors in science and engineering join the team each year. A total of 35 top schools at many state-funded universities set up software engineering schools in a joint effort with IT enterprises to deliver market-oriented training programs for software engineering. The Chinese government also encourages the establishment of private universities and gives strong support to software education. For example, Neusoft, as a corporation focusing on software and services, has set up three IT institutes in China. Currently, 20,000 students enrolled by these institutes are enjoying the first-class teaching facilities and environment. They may not only learn the most advanced technologies in labs set up by leading Multinational Companies (MNCs), but also run virtual companies founded with the Students Office & Venture Office (SOVO). Besides, they may take industry-based training (IBT) programmes jointly designed by Neusoft and its enterprise customers and partners in the last two years and even win job opportunities – if they perform well. In conclusion, China is now focusing on the high-quality training of talent to meet its economic development, which in turn will attract more investment.

After China becomes an integral part of economic globalisation, its large population – that used to be considered a heavy burden – will become valuable assets to be shared by the world, contributing to the miracle of *"Made in China"*. Also, in the IT and service industry, China possesses the impressive competitive advantage of higher-quality and lower-cost human resources. The average annual income of IT professionals in major Chinese cities ranges from $4,000 to $9,000 (USD), far from that of the developed countries. For MNCs engaged in IT services in Asia from Europe and the United States, China is the best choice. One reason is that China has the biggest population who can speak Japanese or Korean outside Japan and Korea and the number of English speakers is increasing very fast. China will render back office services to the world at a competitive price. In Dalian, a Chinese city full of Japanese-speaking talent, nearly a hundred MNCs such as IBM, HP, SAP, GE, DELL, TOSHIBA, and SONY have set up their service centres to serve the market of Northeast Asia in less than five years. Currently, hundreds of enterprises in Dalian are engaged in offering software development and BPO services, making the city the number one in terms of IT cooperation with MNCs in the software and BPO business in China.

China will, with its huge population, continue to provide high-quality manufacturing and service talent with a low cost a long period of time into the future. According to the China National Report on Human Resource Development, China will retain a labour force of 700 million people between the age of 18 and 60 by 2050, suggesting that the HR cost in China will not go up in the short to mid term.

Second, China is also a huge consumer market rather than just a low-cost talent and service provider. As the middle class has increased, the proportion of consumption to GDP will continue to rise – up to 65 per cent in 2010 and 71 per cent in 2020, close to that of the developed countries. Taking consumer electronic products for example, IDC predicts a market value of 15 billion US dollars by 2008 in the Chinese market. According to McKinsey, the annual direct and indirect consumption of children and teenagers in urban China has reached $36 billion US dollars. Chinese people have changed their major consumption patterns from food to computers, autos, housing and so on.

MNCs are shifting their offshore manufacturing and operations to China for its huge consumer market and at the same time this causes the shift of IT services. Information technologies have also been widely used in many products, causing increased IT R&D and the needs of relevant services. Without a doubt, it is a good opportunity for China to develop its IT service industry as the MNC investment creates a need for this service in China. China will attract more and more global services business, such as finance, retail, and insurance, and in turn this will create more and more IT services business.

Third, the development of China's manufacturing base will give rise to more software development and BPO services. Software has been widely used in many types of equipments such as communication facilities and home appliances. China will become a software components provider as an extension of manufacturing, and deliver more and more embedded software in devices. At present, the embedded software outsourcing service in China is developing at a very high speed, especially those for Japanese companies engaged in mobile phones, home appliances, autos, electronics, semiconductors, and so on. The Japanese electronic manufacturing and Chinese software industry have maintained a good, and complementary, partnership.

The Chinese government, a key player in the second shift, has made huge inputs in social infrastructure in addition to its increased investment in education for the supply of high quality human resources. China's complete infrastructure and advanced communications and information facilities have been attracting many MNCs and investors. Also, the Chinese government provides many favourable policies for the IT service industry. After China's admission into the WTO, Chinese corporations have learned to run an international business according to the international practices and standards expected of them. All these factors will help China to become an important component of the international value chain. Consequently, in the coming decade, China will become the owner of both the biggest manufacturing capacity and one of the largest IT service industries in the world.

## The Time of Integration

The exact definition of the term "offshore" has exceeded its original meaning of outsourcing business services from one country to another. With the revolution of international trade and the rise of offshore manufacturing and operations, the MNCs have promoted the shift of jobs from one country to another, eliminating the usual boundaries of shores. Enterprises are becoming more and more integrated, indicating the arrival of a new era of business cooperation and resource consolidation around the world.

For instance, in a visit to Alpine's R&D Centre in Dalian, you may find difficult to tell which employees are from Alpine or Neusoft, for all of them are dressed in the same uniform and most of them can speak Japanese. In this three-floor building, the third floor is the hardware design centre of Alpine, the second is the software design and R&D centre outsourced by Alpine to Neusoft, and the first is the product testing centre of

Alpine. This is a brand new offshore outsourcing system. The "shore" is right in one single building. By seeing this all in one place, we have to say, it is a small world – a flat world.

As China opens up to the world and many of its companies succeed in offering services to the global market, China is no longer an offshore outsourcing service provider only, but also the originator of work, producing many offshore businesses in many sectors. The miracle of "Made in China" helps many Chinese corporations seize high market shares worldwide, allowing them to outsource the derived localisation service to local corporations in some countries and regions.

This phenomenon is well explained by the manufacturing and sales of Neusoft's sophisticated medical imaging equipment. As we know, sophisticated medical imaging equipment works with high-end embedded software. We develop and produce software by ourselves while outsourcing hardware manufacturing to leading corporations worldwide – enhancing the core value of our products. Moreover, we outsource some services rising from products sold overseas to local corporations so as to guarantee timely and good service delivery.

In this sense, the offshore cooperation has gone beyond its traditional shifting from the developed nations to the developing ones. Many "Made-in-China" products are delivered by the MNCs in China including some parts and components manufactured in other countries. The delivery of a product may contribute to cooperative efforts by more than one company from many parts of the world. The logistical integration of these global resources, enterprises, and technologies has become a major trend.

For such global integration, language proficiency is becoming a requisite. Just like India providing outsourcing services for the United States thanks to its good command of English, China has become an outsourcing centre of excellence in Northeast Asia thanks to its linguistic advantages in Japanese and Korean.

The number of Chinese-speaking people ranks second in the world following English. Many Chinese people are living abroad while some others travel all over the world due to the opening up of trade and tourism. The number of people learning Chinese is rapidly increasing overseas. Some linguists believe that by 2050, the number of non-native Chinese speakers would have been equal to that of native speakers. In line with this trend, there will be a portfolio of Chinese language based outsourcing services to serve the Chinese-speaking and learning people all around the world. It will definitely be a huge potential market for the future.

At the same time, China possesses the largest number of Japanese-speaking people besides Japan and Korea, which makes China the largest outsourcing partner of Japan. In addition, China has become the R&D and service centre of many MNCs from the rest of the world for the Japanese market – delivering software development and BPO services to Japan.

English is becoming the most popular language among young Chinese. From primary schools to universities, English is the first foreign language as a compulsory course. With more and more Chinese talent returning to China after years of study in US and Europe, China will be able to offer a large pool of talent with diversified linguistic capacities who can provide services in Chinese, English, Japanese, Korean and many other languages.

In conclusion, the concept of "offshore" is constantly expanding and evolving. In the process of economic cooperation, the concept of the nation state is fading. Enterprises may enter into partnership by more flexible means. More products are delivered via cooperation, and open innovation has become a new ideal choice for enterprises to grow faster. Cultures merge more quickly as well. If it is said that the first shift of industry promoted the manufacturing capacity in the process of economic globalisation, the second shift of information technology and service will definitely promote further integration of our different cultures, technologies, the people, and their ways of work.

# Conclusion

*Mark Kobayashi-Hillary*
*National Outsourcing Association, London, UK*

This has been quite a journey. It's like a whirlwind tour through the BRICs with some of the leading service company chief executives from those four nations. In summary, what can be concluded from the contributions of the authors contained in this volume? I'd like to briefly take a moment to examine some of the key points raised by these essays, quoting a point of interest raised by each author.

## Brazil

First, Dalton Luz at Politic highlighted some of the issues faced by Brazil in building their economy when contrasted against the other members of the BRICs:

- *Brazil is much less open to trade.* The tradable goods sector in China is almost eight times larger than in Brazil, when measured by imports plus exports.
- *Investment and savings are lower.* Savings and investment ratios are around 18-19% of GDP compared to an investment rate of 36% of GDP in China and an Asian average of around 30%.
- *Public and foreign debt is much higher.* Without a deeper fiscal adjustment and lower debt to GDP ratio (currently at 57.7% of GDP on a net basis and 78.2% of GDP on a gross basis), the private sector is almost completely crowded out from credit markets. China's net foreign debt and public debt are both significantly smaller.

Of course, Brazil also has many points in its favour. Thiago Turchetti Maia at Vetta Technologies focused on potential sources of differentiation. It would be hard for any region to rival the industrial nature of the Indian software industry now, so Thiago outlined where he feels Brazil can make a difference:

An alternative approach, which we strongly believe, is that Brazil should look at higher-value opportunities, where companies will be able to differentiate their offer and earn rates compatible with the country's own domestic rates. A possible consequence, should this strategy work to secure some market share, will be an increasing tendency towards specialisation and verticalisation of the Brazilian offer. If all goes well, Brazilian companies will increasingly dominate selected niches where their offer is strong and their value proposition is superior to those of other offshore locations. In time, the successful consolidation of several niches dominated by Brazilian providers will increase the country's global market share, and eventually promote Brazil to the status of global player.

## Russia

So a higher-value niche-oriented approach – a focus on Knowledge Process Outsourcing (KPO) might appear to be one route forward for Brazil, though not the only one as Brazil surely has the capability to offer ITO and back-office services to both American continents. In Russia, Arkadiy Dobkin of EPAM believes the fast market growth there will continue for some time to come, and that costs will only rise slowly in the near term:

If we take this "brick" out of the BRICs to scrutinise it, the immediate and biggest fact about Russia is that its IT sector develops at the staggering pace of 25 per cent annually, making IT the fastest growing economic sector of the country. I believe this positive trend is likely to continue in the coming years, as there are all the makings of progress in the Russian legislative and economic field, which stimulates domestic and foreign demand for IT services. Russia is one of the countries with the most skilled and highly qualified labour pools in the world. Given the fact that Russia's IT sector is still in the development stage, the IT labour force costs rise at a relatively slow rate compared to those of the happier Indian IT industry. This brings tangible cost savings to the customers.

Dmitry A. Loschinin at Luxoft takes the view that Russia can actually focus on a very different area of software development to that pioneered in India. India developed a reputation for high quality software development by focusing on the use of various international quality frameworks – most notably the CMMi standard created by the Software Engineering Institute at Carnegie Mellon University. By their very nature, these frameworks promote quality, but can be a restriction on the software lifecycle, making the iterations between specification, coding, and testing long – but without error. Dmitry believes that the use of alternative software development methodologies, such as Agile, where there is more of a focus on making quick changes and testing rapidly could be an area of focus for Russia:

Smaller software and product companies have tremendous success outsourcing to Russia because leading vendors have already demonstrated that Russia can play at the high end. The *Agile* software development methodology is an increasingly popular approach that shifts the traditional focus away from documenting and planning to communication and continual change. Product companies appreciate the proprietary client-centric engagement model Luxoft has developed, for example, to identify whether Agile will work for them. If Agile does make sense for the client, our process maps out the development and project management process every step of the way, ensures every single change is addressed, and mitigates any hidden risks.

They also appreciate the technology expertise that Russia brings to the table. Platforms such as Java and Microsoft .NET are second nature to Russian developers. This familiarity with the development platforms makes it easier for product companies to outsource to Russia.

The whole notion of Agile, the facility with common development platforms and ongoing changes in development style will shape the outsourcing market in the future. Traditional methods will not go away; but collaboration methods such as Agile will enable people to work together better – whether they are 1,000 miles apart or even in the next cubicle.

At Reksoft, Alexander Egorov believes that branding of Russia itself is key to a change in the fortunes of the industry. His view that Russia is often perceived through a filter of prejudice is correct and though other regions – India possibly the most notable – still have their own issues, they have achieved a good level of brand reputation:

It is obvious to every industry insider that the situation in the Russian IT export sector has improved dramatically over the past four years. However, these changes are often not obvious to the outside observer. Russian companies have to communicate with the market in a more professional manner to avoid old prejudices and eliminate the negative effects, which may arise from them in sales channels. Russian pioneer companies achieved some results in creating a totally new sector of Russian exports, but they could not demonstrate the growth achieved by the world market of IT services so far. However, the appearance of Russian suppliers in the reports of the leading analytical houses in 2002-2005 gives them a chance to play big.

Dmitry Ponomarev at Mera Networks echoes Dmitry at Luxoft in his view that Russia needs to be more selective in the areas of focus chosen by service companies in the technology sector. Higher-value specialised services lend themselves better to the Russian environment:

The Russian IT export industry leaders keep questioning the world-recognised offshore outsourcing experts and gurus if Russia needs to expand its offering and what domains it needs to expand its offering into. The answer to this question lays right in the BRICs projections. According to BRICs analysis Russia would most likely drop out of low-cost destinations for offshore outsourcing within next 15-20 years. Therefore, it is not advisable for Russia to consider expanding into IT services such as ITO and BPO which clearly fall into category of non-core activities for which low-cost will always be one of the top decisive factors. The BRICs projections hence reinforce the importance for the Russian IT export industry to keep its current focus on R&D intensive IT industry niches such as cutting-edge software R&D services. In contrast to ITO and BPO, software R&D services could be attributed to core activities such as creation of innovation. The latter is the key to staying competitive in today's fast paced IT business environment. It is availability of brilliant and ample labour force capable of thinking outside of the box rather than low cost that drives the decision to offshore outsource software R&D services. Hence, the current industry's focus on software R&D services is well justified and BRICs projections imply that it will be a viable choice throughout years to come.

## India

In the market leader India, there is intense debate over the way forward. How to maintain the outsourcing lead and avoid a loss of business to other regions in the BRICs and beyond are perennial concerns. One of the industry giants, Shiv Nadar of HCL, argues that they must use their present advantage to move further into strategic partnerships:

The lesson to be learnt here is a simple yet critical one – it is better that industry works proactively towards moving relationships up the value chain, from *tactical* to *strategic*, engaging deeper with the customer. Only this will demonstrate to enterprises worldwide that they can leverage the service capabilities and competence of Indian IT companies to create significant competitive differentiators for themselves.

If we look closely at the fine print, and beyond the heady growth numbers that the IT industry has been witnessing again after suffering some nervous hiccups between 2000 and 2002, the industry stands at an inflection point. Sure, India and Indian firms are ready to leapfrog into the big league, particularly so as they hold out the potential of transforming not only the global IT landscape but also the very roots of businesses worldwide. For that, however, some serious thought needs to go into delivery, product offerings, and the very way in which we operate.

At Infosys, Nandan Nilekani makes an interesting case that moves somewhat beyond the concerns of the Russian organisations. He feels that India as a destination has earned its good name – the brand has been built through the consistent efforts of the industry and Nasscom since the 1980s. Now there must be considerably more effort in building individual and trusted brand names – such as Infosys – and to move the perception of those brands beyond being just Indian companies to being considered global:

In the early years of offshore outsourcing Infosys and other Indian service providers collaborated to build a country brand image while still competing with one another. Through a combination of entrepreneurial drive, technology expertise, a large pool of skilled labour, and the disruptive force of global delivery, this effort resulted in India being synonymous with IT and business process service excellence.

Today, Infosys is a recognised brand in its own right and India is the world's largest IT and business process global sourcing destination. However, in a flattening world the role of countries is becoming less important than the client/vendor relationship. Companies are looking beyond India, China, and other established locations for a variety of reasons and they are looking to trusted service partners to help them in their quests.

From a geography standpoint becoming a flat world service provider means expanding beyond the boundaries of primary locations to acquire and apply the skills of a worldwide talent pool. Although this may sound like the standard definition of a multinational business, there are significant differences between it and a flat world company.

Ananda Mukerji at FirstSource makes a bold assertion about corporate strategy in general, in his belief that the support for outsourcing as a strategy has only just started:

In the future, hardly any back office processes will be carried out in house. Just as it has become natural to outsource catering and cleaning services, administrative processes that can be broken down into logical components will generally be outsourced. These standardised services will be provided in mass volume by a handful of global Indian operators with large hubs in India, but supported by their subsidiary delivery centres worldwide. Thus delivering the right outsourcing solution in the right location for the client's specific process requirements.

There will also be enormous growth in higher value, more complex work going to India. This section of the outsourcing industry has come to be known as Knowledge Process Outsourcing (KPO). Research from Frost & Sullivan shows that the Indian KPO industry generated $405.2 million in 2005, representing a 59 per cent increase on the previous year, and could be worth $5.5 billion by 2019. Retail banks and insurers are starting to offshore higher value work, including financial analysis, statutory and regulatory reporting, and risk assessment.

India is the natural home for knowledge process outsourcing due to its pool of highly educated graduates who can carry out complex analysis and reporting at a fraction of the cost of carrying out such processes in western countries. The banks are making huge savings in labour – Wall Street banks pay their Indian staff about $20 an hour, compared to about $100 an hour for juniors in the US.

Rajendra Pawar at NIIT highlights a very thoughtful essay by stepping back somewhat from the debate over outsourcing, offshoring and global business to consider the wider context of social change presented by more pervasive knowledge. We are actually structuring a new man-machine relationship in the construction of this knowledge society and it can be of interest to consider the wider ramifications of this change:

It was the transistor, perhaps the most important invention of the $20^{th}$ century – which represented changing information through zeros and ones – that sowed the first seeds of the Knowledge Society. The transistor marked the big leap from the Industrial to the Digital age. It kick-started the arrival of the post-industrial society, the service economy, and the knowledge era.

In a departure from the past, when man was taking a back seat and letting machines take over, the end of the $20^{th}$ century signalled the return of the Mind, as the centre-piece of the universe.

For two centuries, Man had been seen as an unnecessary appendage in the entire wealth creation process. One can recall the unsettling images of the "ghost factories," which became symbolic of the industrial age and conjured up bone-chilling visions of highly automated and mechanised facilities, where computers performed with clockwork precision, un-manned, unwatched and untouched by human hand.

With the arrival of the Knowledge Era, the balance is once again restored and Man has been placed back in the driving seat. From a time, when Man was an appendage to machines, we have moved into a phase where the computer, and more specifically information technology, has become a tool in the hands of Man.

The Century of the Mind has also been accompanied by other key developments, the most important among them the end of the cold war and the surge of democracy. The fall of the German wall, *Perestroika* in Russia, and the cry for more open and free governance by citizens, has led to democracy becoming the preferred political structure around the globe, a movement that is transforming the world.

## China

In China, Remi Vespa of the Venus Software Corporation, believes that the huge international Diasporas of countries such as China can play an active role in helping those regions grow within this industry:

An important element in bringing business to a country is the Diaspora, i.e. the people living abroad.

According to statistics provided by the Overseas Chinese Affairs Commission of Taiwan, the Chinese Diaspora (Chinese people leaving outside Mainland China and Taiwan) represents today 35 million of individuals – the largest in the world.

The Russian Diaspora is probably the second largest one: about 20 million Russian people live in the CIS-countries (the former republics of the USSR), including 8 million in Ukraine, and another 10 million living in foreign countries.

The third largest Diaspora is from India with a little over 20 million individuals living abroad, according to the Indian Ministry of External Affairs.

The U.N. Population Fund estimated that between 3 million and 4 million Brazilians live outside Brazil; 70 percent of them are in the United States, Paraguay and Japan.

If we exclude the Russian Diaspora living in the CIS-countries, the Chinese Diaspora alone is larger than the combination of the Russian, Indian and Brazilian Diasporas!

The *Huaren* (Chinese living outside China) are playing a key role in helping Chinese companies capture world leadership within the next 7-10 years. For instance in California, a state that has close economic ties to China and where the IT industry is dominant, hundreds of business associations exist that help American businesses smoothly outsource their IT to China.

Dr. Jiren Liu of Neusoft makes the point that China is an attractive market as a consumer of services, and so the investment patterns will often reflect this, meaing that organisations may not just seek to outsource part of their supply chain to China, they will also explore how to sell their own products or services within China simultaneously as part of a wider 'China strategy':

China is also a huge consumer market rather than just a low-cost talent and service provider. As the middle class has increased, the proportion of consumption to GDP will continue to rise – up to 65 per cent in 2010 and 71 per cent in 2020, close to that of the developed countries. Taking consumer electronic products for example, IDC predicts a market value of 15 billion US dollars by 2008 in the Chinese market. According to McKinsey, the annual direct and indirect consumption of children and teenagers in urban China has reached $36 billion US dollars. Chinese people have changed their major consumption patterns from food to computers, autos, housing and so on.

MNCs are shifting their offshore manufacturing and operations to China for its huge consumer market and at the same time this causes the shift of IT services. Information technologies have also been widely used in many products, causing increased IT R&D and the needs of relevant services. Without a doubt, it is a good opportunity for China to develop its IT service industry as the MNC investment creates a need for this service in China. China will attract more and more global services business, such as finance, retail, and insurance, and in turn this will create more and more IT services business.

## Outsourcing Developments

Open your web browser now and punch 'outsourcing' into Google – or your search tool of choice – then see what it returns. The last time I tried, it offered a choice of over 100 million articles. Some links are for credible organisations that might be able to offer advice; the National Outsourcing Association in the UK is a good example that turns up high in the Google rankings – and I am on their board so that's a good thing! Other search recommendations are not so useful though, page after page of 'consultants' located everywhere from Argentina to Zambia.

There are now so many diverse flavours of outsourcing it really is becoming a moveable feast. It can be quite dazzling when faced with 100 million pages of information and the temptation is just to ignore the advice and plough on with your own idea of how an offshore project should work, which can be a costly mistake.

It is possible to find an offshore company to partner with and therefore to outsource in the true meaning of the term. It is also possible to just consider offshoring, where you open a facility in a lower-cost environment and hire your own employees. The do-it-yourself route is often termed the 'captive' model, a rather disconcerting title for a business strategy.

The most common forms of outsourcing described in this book are Information Technology Outsourcing (ITO) and Business Process Outsourcing (BPO). Software developers, infrastructure engineers or technical support teams can provide a service from an offshore location in much the same way as a local team, provided a standard process is in place to manage the relationship between sites.

BPO is the trailblazing practice of working with a Business Service Provider in the offshore location, so an entire service – or business process – can be outsourced. This is the form of outsourcing that is most frequently featured in the media as it often involves complete services such as contact centres or back-office administration.

The first five questions to consider before you go any further in any outsourcing programme are:

1. **Why do I want to outsource a process?**
   What is the strategy driving this process? If it is a cost-reduction measure then what are the targeted savings? Has the risk/benefit ratio been considered so a potential project failure is considered?

2. **What do I want to outsource?**
   Is it a short time-bound technical piece of work or the handover of a complete, ongoing process that is critical to the daily running of the business?

3. **Do I want to outsource or just go offshore?**
   Have you considered the difference between partnering with another company and outsourcing the tasks or just setting up your own offshore facility? Clearly the BRICs are being focused on here, but there are some other regions offering specialist skills in other areas. This book is focused on the BRICs, but there are many other regions offering specialist skills that may work for your organisation.

4. **Which company should I partner with?**
   If you need a partner then how do you select a company you can trust? Especially if the region where they are based is not somewhere you are used to working in. Perhaps there are also cultural and linguistic barriers to overcome in working with a different region even if the company itself can interact with you?

5. **In which country should I operate?**
   Everyone talks about India, but there are so many regions starting to offer credible offshore services at various prices including all of the BRICs players featured in this book; some regions are now becoming specific centres of excellence.

You should be able to consider these questions without external advisors. It is understandable that some of the options may be confusing if you have very limited experience of working offshore, but books like this one and those listed at the end of this chapter should contain enough information for you to understand at least why outsourcing may or may not work for your situation.

Beyond that understanding, you may need advice and so a consulting firm is likely to be the best option, especially once you start digging into the specific processes that are candidates for outsourcing. So, to understand the steps required to go offshore, first you need to understand the process and outsourcing options.

## Process Requirements

Initially you need to examine the processes within your company that you are considering. By undertaking the following five steps (Cullen & Willcocks 2003) you can determine what is feasible, difficult and where any priorities exist:

1. Map the existing services you are considering: Break out the different services into a list of what is performed and where.

2. Establish the criteria: Identify the short and long term rationale for outsourcing and also the barriers that may prevent it.

3. Apply each criterion for outsourcing: Map the reasons for outsourcing against each service that you want to move offshore, one reason at a time.

4. Aggregate the results of potential services and reasons: Produce a map that shows all the services and criteria or blockers mapped in a grid.

5. Determine priorities and service bundles: Organise the information so outsourcing phases can be created by bundling easy, medium and hard services – discarding the possibility of outsourcing any blocked service.

So by undertaking this exercise you can create a map of all the services you are considering, with reasons for outsourcing and difficulty estimates for each one. This approach allows you to bundle the processes into groups by service-type or priority with a clear distinction between what can and cannot be outsourced. Taking these steps protects you from outsourcing the wrong process. By listing every service with its required criteria and blockers, it becomes possible to remove tasks that are considered as core competencies or those that offer some advantage over the competition. If the service adds a competitive advantage to your business of contains a very high amount of intellectual property then you should question why you want to outsource it to another organisation.

Those tasks that remain can be prioritised by the potential ease of transfer, so the easiest tasks – or 'low-hanging fruit' in consulting parlance – start moving offshore first. Creating this map of tasks, priorities, blockers and potential transition phases is an essential prerequisite to consideration of the appropriate outsourcing strategy.

These are the most basic high-level strategic choices:

- Tactical Outsourcing
- Strategic Outsourcing
- Transformational Outsourcing

## Tactical Outsourcing

This is the practice of outsourcing a very specific problem or task. It is usually applied where in-house resources cannot immediately deliver what is required and can be mixed with in-house services creating a blend of in-house and outsourced services. As such, it can be viewed as a short-term approach though the effects are immediate.

Commenting on tactical outsourcing, Elizabeth Sparrow, author of *A Guide to Global Sourcing* said: "In recent years many companies have adopted tactical outsourcing solutions to contract out the development of web sites and services, using small innovative companies to gain rapid access to new technical skills." (Sparrow 2004)

At the opposite end of the innovation scale to new web sites is the maintenance of legacy technology systems. For many software developers, programming languages such as COBOL are archaic relics from a bygone age. However, there are systems across the world still using this legacy technology – the stuff still works. Even where an organisation has its own internal technology team, it is quite common to use tactical outsourcing as a tool for managing the legacy part of an operation.

A Facilities Management (FM) contract can be considered as an example of tactical outsourcing. FM is the practice of paying a vendor to manage your equipment, though you retain ownership of that equipment.

The main reasons for choosing a tactical outsourcing solution are:

- Resources with the correct skills are not available internally to launch and run a specific project.

- Ongoing maintenance of an existing service is difficult due to a lack of suitable resources.

- There is a need to quickly reduce or control spending on a particular service or function.

## Strategic Outsourcing

With strategic outsourcing business strategy enters the equation and the overall corporate 'big picture' has to be considered, rather than individual projects or required skill-sets.

This form of outsourcing allows the company to step back from the debate over whether to outsource or not and to consider what it does best and how. Strategic outsourcing can be an opportunity for the senior management of a company to do some serious re-engineering on the products and services offered.

This business process reengineering effort needs to consider why the company exists, what competitive advantages it has and how to best take advantage of this in the marketplace. Strategic outsourcing is a powerful tool for an organisation that truly wants to shift focus to the things that matter, intelligence and intangibles.

In *Funky Business*, Jonas Ridderstråle and Kjell Nordström, explain: "Things that were in demand used to consist of a little knowledge and a lot of stuff. The new valuables are made up of a little stuff and a lot of knowledge. The average weight of a real dollar's worth of US exports has more than halved since 1970." The funky academics add: "Today, competitive advantages weigh no more than the dreams of a butterfly." (Ridderstråle & Nordström 2001) These Swedish academics apparently give lectures on economics to a soundtrack of *The Prodigy* – I would love to hear the theory of competitive advantage explained with *Hotride* blasting from a Bose stereo!

So if your competitive advantage depends on your ability to get a new product to market quickly, but your management team is forever tied up with IT, accounts, customer services or other essential, but baseline, services then it might be time for a strategic review.

Elizabeth Sparrow believes that a critical issue when planning any form of strategic outsourcing is to focus on the end-result, not how the company gets there. She said: "Managers will need to adopt a new perspective on control and are likely to be more successful if the focus is on outputs rather than inputs."

This is an important point to consider as most managers are more familiar with managing daily activities than planning services, measuring targets and managing a partnership.

The main reasons for choosing a strategic outsourcing solution are:

- To provide access the best resources in the business by ensuring that only leading experts work on your projects.

- Internal resources can be freed from non-core activities and allowed to focus on revenue generation.

- It allows the business to focus on its core competencies rather than reinventing the wheel.

## Transformational Outsourcing

As the name suggests, transformational outsourcing goes beyond strategic considerations and works on the basis of how you might run the business if you could start over again.

This complete business redesign would use outsourcing as a strategic tool to ensure that the benefits of strategic outsourcing are achieved as a new way of doing business is created. This is a complete corporate overhaul and has far-reaching long-term consequences.

Transformational outsourcing might typically be used when a company is being spun-off from a parent firm or when a new product or service is created that is so different from previous offerings that only a corporate transformation will suffice.

Innovation leads to transformation. Love it or hate it, today every manager knows the story of 'Who moved my cheese?' Outsourcing can be the guide that allows your company to navigate the maze and transform into a true innovator. In this global knowledge-based economy differentiation has become critical to success and differentiation cannot be achieved by a company that does not focus one hundred per cent on how to best leverage its competitive advantage.

Gary Hamel argues this point in *Leading the revolution:* "Without radical innovation, a company will devote a mountain of resources to achieve a molehill of differentiation. The amount spent on advertising indistinguishable soft drinks, the legions of telemarketers trying to induce customers to switch from one mediocre long-distance carrier to another, the millions of 'free' miles given away by airlines to induce customers to remain 'loyal' despite uniformly awful service, the marketing investment needed to get investors to pay attention to any one of the more than 3,500 mutual funds available in the United States, the resources expended in producing half a dozen look-alike television newsmagazines, the 'incentives' car companies have to pay to move indistinguishable autos off dealer lots – these are just a few examples of the high-cost, low-impact futility of carbon copy strategies." (Hamel 2002)

However it should be noted that transformation can be dangerous and managers are afraid of organisational change. They need to be aware that the twenty-first century consumer does not tolerate average companies. Transformational outsourcing may be your first step to long-term survival.

The main reasons for choosing a transformational outsourcing solution are:

- To redefine the supply chain; creating new and better relationships with suppliers and customers.
- To enter new markets.
- To overhaul the time-to-market process for new products and services.

## The Key Drivers of Outsourcing Today

So why is BPO and global outsourcing so important now? It's a topic that hardly ever seems to exit the business press these days and this book is exploring the potential development of Brazil, Russia, India, and China within this market. Every time a company anywhere makes a new strategic sourcing decision, the discussion is about outsourcing all over again, good, bad or just wrong.

I checked 'BPO' as a search term on Google news on a weekend in May 2007; the website returned 5,923 news articles from around the world. It's true that some of those may be the latest news on the 'Buffalo Philharmonic Orchestra' or the 'Baltic Ports Organisation' or even the 'Bulgarian Patent Office', however from the headlines it would appear that almost all of them are talking about Business Process Outsourcing. Nearly 6,000 news stories, constantly debating this business strategy; that's a lot more than 'keiretsu' rates on the same day (1,193 more to be precise), but who can forget having to write all those essays at business school on Japanese corporate relationships as the future for Europe?

Outsourcing has become such a staple of modern corporate strategy that it would now be unusual to consider hiring employees for some tasks. Can you imagine a company that would employ their own window-cleaners? Probably not. It just isn't done that way anymore, but why now?

Cost reduction is usually the primary reason for offshore outsourcing and especially BPO, as ongoing services have ongoing costs and therefore larger savings as you extrapolate all those reduced costs into the future. However money was just as valuable to corporate executives twenty or thirty years ago, so why were they not jetting back and forth to India or South Africa, setting up contact centres then? South Africa has a different answer as most Britons were not even buying Cape fruit during the apartheid era, but how has the approach changed and what are the key drivers today?

I outlined my CCC thoughts in the introduction to this book, but also I believe that there are four more general drivers changing the business landscape and allowing BPO to grow exponentially today:

- **Government Policy**
- **Globalisation and the International Knowledge Economy**
- **Technology**
- **Corporate Strategy**

Government Policy

As the speed of improved communications and the Internet decreases the size of the globe (Thomas Friedman's 'Flat World'), it is becoming more common for people themselves to migrate throughout the world seeking work and many governments are encouraging the arrival of skilled labour.

Manuel Castells, Professor Emeritus at the University of California Berkeley, believes that people with the right 'knowledge' skills are already above the laws of immigration policy: "There is, increasingly, a process of globalisation of speciality labour. That is, not only highly skilled labour, but labour which becomes in exceptionally high demand around the world and, therefore, will not follow the usual rules in terms of immigration law, wages, or working conditions. This is the case for high-level professional labour: top business managers, financial analysts, advanced services consultants, scientists and engineers, computer programmers, biotechnologists, and the like. But it is also the case for artists, designers, performers, sports stars, spiritual gurus, political consultants, and professional criminals." (Castells 1996)

So it would appear that we are already in a situation where huge numbers of illegal immigrants move in search of a better life and those with the right qualifications of experience need not worry about the process as they will be welcomed. As Castells says: "Anyone with the capacity to generate exceptional value added in any market enjoys the chance to shop around the globe."

Several US states have attempted to introduce bills that would prevent the state from outsourcing any of their activities offshore. The view of the UK government is rather more supportive, though it is worth remembering that introducing populist bills is a far cry from actually establishing new legislation. The UK Department of Trade and Industry (renamed in 2007 to the Department for Business, Enterprise and Regulatory Reform) has published several research reports investigating the effect of offshoring on the UK economy and has remained supportive of the strategy, through a belief that the UK is stronger if companies are allowed flexibility.

Many governments in the developed world are now struggling to deal with the challenges of an older population and state pension demands. The nears future in the UK could be summarised as a continuation of declining birth rates, a sharp increase in the number of over-65s and demand for skilled workers increasing.

Government policy on the migration of labour will become a key manifesto issue for developed governments and will be closely linked to the official line on offshore outsourcing.

## Globalisation and the International Knowledge Economy

The globalisation of business and government is affecting every person on earth and not only those who work in major corporations seeking offshore outsourcing relationships. Coke is the 'real thing' in almost every country you can name and no British High Street would be complete without its Indian takeaway offering the rite-of-passage combination of Cobra beer and a mutton vindaloo.

Globalisation as a phenomenon has a somewhat chequered history and status. Detractors, of which the most prominent is probably the economist and Nobel Laureate Joseph Stiglitz, argue that it has a negative effect on society. These arguments range from Mr. Stiglitz, who essentially believes that globalisation *could* work, but not the way it is controlled at present (Stiglitz 2002), to the brick-throwing thugs who believe it is an ideological statement to burn down their local Starbucks. The English singer-songwriter Billy Bragg is famous for his rambling monologues between songs, often there is more speech and opinions at his shows than music. I was listening to one of his live shows just after the 1999 'battle in Seattle' – the riot in opposition to a meeting of the World Trade Organisation. In Bragg's rambling monologue he criticised the violent anarchists and said if any of the protestors was serious about changing global capitalism they would make a concerted effort to unionise McDonald's.

Despite the ongoing protests, there is no way to ignore the fact that the world is becoming a smaller place and this trend is allowing the idea of offshore outsourcing to gradually become accepted as a 'normal' business tool. In fact, as suggested throughout this book, the use of terminology such as 'global sourcing' and 'transnational' is starting to replace the term 'outsourcing'.

The major benefits of globalisation for the consumer are:

- Business services and products are subjected to greater transparency when used across many nations.
- Choice of suppliers becomes more attractive when any global supplier can be chosen, rather than just local service providers.
- Competition is created by this choice, ensuring an improved service and better pricing.

Countries and companies are becoming more alike. This makes it much harder to defend the argument that a local firm is needed to service the requirements of your organisation. The distance is becoming irrelevant. All that matters is whether they can do the job in hand. There is less consumer nationalism. The English may want to buy English motor vehicles, but the Chinese bought the Intellectual Property Rights to Rover vehicles and BMW now manufactures the classic 'Mini', a car that remains as English as Michael Caine or Noël Coward.

Brands, beer and 'Freddie' Flintoff; they encircle the world and make it easier for one country to interact and do business with another. Never before has knowledge and information been valued so highly, but just a single glance at the companies of today demonstrates that 'knowledge economy' is not the catch-phrase of dry academicians. It is a mantra for any business that wants to survive in a world that lives on Internet time.

## Technology

The world would not be declining in perceived size if we could not use email, instant messaging, video conferencing and the telephone itself to keep in touch. The unrelenting progress of technological advancement is driving a new way of thinking. Who remembers when it was a big deal to leave the city for a weekend? Now divers are leaving Europe for a weekend diving in Thailand and remaining in touch thanks to the global roaming facility on their mobile phone. People used to arrange to meet in a specific location at a specific time, now they just make a vague arrangement and home in on each other using the mobile.

On September 12, 2005 the global auction company eBay announced its plan to acquire Internet telephony company Skype for USD 2.6 billion, plus an additional USD 1.5 billion in rewards if goals are met by 2008. eBay will pay half in cash and half in stock options. This was an important acquisition as it underlines the growing stature of Voice over Internet Protocol (VoIP) technologies. The Skype domain name was only registered on April 23, 2003 and version 1.0 of the software was published on July 27, 2004. This must be the fastest four billion ever earned for the two founders of Skype.

Without the current low price of global telecommunications, outsourcing could not have exploded in importance the way it has. What is so amazing to a detached observer is the exponential increase in capacity and speed. Any technology undergraduate can describe Moore's Law; the concept first described by Gordon Moore of Intel in 1965 where he predicted that the number of transistors on an integrated circuit would double every couple of years. Moore was right, even though commentators have predicted for many years that computing speed and power cannot continue to grow at its present rate. The development of atomic computing will ensure Moore's legacy lives on a little longer.

This concept of the technology driving the business, rather than just being a tool of the business creates a virtuous circle. The business leaders can use technology in order to gain a competitive advantage over their rivals, while the technologists can continue to improve their systems knowing that the improvements will find a waiting market.

The technology available to companies today will radically alter their supply chain. Search technologies, such as Google, should eventually be integrated right through to company inventory and connected back to consumers via their telephone. Consumers should be able to pull knowledge, rather than see useless information pushed to them. The management writer and former McKinsey director Kenichi Ohmae (Ohmae 1995) believes there are three broad themes where technology benefits the organisation:

- Information can flow freely throughout the world instantaneously.
- It is possible to track information about people, products and services in real time.
- The customer can compare and contrast your service with other firms throughout the world.

Twenty or even ten years ago these were difficult issues for any senior executive to contend with. The technology was not good enough to allow a global market in information, yet today there is a considerable infrastructure available in the Internet and this is improved at an accelerating rate.

Ohmae's thematic vision is real and affects us all.

The Internet is the fifth network of the modern age; the first four networks were the telegraph, the railroad, the telephone, and the electric network. Those commentators who fail to rate the effect on society of the Internet on a par with electricity simply fail to see how we will live our lives in 20, 30 or 50 years. Each of these networks had an enormous impact on how people live, work and communicate, and the Internet is no exception. The creation of a ubiquitous network and digitisation of information is leading to unprecedented innovation and opportunity. There are hundreds of ways in which technology is now driving change in our personal lives as well as in corporate life. Outsourcing is being enabled by this surge in global connectivity and the opportunities are unlimited.

## Corporate Strategy

Though outsourcing was observed in earlier decades, it really entered into the strategic arsenal of executives in the 1980s. Machiavelli wrote about freelance (free-lance) armies ready to fight for the right price and every sensible person has used a plumber to fix bathroom troubles since Thomas Crapper first popularised the flush toilet. Two academics can share the credit for popularising the concept of outsourcing as a tool for gaining competitive advantage, though in different ways.

Professor Michael E. Porter has published a series of books focused on competition in which he dissected the corporate value-chain (Porter 1981, 1985, 1990). Porter urged managers to understand how their company works and where it really adds value to the service or product it produces. Charles Handy, a writer and founding professor at London Business School, published his 'shamrock' theory in *The Age of Unreason* (Handy 1989). The shamrock is the Irish national emblem. It was used by St. Patrick to symbolise the holy Trinity. Charles Handy uses it to describe the three groups of people within an organisation.

- Core workers for essential and managerial tasks.
- Contract employees for non-essential work.
- Flexible workers, temporary, part-time and occasional labour.

Handy described how companies would employ an essential core team, around which they would hire contracted expertise for specific time-bound projects. In addition, there would be the flexible labour needed for maintenance, sorting the mail and cleaning the office.

It sounded like a radical idea, but look around your own company now. Isn't there a core team of essential people? Don't they hire contract teams or outsource non-core activities and are the cleaners and mail-room staff still employed by the company you work for?

Professor Porter describes the value chain in *Competitive Advantage*: "These activities can be represented using a value chain. A firm's value chain and the way it performs individual activities are a reflection of its history, its strategy, its approach to implementing its strategy, and the underlying economics of the activities themselves." (Porter 1985)

Porter advises that value added activities should be identified by management. He said: "Identifying value activities requires the isolation of activities that are technologically and strategically distinct. Value activities and accounting classifications are rarely the same. Accounting classifications (e.g. burden, overhead, direct labour) group together activities with disparate technologies, and separate costs that are all part of the same activity."

The concept of 'core competence' has become a management mantra today to the point at which there is an endless debate about where the concept begins and ends. Outsourcing should allow executives to focus on the core business while resolving skills shortages or resource problems, reducing costs, and fundamentally transforming how an organisation thinks, acts and operates. The management should focus on the core of their organisation, where value is created, and leave other tasks to partner organisations.

The strategy of focusing on core competences as detailed by commentators such as Charles Handy and Professor Porter naturally fits the outsourcing model. Look into your value chain and focus on what you are good at. Let the experts worry about the remaining tasks.

We are living right now in one of the most exciting periods in history. It's true that there are many negatives to the present; the horrifying tsunami in Asia back in 2004 and the 2005 Louisiana flooding as hurricane Katrina wreaked havoc on the richest country in the world are some of the more memorable natural tragedies that have occurred recently. The manmade catastrophes of 9/11 in the US and 7/7 in the UK have created a sense of fear and increased our mistrust of established government.

Yet, through all this maelstrom of disaster there is the positive. The thrill of watching developing nations grow stronger and more confident, to see them engaging fully on a world stage. The amazing advances in global healthcare championed by the Bill and Melinda Gates Foundation are astounding. To the critics of Mr. Gates and his company, ask yourself 'has any single person saved more fellow humans from a wretched death through a malarial infection?'

Global services are extending our reach as humans in this same way. Long ago we saw how toys could be manufactured in China and shipped to Europe for less than the cost of local production. Now it is becoming clear that the technology required to share intellectual property and skills is available – this is no longer about science fiction. When the historians of the future look back in the archives of the British library and see the flurry of books published on outsourcing at the turn of this millennium, they may well wonder what the fuss was all about.

## Outsourcing – Recommended Reading

BPO is the hot ticket in outsourcing in this early stretch of the twenty first century. Though the idea of BPO has been with us for many years, the advent of inexpensive global telecommunications and the Internet has paved the way for complex services to be provided from anywhere, yet this opens up a new area of business complexity that has to somehow be managed.

As outlined throughout the cases in this book, BPO generally means that an entire function, including computer systems, corporate assets and employees, are transferred to a service provider. Many services are being delivered from remote locations in this way, for example:

- Call and contact centres.
- Email and chat-based customer service.
- Document processing.
- Payroll management.
- Human Resources management.
- Accounting services.
- Financial service processing and operations.
- Airline ticketing.
- Market research.
- R&D.

Each month new services spring up, stretching the very limit of where people thought a remote service might be able to go. When my doctor was conducting a physical examination prior to his attempt on the London marathon run, it was no surprise to hear him declare that he has founded a BPO firm in India dedicated to the transcription of medical dictaphone messages.

BPO is growing in complexity and value as more companies realise the benefits it has to offer. The value to a client of letting a vendor manage and improve business processes is far beyond the earlier use of outsourcing for the management of technology infrastructure. Accenture call their service Business Transformation Outsourcing for a good reason – the vendors usually improve what the client is already doing.

Just a few years back, who would have imagined that an offshore firm such as Office Tiger could handle your tax return – and word processing in multiple languages? In the equity boom at the close of the millennium, who could have predicted that major investment banks would be turning to Evalueserve for stock market analysis? These are examples of where BPO has gone today, and the possibilities are increasing as experience grows and more complex offshore services become commonplace.

Clearly there is an extensive list of questions to ask before you consider offshore outsourcing, but this book and those listed can get to you to a position of knowing what you want and where the market across the BRICs region is headed – then it's best to turn to an advisor with experience of the market.

- **A Guide to Global Sourcing (BCS 2004),
  Elizabeth Anne Sparrow, ISBN 1-902505-61-1**
  This is an excellent overview of the risks and management processes needed for offshore outsourcing, though it may seem like a shameless plug for another BCS title it has an excellent country comparison section that looks at the benefits and drawbacks of offshoring in 18 different countries.

- **Outsourcing to India: The Offshore Advantage (Springer 2004, 2005), Mark Kobayashi-Hillary, ISBN 81-8128-290-6**
  I need to mention my earlier book on India, which was completely revised for the second edition published in 2005. It is a complete overview of outsourcing to the most popular offshore destination, including information on history, regions within India and how to start working with Indian companies.

- **Technology and Offshore Outsourcing Strategies (Palgrave 2005) Peter Brudenhall, ISBN 1-4039-4619-1**
  Peter Brudenhall is a London-based partner in law firm Simmons & Simmons, with expertise in outsourcing law. This is a collection of essays connected by a strategic theme, so it is more useful when initially considering an offshore move, rather than trying to pick up the pieces of a failed venture.

- **The Outsourcing Revolution (Dearborn 2004)
  Michael F. Corbett, ISBN 0-7931-9214-5**
  This is one of the best 'all-round' guides to outsourcing, outlining business strategy and the practical steps managers need to take to control offshore projects, all in a single volume.

- **Global Services: Moving to a Level Playing Field (BCS 2007) Mark Kobayashi-Hillary and Richard Sykes, ISBN 1-902505-83-2**
  Richard and I put this book together as a big picture overview on the outsourcing process and how it is actually the globalisation of the service economy that is the important question, not how particular service companies behave alone.

## A Final Word

Those are the key themes in summary. It's been a pleasure to collect together the thoughts of these twelve industry leaders for the book.

This book represents one small step on the journey to success in IT and IT-enabled services. The companies documented within these twelve essays are all leaders in their particular field of services. A decade from publication it's almost certain that at least some of the companies documented in this book will be talking of themselves as world leaders, and not just leaders in their particular corner of the BRICs.

This book presents a view from the service companies themselves; there are no service buyers or advisors here. This might colour the judgement of those featured, but essentially those who are selling to multiple clients in multiple locations generally have a vision of where their own industry is headed. Only time will tell if their views within this book are borne out by the reality of what happens to the BRICs over the coming decades.

# Bibliography

Manuel Castells, The Rise of the Network Society, Blackwell (1996)

Sara Cullen and Leslie Willcocks, Intelligent IT outsourcing, Elsevier Butterworth Heinemann (2003)

Thomas Friedman, The world is flat: A brief history of the twenty-first century, Allen Lane (2005)

Gary Hamel, Leading the Revolution, Harvard Business School Press (2000)

Charles Handy, The Age of Unreason, Arrow Books (1989)

Spencer Johnson, Who Moved My Cheese?, Vermilion (1999)

Mark Kobayashi-Hillary, Outsourcing to India: The Offshore Advantage 2nd Edition, Springer (2005)

Mark Kobayashi-Hillary & Dr Richard Sykes, Global Services: Moving to a Level Playing Field, BCS (2007)

Kjell Nordström and Jonas Ridderstrale, Funky Business, FT Prentice Hall (2000)

Kenichi Ohmae, The end of the nation state, The Free Press (1995)

Michael E. Porter, Competitive Advantage, The Free Press (1985)

Michael E. Porter, Competitive Strategy, The Free Press (1980)

Michael E. Porter, The Competitive Advantage of Nations, Palgrave (1990)

Elizabeth Anne Sparrow, A Guide to Global Sourcing, British Computer Society (2004)

Joseph Stiglitz, Globalization and its Discontents, Allen Lane (2002)

Don Tapscott & Anthony D Williams, Wikinomics: How Mass Collaboration Changes Everything, Portfolio (2006)

Bibliography

# About the Editor

**Mark Kobayashi-Hillary MBA MBCS CITP**

Mark is a British corporate advisor, writer, and researcher based in London where he lives with his wife Nobumi and a Staffordshire bull terrier named Matilda.

Mark is the author of 'Outsourcing to India: The Offshore Advantage' first published by Springer in 2004 and updated to a new edition in 2005. He contributed a chapter on offshoring to Peter Brudenall's book 'Technology and Offshore Outsourcing Strategies' (Palgrave 2005). Mark co-authored 'Global Services: Moving to a Level Playing Field' (BCS 2007) for the British Computer Society with Dr. Richard Sykes of the British hi-tech trade association Intellect.

Mark is the offshoring director of the UK National Outsourcing Association (NOA) and is a founding member of the British Computer Society working party on offshoring. He is a visiting lecturer at London South Bank University, focused on teaching outsourcing to MBA students. Mark is a non-executive director of foreign exchange firm FXA World. Mark has an MBA from the University of Liverpool.

Mark writes a regular blog titled 'Talking Outsourcing' for the leading technology magazine 'Computing', is editor of the NOA podcast, and occasionally writes other media features when he can find the time.

*www.markhillary.com*

# About the Contributors

The contributors to the book are listed here in the order in which the chapters are featured in the book; Brazil, Russia, India, then China.

**Dalton Luz** is the CEO of Politec USA. He has been Chief Executive Officer of Politec USA since 1998. He has more than 21 years of experience with outsourcing, including application life-cycle services, large-scale systems integration projects employing business process automation, electronic document management, imaging, forms processing, and identity and access management implementations. Mr. Luz has a degree in Business Administration from the Catholic University of Goiás in Brazil and he is also an alumnus of IMD (International Institute for Management Development) in Lausanne, Switzerland.

*www.politec.com*

**Thiago Turchetti Maia** is founder and Chief Executive Officer at Vetta Technologies, a Brazilian services company specialised in offshore outsourcing with businesses worldwide. He is also member of the Board of Directors of Fumsoft, an association of software development organisations where he orchestrates a consortia of Brazilian companies to meet large-scale international and domestic demands. He holds a bachelor's degree in Computer Science, a master's degree in Electrical Engineering, a doctor's degree in Electrical Engineering (emphasis on computational intelligence), and an MBA in Finance.

Before founding Vetta, he worked at Webmind's headquarters in New York, where he led artificial intelligence research and development projects in the United States, Australia, New Zealand, and Brazil. In 2001, he returned to Brazil to incorporate Vetta Technologies, focusing on providing offshore services first in North America, and then in Europe and Latin America. Three years later, in 2004, Vetta Technologies received an award by the Brazilian Government for being amongst the top-20 Brazilian exporters of the year.

*www.vettatech.com*

**Arkadiy Dobkin** is the CEO and President of EPAM Systems. Under Mr. Dobkin's leadership, EPAM Systems has grown to be one of the world's leading software engineering services firms. Mr. Dobkin began his career in Minsk, Belarus where he worked for several emerging software companies. After immigrating to the United States, he held thought and technical leadership positions in Colgate-Palmolive and SAP Labs.

Mr. Dobkin has been a speaker at various international industry and technology events, such as Gartner Outsourcing Summits, Forrester's Giga-World IT Forum Europe, Russian Outsourcing & Software Summits, SAP TechEd, etc. In 2004, along with the CEOs of Wipro Technologies and CGI Group, Arkadiy Dobkin was spotlighted as a key industry influencer in the Foreign Relations category of CRN's 'Top 25 Executives' issue. In 2006, Mr. Dobkin was named one of the 'Top 25 Most Influential Consultants' by Consulting Magazine.

Mr. Dobkin holds an MS in Electrical Engineering from the Byelorussian National Technical University.

*www.epam.com*

**Dmitry A. Loschinin** is the President and CEO of Luxoft. He has led Luxoft from its inception in April 2000. With over 15 years of IT experience Dmitry has built a superior team of professionals and has led Luxoft to a leading position in the international software development market. Under Dmitry Loschinin's stewardship Luxoft has enjoyed exponential growth, became the world's only company to achieve both CMM and CMMI Level 5 certification simultaneously, and has climbed to the top of the Russian software services industry by building a loyal client base of world's most successful companies.

Dmitry started his professional career as a software engineer in the late 1980s. In a short period of time he achieved management roles within leading multinationals such as MCP GmbH, KED GmbH and IBM. In 1998 Dmitry joined the IBS Group where he successfully established their SAP R/3 implementation practice before taking charge of the IBS initiative to offer offshore software services. This initiative eventually became Luxoft. Dmitry is a Chairman of RUSSOFT, Russia's largest and most influential software development trade association representing 80 companies from Russia, Ukraine, and Belarus and more than 7,000 highly qualified programmers and software engineers with advanced graduate level degrees in technology and computer science.

Dmitry Loschinin graduated with honors from the Computational Mathematics and Cybernetics department of Moscow State University.

*www.luxoft.com*

**Alexander Egorov** is the CEO and Co-Founder of Reksoft. He co-founded the company in 1991 and has served as CEO since its inception. Along with his duties at Reksoft Mr. Egorov co-founded and served as a member of the board in a number of successful IT ventures such as Ozon.ru (1998, the largest Russian online-bookstore) and Assist (1999, Russia's leading Internet Payment Gateway).

Mr. Egorov repeatedly enters the 'IT TOP 100' rating presented by the largest Russian nationwide business newspaper 'Kommersant'. In April 2003 – February 2004 he served as Chairman of the Board of the Russian Software Development Association RUSSOFT and has been elected to the board three times since. Mr. Egorov is a frequent speaker at major conferences and events, recently included events hosted by Gartner, Forrester Research, ETRE, and the International Association of Outsourcing Professionals.

Mr. Egorov holds an MBA degree from the Stockholm School of Economics.

*www.reksoft.com*

**Dmitry Ponomarev** has served as President and Chairman of the Board of Directors of MERA Networks since the day of its inception in 1989. Dmitry has built MERA Networks from a small software development company with a handful of employees to a global software development leader providing full lifecycle software development services in cutting-edge technology areas. His entrepreneurial spirit is the driving force behind the creation, growth and ongoing success of MERA Networks. The company owes much of its leadership in the Russian software development outsourcing market to Dmitry's personal commitment and contribution.

Prior to starting his entrepreneurial career in 1989, Dmitry was a Professor at the Nizhny Novgorod State Technical University. He earned his Master's degree in Telecom Engineering in 1974 and PhD in 1979 from the Nizhny Novgorod State Technical University. He is an author of 70+ publications in scientific and technical journals and a holder of 12 patents. Dmitry Ponomarev is also a co-founder of other several successful Russian and international telecom companies.

*www.meranetworks.com*

**Shiv Nadar** is the founder of HCL and Chairman and CEO of HCL Technologies. From modest beginnings three decades ago, Shiv Nadar entered the Forbes List of billionaires in the year 2000. In 2006 he was ranked 168 globally and among the top ten in India. Business Standard ranked him 4$^{th}$ in the billionaires club and he is amongst the top 20 Indian personalities as per the Business Today / Cirrus survey. During this process, he has not only created wealth for himself but also for his customers, partners, employees, and investors.

In January 2005, Shiv Nadar received the CNBC Business Excellence award from the Prime Minister of India. In February 2005 he was listed by 'India Today' in the Power List of India's leaders from all walks of life, for building a global IT enterprise from scratch in 3 decades, creating valuable joint ventures with partners such as Deutsche Bank, and creating jobs in Belfast when India was being criticised for doing the opposite. When the UK Prime Minister, Tony Blair, visited India in September 2005 he recognised Shiv Nadar for his contribution in creating 2,300 jobs in the UK.

Shiv Nadar firmly believes that "If you want to empower people, give them the tools. There's enough entrepreneurship in India to take care of the rest."

*www.hcltech.com*

**Nandan M. Nilekani** is the Co-Chairman of the Board of Directors of Infosys Technologies Ltd. He has served as Chief Operating Officer and as a director on the company's board since its inception in 1981. In 2006, Nandan became one of the youngest entrepreneurs to join 20 global leaders on the prestigious World Economic Forum Foundation Board. Nandan was named the Businessman of the Year 2006 by Forbes Asia. He was listed as one of the 100 most influential people in the world by Time Magazine in 2006. He received Fortune's 'Asia's Businessmen of the Year 2003' award and was named among the 'World's most respected business leaders' in 2002 and 2003, in a global survey by the Financial Times and PricewaterhouseCoopers. In 2005, Nandan was awarded the prestigious Joseph Schumpeter prize for innovative services in the fields of economy, economic sciences and politics.

Nandan is the Vice Chairman of The Conference Board, a member of ASPEN Institute's Business and Society Advisory Board, and serves on the London Business School's Asia Pacific Regional Advisory Board. In 2006, Nandan was conferred the Padma Bhushan, one of the highest civilian honours awarded by the Government of India.

*www.infosys.com*

**Ananda Mukerji** is the Managing Director and Chief Executive Officer of FirstSource. Ananda Mukerji has over 17 years experience, working in a number of areas including project finance, corporate finance and investment banking. At ICICI Bank he set up and/or managed a number of new businesses including the Infrastructure, Structured Finance and Advisory businesses. Ananda Mukerji joined ICICI OneSource (the earlier name used for FirstSource) in January 2002 as the Managing Director and CEO. Ananda Mukerji has also been CFO of Enron India Limited and Group CFO of BPL Communications Ltd.

Ananda Mukerji has a Post Graduate Diploma in Management (PGDM) from the Indian Institute of Management (IIM), Kolkata and a Graduate degree from the Indian Institute of Technology (IIT), Kharagpur.

*www.firstsource.in*

**Rajendra S. Pawar** is Chairman and co-founder of the NIIT Group, which encompasses two businesses – NIIT Technologies Limited, the software and services arm and NIIT Limited, the Learning Services organisation. Set up in 1981, NIIT pioneered the computer education market in India.

Mr. Pawar has played a leadership role in nurturing NIIT Limited and building it into Asia's largest IT education and knowledge corporation. Spearheading NIIT's globalisation endeavours, he has helped the company establish a presence in nearly 30 countries and touch nearly 1.8 million students, annually.

Mr. Pawar broadened NIIT's horizon in the early 1990s, leading the company's foray into the software and services market and creating one of India's premier IT and BPO organisations. NIIT Technologies offers SEI-CMMi 5 assessed services in 14 countries. Actively involved in India's key Chambers of Commerce, Mr. Pawar has led several ICT industry initiatives, giving voice to the sector's aspirations and goals. He is a founder and member of the Executive Council of NASSCOM, and a member of the International Business Council of the World Economic Forum. Mr. Pawar has served on the Prime Minister's National Task force, which aims at making India an IT Superpower by 2008.

Recognising his pioneering and entrepreneurial work in the education and software sectors, Ernst & Young conferred on Mr. Pawar its prestigious Master Entrepreneur of the Year Award in 1999. His contributions to the IT industry in India have also earned him the IT man of the Year award instituted by IT industry journal, *Dataquest*.

Mr. Pawar studied at the Scindia School, Gwalior and graduated from the country's prestigious engineering institution, the IIT, Delhi in 1972. At

IIT, he pursued the B.Tech program in electrical engineering and received the Distinguished Alumnus Award of IIT in 1995.

*www.niit-tech.com*

**Remi D. Vespa** is the VP of Market Development at Venus Software Corporation. Remi has a proven track record of 25 years in the software and semiconductor industries, including more than 10 years of experience at the executive level. He has solid knowledge of all aspects of company management, with special emphasis on business development and operations management.

Mr. Vespa acquired his in-depth experience in the major market places (North America, Europe and Northern Asia), where he promoted breakthrough solutions to a wide range of companies, ranging from small start-ups to Fortune 500. His former positions include founder and President of Favic LLC, a consulting company based in San Francisco, President and CEO of Silicon Recognition, a semiconductor company located in the Silicon Valley, Senior Vice-President at Dynasty Technologies, a Texas-based leading provider of high-end software solutions for mission critical applications, and Vice President of Groupe IBSI, the then arm of France Télécom in the Systems Integration arena.

He is the creator of a software tool (CONCEPTOR) that became a leading solution for the analysis and design of large projects, with thousands of users worldwide. Remi holds a Master of Science in mathematics from the University of Nice, France.

*www.vsc.com* (Chinese and Japanese)
*www.outsourcing-vsc.com* (English)

**Dr. Jiren Liu** is the founder; Chairman and CEO of Neusoft Group Ltd. Dr. Liu started his entrepreneurial career in 1991 when, together with two other teachers, he set up the laboratory in Northeastern University. Now Neusoft has grown to become a leading software and solutions provider in China. At present, Neusoft has over 13,000 employees, with over 8,000 customers at home and over 30 outsourcing customers abroad.

Dr. Jiren Liu is also currently the Vice President and Professor of Northeastern University, Deputy Chairman of the China Software Industry Association (CSIA) and China Society of Image and Graphics (CSIG). He was formerly Deputy Chairman of the Internet Society of China, and member of APEC Business Advisory Council (ABAC). He is now working as senior editor for 'Journal of Software' and 'Acta Electronica Sinica' of China.

In recent years, he has achieved many national-level top prizes including 'China IT Annual Figure', 'China Software Outstanding Contributions', and 'China Information Industry Annual Economic Figure'. Dr. Liu was born in Dandong City, Liaoning Province in 1955. He graduated from Northeastern University with a major in Computer Applications, and was conferred the degrees of Bachelor and Master successively. He achieved his Doctoral degree in 1987.

*www.neusoft.com*

Printing: Krips bv, Meppel
Binding: Stürtz, Würzburg